ReFocus: The Films of Denis Villeneuve

ReFocus: The International Directors Series

Series Editors: Robert Singer, Stefanie Van de Peer and Gary D. Rhodes

Board of advisors:
Lizelle Bisschoff (Glasgow University)
Stephanie Hemelryck Donald (University of Lincoln)
Anna Misiak (Falmouth University)
Des O'Rawe (Queen's University Belfast)

ReFocus is a series of contemporary methodological and theoretical approaches to the interdisciplinary analyses and interpretations of international film directors, from the celebrated to the ignored, in direct relationship to their respective culture – its myths, values and historical precepts – and the broader parameters of international film history and theory.

Titles in the series include:

Susanne Bier Edited by Missy Molloy, Mimi Nielsen and Meryl Shriver-Rice

Francis Veber Keith Corson

Jia Zhangke Maureen Turim

Xavier Dolan Edited by Andrée Lafontaine

Pedro Costa: Producing and Consuming Contemporary Art Cinema Nuno Barradas Jorge

Sohrab Shahid Saless: Exile, Displacement and the Stateless Moving Image Edited by Azadeh Fatehrad

Pablo Larraín Edited by Laura Hatry

Michel Gondry Edited by Marcelline Block and Jennifer Kirby

Rachid Bouchareb Edited by Michael Gott and Leslie Kealhofer-Kemp

Andrei Tarkovsky Edited by Sergey Toymentsev

Paul Leni Edited by Erica Tortolani and Martin F. Norden

Rakhshan Banietemad Edited by Maryam Ghorbankarimi

Jocelyn Saab: Films, Artworks and Cultural Events for the Arab World Edited by Mathilde Rouxel and Stefanie Van de Peer

François Ozon Edited by Loïc Bourdeau

Teuvo Tulio Henry Bacon, Kimmo Laine and Jaakko Seppälä

João Pedro Rodrigues and João Rui Guerra da Mata Edited by José Duarte and Filipa Rosário

Lucrecia Martel Edited by Natalia Christofoletti Barrenha, Julia Kratje and Paul Merchant

Shyam Benegal Edited by Sneha Kar Chaudhuri and Ramit Samaddar

Denis Villeneuve Edited by Jeri English and Marie Pascal

edinburghuniversitypress.com/series/refocint

ReFocus:
The Films of Denis Villeneuve

Edited by Jeri English and Marie Pascal

EDINBURGH
University Press

Edinburgh University Press is one of the leading university presses in the UK. We publish academic books and journals in our selected subject areas across the humanities and social sciences, combining cutting-edge scholarship with high editorial and production values to produce academic works of lasting importance. For more information visit our website: edinburghuniversitypress.com

© editorial matter and organisation Jeri English and Marie Pascal, 2023, 2024
© the chapters their several authors, 2023, 2024

Edinburgh University Press Ltd
The Tun – Holyrood Road
12 (2f) Jackson's Entry
Edinburgh EH8 8PJ

First published in hardback by Edinburgh University Press 2023

Typeset in 11/13 Ehrhardt MT by
IDSUK (DataConnection) Ltd

A CIP record for this book is available from the British Library

ISBN 978 1 4744 9738 1 (hardback)
ISBN 978 1 4744 9739 8 (paperback)
ISBN 978 1 4744 9740 4 (webready PDF)
ISBN 978 1 4744 9741 1 (epub)

The right of Jeri English and Marie Pascal to be identified as editors of this work has been asserted in accordance with the Copyright, Designs and Patents Act 1988 and the Copyright and Related Rights Regulations 2003 (SI No. 2498).

Contents

List of Figures	vii
Notes on Contributors	ix
Introduction *Jeri English and Marie Pascal*	1
1 Denis Villeneuve, Québécois and Citizen of the World *Amy J. Ransom*	5
2 Science Fiction, National Rebirth and Messianism in *Un 32 août sur terre* *Kester Dyer*	23
3 Close-ups and *Gros Plans*: Denis Villeneuve the Macrophage *Marie Pascal*	41
4 Reproductive Futurism and the Woman Problem in the Films of Denis Villeneuve *Brenda Longfellow*	59
5 Filming Missing Bodies: 'Bodiless-Character Films' and the Presence of Absence in Denis Villeneuve's Cinema *Emily Sanders*	76
6 Life, Risk and the Structuring Force of Exposure in *Maelström* *Terrance H. McDonald*	93
7 The Self as Other and the Other as Self: Identity, Doubling and Misrecognition in *Incendies*, *Enemy* and *Blade Runner 2049* *Jeri English*	110
8 Villeneuve's Hidden Monsters: Representations of Evil in *Prisoners* and *Sicario* *Alex Frohlick*	126

9	Beyond Complexity: Narrative Experimentation and Genre Development in *Enemy* *Melanie Kreitler*	143
10	Subjectivity and Cinematic Space in *Blade Runner 2049* *Christophe Gelly and David Roche*	161
11	Mere Data Makes a Man: Artificial Intelligences in *Blade Runner 2049* *Kingsley Marshall*	178
12	Shortening the Way: Villeneuve's *Dune* as Film and as Project *Trip McCrossin*	194

Filmography	209
Bibliography	210
Index	226

Figures

1.1	Morille before his make-over by Tekno	10
1.2	Morille after his make-over by Tekno	10
1.3	Val returns to consciousness after the attack	12
2.1	Simone awakens on August 32nd	26
2.2	Philippe mimicking the effects of weightlessness	28
3.1	What are you thinking about, Anthony?	45
3.2	What do you feel, Loki?	47
3.3	The Killer writing the hate-letter	51
4.1	Hannah, the precocious child	66
4.2	Louise floats in the Heptapod atmosphere	69
4.3	The Heptapod Costello and Louise meet	70
5.1	The dying fish/the narrator giving voice and form to Bibiane's abortion	81
5.2	Nawal leaves her village	84
5.3	Jeanne retraces her mother's steps	85
6.1	The dying fish narrator	97
6.2	Bibiane with her bare feet exposed	101
7.1	Simon blindfolded	115
7.2	Adam covering his eyes	119
7.3	K with Dr Stelline's face reflected onto his	122
8.1	Matt seen head-on in the car	132
8.2	Matt's eyes reflected in the rear-view mirror	132
8.3	Alex in Keller's torture chamber	136
9.1	A giant spider looms over the Toronto cityscape	145
9.2	Adam/Anthony's confusion during a conversation with his mother	146

9.3	Helen's transformation into a spider	152
10.1	Reality and its virtual representation	165
10.2	Thwarted verticality	167
10.3	Joi's giant hologram as the sign of a deceptive subjectivity	172
11.1	A pixellated Joi	180
11.2	The inscription 6.10.21 that K remembers as his birth or incept date	182
11.3	Niander Wallace and the simulacrum of Rachael	187
12.1	Paul's lowered gaze and knowing expression	195
12.2	Paul, shrouded in mist, as seen by his mother	199
12.3	Chani as imagined by Paul in the final scene	206

Notes on Contributors

Kester Dyer is an Assistant Professor in Film Studies in the School for Studies in Art and Culture at Carleton University (Canada). His teaching and research focus on Québec and Indigenous film and media and he has published several articles and book chapters on these topics. His current book project, *Otherworldly Incursions: The Supernatural in Québec Cinema*, comprises a broad exploration of the Québec film corpus since the 1990s. *Otherworldly Incursions* analyses how supernatural tropes across genres reveal key information about the Québec social imaginary's struggle to delineate relationships between historically dominant and more marginalised groups.

Jeri English is an Associate Professor of French and Women's & Gender Studies at the University of Toronto Scarborough (Canada). Her teaching and research areas include feminist literary, film and cultural theories, contemporary French cinema and twentieth- and twenty-first-century French women writers. She recently published a chapter entitled 'Youth and Gender Panic in *Ma vie en rose* and *Tomboy*' in the book *Screening Youth: Contemporary French and Francophone Cinema* (Edinburgh University Press, 2019) and has an article forthcoming in *Dalhousie French Studies* on abjection in Léos Carax's *Holy Motors*. Her current research project examines the monstrous, the abject and the uncanny in contemporary SF films.

Alex Frohlick is a PhD researcher at Goldsmiths University of London (United Kingdom) in the department of Media, Communications, and Cultural Studies. Alex's research explores current and future intersections between filmmaking and artificial intelligence and the implications for film studies and film theory. Alex holds an MA from King's College London in

Film and Philosophy as well as a BA from Solent University in Film and Television Production. His research interests include filmmaking innovation, film-philosophy, artificial intelligence, and representations of technology.

Christophe Gelly is a Professor of British literature and film studies (Université Clermont Auvergne, France). He has worked mainly on film genre, film noir and adaptation, and has published two book-length studies on Arthur Conan Doyle and Raymond Chandler, as well as co-edited a book on reception theories in cinema and literature. He also edited the issue of the journal *Écrans* devoted to French literary realism and film adaptation (*Écrans*, no. 5, 2016 – 1) and co-edited several collections of essays published online (*Mise au Point*, *La Furia Umana*). He has recently oriented his research towards digital culture and post cinema, through an article dealing with Spike Jonze's *Her* (in *Ekphrasis*), and is currently completing a book on dystopia in literature and film.

Melanie Kreitler is a graduate student at the Justus-Liebig-University in Giessen, Germany. Her PhD thesis, *Fictions of Experience: Mental Illness in Puzzle Films and Complex Television*, considers the impact of narrative complexity on meaning-making and viewers' understanding of lived experiences of mental illness. She has published on complex film, videogames, the television musical, and the intersections of medical and medial discourses, and co-edited a special issue on 'Illness, Narrated' in 2021.

Brenda Longfellow is a Professor of Cinema and Media Studies in the Department of Film, York University (Canada). She has published articles on documentary, feminist film theory and Canadian cinema in *Public*, *CineTracts*, *Screen*, *Camera Obscura* and the *Journal of Canadian Film Studies*. She is a co-editor (with Scott MacKenzie and Tom Waugh) of the anthology *The Perils of Pedagogy: The Works of John Greyson* (2013) and *Gendering the Nation: Canadian Women Filmmakers* (1992). She produces and directs documentary and interactive projects with a strong social justice and feminist focus. She recently produced *What Fools These Mortals Be*, a public art collaboration with visual artist Adad Hannah and fifteen formerly incarcerated women and *Intravene*, an immersive audio experience on the overdose crisis in Vancouver.

Kingsley Marshall is Head of Film & Television and a film producer, through the Sound/Image Cinema Lab at Falmouth University (United Kingdom), and independent production company Myskatonic. As a filmmaker, Kingsley served as executive producer on the feature films *Wilderness* (Justin John Doherty, 2017), *The Tape* (Martha Tilston, 2021), *Long Way Back* (Brett Harvey, 2022) and *Enys Men* (Mark Jenkin, 2022), produced *Backwoods* (Ryan Mackfall, 2019) and *The Birdwatcher* (2022), and composed the scores for *Hard, Cracked the

Wind (Mark Jenkin, 2019) and *Dean Quarry* (Rachael Jones, 2021). His academic research is focused on filmmaking practice of film and television production, the representation of history, and the notion of an 'emotive' artificial intelligence.

Trip McCrossin is a member of the Philosophy Department at Rutgers University (United States) working in various ways on the history and legacy of the Enlightenment in philosophy and popular culture, writing both academically and popularly on the subject, including periodic contributions to collections in the Open Court and Blackwell *Popular Culture and Philosophy* series, Edinburgh University Press' *ReFocus: The American/International Directors* series, and Lexington Books' *Critical Companion to Contemporary Directors* series.

Terrance H. McDonald is a Sessional Lecturer II of Cinema Studies at the University of Toronto Mississauga (Canada). Film philosophy, film genre, and feminist media studies are their main research areas, which includes a primary focus on Hollywood, Indigenous, and Canadian cinemas as well as a secondary focus on popular cinemas in a global context. Their work is published in *Men and Masculinities*, *NORMA: International Journal for Masculinity Studies*, and *Symposium: Canadian Journal of Continental Philosophy*, among other venues. Also, they are a co-editor of *From Deleuze and Guattari to Posthumanism* (2022). Currently, they are working towards the completion of a monograph: *Posthuman Cinema: Film Philosophy for Life Yet to Come*.

Marie Pascal is an Assistant Professor of French and Québec literature and film at King's University College, Western University (Canada). One of her main centres of interest deals with the question of the Other in the arts. She has also written on the reception of cinematographic adaptations – which she calls 'transcreations' – in the Québec canon. Her most recently published works are: 'La mère abjecte dans la transcréation Québécoise', *Cinémas, Revue d'études cinématographiques/Journal of Film Studies*, Montréal, no. 30 (2020); 'Xavier Dolan: Transcreating *Tom à la ferme* and *Juste la fin du monde*', *ReFocus: The Films of Xavier Dolan* (2019). She is currently directing an issue of *Dalhousie French Studies* dedicated to the concept of abjection in literature and cinema.

Amy J. Ransom, Professor of French at Central Michigan University (United States), is the author of *Science Fiction from Québec: A Postcolonial Study* (2009) and *Hockey, PQ: Canada's Game in Québec's Popular Culture* (2014), and three dozen articles on Québec's popular literature and film. In addition, she has published on Kubrick's *Eyes Wide Shut*, Bollywood sport and science fiction film, and a study of film adaptations of *I Am Legend*

(McFarland, 2018). She is currently working on a book on twenty-first-century Québec film.

David Roche, a 2022–7 IUF member, is a Professor of Film Studies at Université Paul Valéry Montpellier 3 (France) and is President of Société pour l'Enseignement et la Recherche du Cinéma Anglophone (SERCIA). He is the author of *Meta in Film and Television Series* (Edinburgh University Press, 2022), *Quentin Tarantino: Poetics and Politics of Cinematic Metafiction* (2018) and *Making and Remaking Horror in the 1970s and 2000s* (2014), and has edited many collected volumes, including *Women Who Kill: Gender and Sexuality in Films and Series of the Post-Feminist Era* (2020, with Cristelle Maury) and *Transnationalism and Imperialism: Endurance of the Global Western Film* (2022, with Hervé Mayer). His articles have appeared in *Adaptation*, *EJAS*, *E-REA*, *Film Journal*, *Horror Studies*, *La Furia Umana*, *Miranda*, *Mise au Point*, *Positif* and *Post-Script*. He is currently writing a book on *Arrival* (Villeneuve, 2016).

Emily Sanders holds an MSc in Film Studies from the University of Edinburgh. She is currently a PhD student in the Screen Cultures and Curatorial Studies Department at Queen's University (Canada). Her research interests include Canadian cinema, gender studies, feminist film theory, psychoanalysis, and film-philosophy.

Introduction

Jeri English and Marie Pascal

Quebec screenwriter and filmmaker Denis Villeneuve's nimble creative spirit is reflected in his varied body of work, which counts ten feature films and seven short films. From the earlier, primarily French-language films that he wrote and directed – *Un 32 août sur terre* (1998), *Maelström* (2000), *Polytechnique* (2009) and *Incendies* (2010) – to the Canadian-Spanish coproduction of the enigmatic *Enemy* (2013), to his critically and commercially successful Hollywood films – *Prisoners* (2013), *Sicario* (2015), *Arrival* (2016), *Blade Runner 2049* (2017) and *Dune: Part 1* (2021) – Villeneuve explores questions of alterity and interculturality, of language and identity, of memory and forgetting, of violence and retribution.

This volume of *ReFocus: The International Directors Series* engages with multiple aspects of Villeneuve's cinematic production, from his earlier auteur films to his major blockbusters. This collection provides a comprehensive analysis of several key aspects of Villeneuve's film production; some of these have not yet been studied by scholars and others are being explored in new ways. These include technical/formal elements representative of Villeneuve's films (sound, score, shots, camera movement, editing, cinematic space, non-linear storytelling, temporality); the cinematic representation of several important themes (national and cultural identity; gender, maternity and reproduction; trauma, embodiment and memory; identity, alterity and subjectivity; time and temporality; monsters, aliens and Replicants); and Villeneuve's position as both a Quebec and Hollywood director.

In engaging with a filmmaker whose output is as varied – linguistically, contextually and with regards to genre – as Villeneuve's, our volume achieves three main goals. Firstly, it comprises a collection of essays that touch on all of his feature films, including the recently released *Dune: Part 1*, in order to investigate the specificity of each of them and, conversely, to see which formal or thematic elements span all of his œuvre. Secondly, it presents several chapters that engage with two or more of Villeneuve's films, as well as two chapters that deal with his identity as a Québécois director, allowing us to examine his position between the two substantially different North American cultural contexts of Quebec and Hollywood. Finally, this volume constitutes a much-needed contribution to film studies in its presentation of the works of a major Hollywood director whose cinematic output has not yet been the object of sustained critical study.[1]

The book contains twelve chapters. The first two chapters situate Villeneuve's cinema in the historical, political and cultural context of Quebec and Hollywood cinema; the following nine chapters deploy different methodological and theoretical tools to engage with important aspects of Villeneuve's films; and the final chapter functions as an opening to future critical reception of *Dune: Part 1*.

In the first chapter, 'Denis Villeneuve, Québécois and Citizen of the World', Amy Ransom analyses Villeneuve's specificity as a Quebec director, linking the identity quests undertaken by characters across his whole filmography to his *québécitude*. Ransom argues that 'Villeneuve's entire corpus remains in touch with his Québécois origins' despite his characters' deterritorialisation that leads to new epiphanies and a certain universalism.

Kester Dyer likewise examines Villeneuve's specificity as a Quebec director in the volume's second chapter, 'Science Fiction, National Rebirth, and Messianism in *Un 32 août sur terre* ', which focuses on the historical and political context of Villeneuve's first feature film. Dyer investigates the reflections of Quebec's religious traditions and failed attempts at independence in *Un 32 août*, arguing that the film fails, finally, 'to radically break from conceptions of nationhood underpinned by linear Eurocentric worldviews'.

Chapters 3, 4 and 5 all engage with several of Villeneuve's films in order to create a deeper understanding of how certain techniques or thematic constructs span his œuvre. In the third chapter, 'Close-ups and *Gros Plans*: Denis Villeneuve the Macrophage', Marie Pascal conducts a detailed analysis of Villeneuve's frequent use of *gros plans* and close-ups from his early Quebec films to his more recent Hollywood blockbusters. In her exploration of how the binaries of largeness/nearness and transcendence/possession, highlighted by the different meanings of *gros plan* in French and close-up in English, play out across Villeneuve's œuvre, Pascal offers 'a typology of the macro' and examines the effects of these shots on the spectator.

In Chapter 4, 'Reproductive Futurism and the Woman Problem in the Films of Denis Villeneuve', Brenda Longfellow focuses on the close association of Villeneuve's female protagonists with a reproductive futurism 'that represents the child, procreation and domestic biological lineage as a utopian and redemptive embodiment of the future'. Longfellow's chapter traces this association with the maternal from *Blade Runner 2049* back through Villeneuve's earlier works with a specific focus on its function in *Arrival*.

In Chapter 5, 'Filming Missing Bodies: "Bodiless-Character Films" and the Presence of Absence in Denis Villeneuve's Cinema', Emily Sanders explores the ways in which the missing body that figures throughout four films (*Maelström*, *Polytechnique*, *Incendies* and *Arrival*) constitutes a particular investigation of trauma. Sanders examines the tropes of motherhood, surrogates and artifactualisation throughout these four films in order to investigate Villeneuve's deployment of an 'absence aesthetics'.

Chapters 6 to 11 all present original analyses of specific elements of one, two or three of Villeneuve's films. Terrance McDonald offers a radical formalist reading of the composition of the visuals in Villeneuve's second film in Chapter 6, 'Life, Risk, and the Structuring Force of Exposure in *Maelström*'. McDonald analyses 'the collapsing of the marked boundaries between inside and outside' in *Maelström*, demonstrating how Villeneuve investigates possibilities beyond those proposed by globalisation, late capitalism and citification 'through exposures and the risks that accompany them'.

In Chapter 7, 'The Self as Other and the Other as Self: Identity, Doubling and Misrecognition in *Incendies*, *Enemy* and *Blade Runner 2049*', Jeri English explores Villeneuve's representations of the Self/Other dialectic in his latest French-language film, his English-language Canadian film and one of his latest Hollywood blockbusters. Focusing on key moments of doubling and misrecognition in these films, English shows how it is 'the protagonists' quests for knowledge of the Other that inevitably lead to a profound shift in understanding of the Self'.

Chapter 8, 'Villeneuve's Hidden Monsters: Representations of Evil in *Prisoners* and *Sicario*', presents a reading of Villeneuve's action films that have, up until now, received little critical attention. Alex Frohlick analyses Villeneuve's use of a series of horror-inspired formal and narrative devices in his construction of 'evil' characters in these films. In his investigation of Villeneuve's '"realistic" human monsters' in *Prisoners* and *Sicario*, Frolick undertakes a 'moral evaluation of characters' capacity for evil through an analysis of their actions, engagements and desires'.

In Chapter 9, 'Beyond Complexity: Narrative Experimentation and Genre Development in *Enemy*', Melanie Kreitler looks into the spatio-temporal incongruities, fragmentation, and metalepses that characterise the 'puzzling mystery' of the film's narrative. By concentrating on the experimental features of *Enemy*'s structure, Kreitler shows how this film compels the spectator to participate in meaning-making and 'explores alternate orders of storytelling'.

Chapters 10 and 11 both deal with Villeneuve's sequel, *Blade Runner 2049*. In 'Subjectivity and Cinematic Space in *Blade Runner 2049*', Christophe Gelly and David Roche link *BR 2049*'s deconstruction of the binary division between interior and exterior spaces to the film's discourse on posthuman subjectivity. Gelly and Roche examine both diegetic and audiovisual space in *BR 2049*, with a focus on 'virtual reality, cinematic space and the relationship between Replicant and AI'; as their chapter argues, Villeneuve's remake deconstructs 'the binary established between the physical and the virtual', between Replicants and AI.

Kingsley Marshall explores how the representation of AI proposes a wider discourse around notions of identity, memory, and the formulation of the human self and subjectivity in 'Mere Data Makes a Man: Artificial Intelligences in *Blade Runner 2049*'. Marshall draws parallels between the representations of biopower in *BR 2049* and our own world 'in a future dominated by corporate power, unbridled consumerism, and biopolitical influence', arguing that K's subjectivity and consciousness should encourage us to 'pay more attention to the technological and global changes occurring in the 21st century through the mechanisms of the fourth industrial revolution'.

Finally, Trip McCrossin's chapter, 'Shortening the Way: Villeneuve's *Dune* as Film and as Project', puts Villeneuve's remake of *Dune* in conversation with all six of Frank Herbert's novels and with Brian Herbert and Kevin Anderson's two sequels, situating Villeneuve's contribution to the *Dune* universe as part of a greater project. McCrossin investigates the intersections between tragedy and optimism in Villeneuve's film and Herbert's novels, positing that the film's departures from the novels suggest 'a premonitory future in the spirit of the Kwisatz Haderach as "shortening of the way"'.

Editing this volume has given us the exciting opportunity to put all of Villeneuve's feature films, including those that have received little critical attention, into conversation with each other. The original analyses the authors provide here, from multiple critical and theoretical approaches (thematic, sociocultural, formal, ontological, feminist, allegorical, narrative, spectatorial, intertextual) offer a broad overview of Villeneuve's contributions to contemporary cinema, both in a Quebec context and with regards to his Hollywood films. Reading the chapters in order can offer perspectives on Villeneuve's progression from Quebec to Hollywood cinema; each chapter also stands alone as an analysis of one or more of his films. We hope that scholars, students and film buffs alike will be drawn into the cinematic world of this complex, intriguing director, whose work ranges from auteur films to genre cinema without ever being limited to either category.

NOTE

1. Villeneuve is a prolific director whose films have won multiple industry awards. His work, however, has not yet been the subject of a monograph in any language, with the exception of two recently published edited collections on *Blade Runner 2049*. See Bunce, Robin and Trip McCrossin (eds). Blade Runner 2049 *and Philosophy: This Breaks the World*. Open Court, 2019; and Shanahan, Timothy and Paul Smart (eds). Blade Runner 2049*: A Philosophical Exploration*. Routledge, 2020.

CHAPTER 1

Denis Villeneuve, Québécois and Citizen of the World

Amy J. Ransom

A successful international director, Denis Villeneuve's specificity as a Québécois nonetheless shapes his entire œuvre, a unified body of work despite its diversity. His Quebec-made auteur films and Hollywood forays into genre consistently engage a protagonist's identity quest, the problem of origins and reproduction, and involve literal and figurative border crossings. This chapter situates Villeneuve in the context of Quebec film, including his identification as a 'nouvelle génération' filmmaker (Chartier 145; Poirier 33n12).[1] It then engages his films' varying degrees of *québécitude* (Quebec-ness),[2] but also their increasing universalism (Privet 15).[3] I frame this discussion with the Deleuzian concepts of territorialisation and deterritorialisation,[4] arguing that Villeneuve's protagonists consistently leave the safety of home and its predetermined notions of identity, crossing borders to achieve a certain epiphany. I conclude that Villeneuve's entire corpus remains in touch with his Québécois origins, but his career trajectory embodies his generation's turn away from their forebearers' preoccupation with the (failed) nationalist project of sovereignty, reflecting a new aspiration to become citizens of the world.

ON THE CUTTING EDGE OF A NEW GENERATION

Quebec has developed a considerable cinematic tradition given its political status as a province of Canada, exceeding definitions of a 'small nation' cinema.[5] It produces both independent auteur films and Hollywood-style mainstream cinema and participates in a nationalist agenda of projecting an image of what it means to be Québécois. Referred to as 'Quebec national cinema',[6] French-language film produced largely in Montreal (although increasingly also in regional settings) feeds a collective 'historical imagination', maps out a specific territory, and reflects identitary models, consistently revealing its *québécitude*. This appears most obviously in locally rooted film settings, dialogue in vernacular Québécois French, references to a common (film) history, and portrayals of conflicted individuals unable to find a clear identity, allegories of their homeland's (post)colonial dynamics and ambiguous national status.

Quebec national cinema's history can be traced back to film's earliest days,[7] with modern filmmaking coinciding with Quebec's Quiet Revolution in the 1960s (Marsolais 16).[8] At first working in documentary, developing the *cinéma direct* style,[9] a generation of pioneers projected an image of the nation and its subjects using institutional frameworks developed by the federal Canadian state.[10] In the late 1960s and early 1970s, a distinct fictional form developed, marrying more-or-less scripted narrative with documentary techniques. In the 1970s and 1980s, partially spurred by provincial and federal funding bodies' demands for profitability, entrepreneurial filmmakers introduced commercial genre films, and Claude Jutra (1930–86) garnered an international reputation by producing Quebec's first 'heritage films'.[11] Turning to local classics, Gilles Carle (1928–2009) invented a form of popular but also critically acclaimed filmmaking, but Denys Arcand (b. 1941) brought contemporary Quebec to the world stage with *Le déclin de l'empire américain* (1986); his Academy Award for its sequel, *Les invasions barbares* (2003), set the stage for Villeneuve's later success. But in the early 1990s another innovator, Jean-Claude Lauzon (1953–97), galvanised film students with a new visual and narrative style that strayed from documentary realism. His *Léolo* (1992) turns one eye inward, playfully depicting the imaginary life of a boy growing up in Montreal's working-class, French-Canadian slums, but it also turns its gaze out onto the world, as Léolo fantastically imagines his Italian origins. This approach appealed to young directors, like Villeneuve, who wanted to break new ground,[12] as he insists: 'Currently, the majority of young Québécois directors have an urgent desire to tell stories with images and not only via the narrative. It's about time that cinema recover its true vocation' (Villeneuve, quoted in Castiel 24).[13]

Poised to take over from the largely self-taught prior generation, young graduates of Quebec's relatively new film programmes released their first fiction shorts and documentaries in the mid-1990s. Indeed, influential producer Roger Frappier's omnibus *Cosmos* (1996) showcased new talents,[14] including Manon Briand (b. 1964), cinematographer André Turpin (b. 1966), and Denis Villeneuve (b. 1967). A year later, Michel Coulombe argued that Quebec national cinema was at a turning point (35)[15] and innovative turn-of-the-millennium films like Louis Bélanger's (b. 1964) *Post mortem* (1999), Villeneuve's *Maelström* (2000), Turpin's *Un crabe dans la tête* (2001), and Briand's *La turbulence des fluides* (2002) fuelled discussions of a 'nouvelle génération'.[16] Born in the mid to late 1960s, they were seen as 'la relève' for the old guard (Privet 15) setting a new 'standard for alluring imagery, innovative narratives, and introspective characterization' (Melnyk 16). Greeted by some with enthusiasm, their visual stylings and elliptical narrative approach were decried by others as superficial.[17] Furthermore, their subject matter – frequently transgressing the boundaries of Quebec's home territory and seemingly uninterested in its collective history – was deemed not Québécois enough, and their commercial success viewed as compromising the integrity of a national auteur tradition.[18]

In this context, Denis Villeneuve rises to the fore of a new generation of Québécois filmmakers who also echo global cinematic trends.[19] A graduate of the Université du Québec à Montréal, Villeneuve began his career at Canada's Office National du Film/National Film Board, like his predecessors. But reviewers soon identified a rupture with the national filmmaking traditions, acknowledging nonetheless his significance as 'a major auteur talent' (Melnyk 17). Producer Roger Frappier jump started his career with a slot in *Cosmos*, 'Le technétium' (1996), and produced his first two fiction features, *Un 32 août sur terre* (1998) and *Maelström*. Although critics (sometimes grudgingly) acknowledged his aesthetic genius, they frequently decried the superficiality of Villeneuve's narrative treatment,[20] accusing him, along with other 'nouvelle génération' filmmakers, of an inappropriate lightness of tone, a fear of being too serious (Loiselle 49). His ludism, magical realism, and fairy tale aspects violate Quebec's tradition of social realism but thus distinguish his early films as pathbreaking. When Villeneuve turned his focus toward dramatic narratives grounded in historical reality in *Polytechnique* (2009) and *Incendies* (2010), some found his aesthetic sensibility morally offensive when applied to the problem of violence.[21] Given the ambivalent response to his work by critics at home in Quebec, Villeneuve must have felt validated when invited to bring his vision to Hollywood.

VILLENEUVE QUÉBÉCOIS

Christa Albrecht-Crane describes succinctly the key concepts derived from the work of Gilles Deleuze that frame this discussion. While on the one hand, '[t]erritorializations provide us with social identities' (Albrecht-Crane 124),[22] deterritorialisation disrupts this process. Rather than viewing this as a form of alienation, however, Deleuze 'argues that it is active, productive and affirmative' and 'makes forms of new thinking possible' (Albrecht-Crane 124). Similarly, as a young auteur, Villeneuve's work remains rooted in the soil of his home territory, but it also suggests that young Québécois must strike out on their own to break free from the national neurosis. He expresses ambivalence to the sovereigntist project, identifying himself as '"a confused separatist" who yearns for a new, positive start' (Monk 135)[23] and his protagonists seem similarly confused about their place in the world. Beginning with 'Le technétium', Villeneuve's work reveals the local preoccupations of contemporary Montrealers but also signals a yearning for the global. As the paths of a series of young Québécois cross through the back seat of a taxi driven by an immigrant chauffer named Cosmos (Igor Ovadis), *Cosmos*'s title and unifying premise mark a developing trend of looking beyond Quebec. Reflective of post-Quiet Revolution filmmaking, *Cosmos* recentres Franco-Québécois identity away from the agricultural past, placing it in the heart of the modern, even postmodern metropolis.

'Le technétium' satirises an earnest young filmmaker's encounter with a crowd of bilingual trendies. Cultural critic Simon Harel interprets its protagonist, Morille Zootrovski (David La Haye), as emblematic of the city itself, 'a character who writes the scenario of a wonky life, as if Montreal, in the aftermath of the 1995 referendum, was trying, once again, to propose some reference points and a way of living that would make it something other than a provincial capital' (65).[24] 'Le technétium' reveals those aspirations but also suggests their futility in its protagonist's alienation even in his home territory. Morille's existential angst appears in its opening sequence, as he vomits from the back seat of a taxi onto the streets of Montreal; his nervousness derives from his insecurity, fear about an inability to articulate himself in an upcoming television interview. His film's plotline reveals both Morille's desire to transcend the local and his inability to leave it behind; set in Cambodia, the adventures of his protagonists – identified in colourful Québécois French as 'un gars pis sa blonde' (a dude and his gal) – were inspired by his own personal experience: '[S]omething similar happened with my ex'.[25]

Morille's migrant-coded surname contrasts with his vernacular Québécois French, signalling an identity crisis reinforced on his arrival at the television studio (ridiculously established inside a hair salon) as its employees repeatedly address him as 'Maurice'. Unable to recognise him properly for who he is – a Québécois who is not called Turgeon, Tremblay, or Thériault – they reveal their own inauthenticity, assuming the stance of trendy bilinguals, plugged into international media trends, despite their residence in a culturally marginal city. *The Tekno Show*'s fast-talking host, Nadja (Audrey Benoit), speaks fluent franglais; her machine-gun delivery of meaningless terms, in which vernacular Québécois French alternates with English, targets young Québécois obsessed with Anglo-American popular culture. She interviews rocker Gilles Ouellette (Stéphane Demers) in (accented) English, purportedly because he doesn't speak French despite his name. Beneath their cosmopolitan façade, they remain culturally colonised French-Canadians.

There is not a little irony in Villeneuve's satire of late twentieth-century Montrealers' cultural aspirations focused entirely on the 'look' (Lahaie 99),[26] given critics' accusations that the beautiful imagery of his films similarly covers a philosophical void. But Morille, too, is a caricature; a bohemian artist with his stubbly beard, tousled hair, oversized coat and turtleneck sweater, he cares not about his appearance, but rather about ideas and emotions, revealing auteurist pretensions to express on film 'fragility, fear, and . . . time stretching out'.[27] But his alienating experience in the MTV-style studio leads to a traumatic break after a makeover by the semi-bilingual anglophone hairdresser/studio owner, Tekno (Carl Alacchi), using David Bowie's hair colour, 'Technétium cuivré 45'. After the reveal shot of his transformation into a trendy hipster with bleached blonde hair, Morille (Figure 1.1, seen as an unkempt Bohemian before and, viewed through a monitor to underscore the mediated nature of this image, after, Figure 1.2, the makeover by Tekno) – armed with electric hair clippers – takes Nadja hostage before fleeing onto the streets of Montreal.[28] In a moment of Jungian synchronicity, he finds refuge in a cab . . . driven by the now familiar Cosmos. Although satire is its vehicle, 'Le technétium' refocuses the Québécois gaze from the past, toward the future, rejecting the idea of settling down in favour of movement and the transitory, as Harel observes of *Cosmos* as a whole (Harel 64).

Un 32 août sur terre features a similarly confused, insecure Québécois male, Philippe (Alexis Martin), but his concerns appear secondary to those of his friend, Simone (Pascale Bussières). Villeneuve's first two fiction features shift their focus onto conflicted Québécoises, invoking contemporary discourses about the postfeminist subject.[29] In addition to their Montreal setting and francophone characters, *Un 32 août* and *Maelström* territorialise themselves by raising the question of reproduction, historically linked to the national imperative to perpetuate the French-Canadian 'race', as it was once conceived. But they also send their female protagonists on deterritorialising journeys – both triggered by automobile accidents – that lead to a *prise de conscience* (a realisation or a new awareness). *Un 32 août*'s title also signals the film's unconventional relationship to time, as Simone re-evaluates her priorities during a week out of time, from August 32 to August 36. Her identity crisis engages evolving notions of femininity, and her 'postfeminist' solution includes becoming a mother, so she asks Philippe to father her child. With the indecision frequently attributed to the Québécois male in film, Philippe expresses reluctance to bring a child into a rapidly evolving world that he cannot understand. Indeed, Villeneuve admits that *Un 32 août* was his 'comment on the Quebec neurosis. Why can't we make a decision?' (Monk 179). Philippe finally agrees, but on the condition that they make love in the desert; the couple cross the US/Canada border together, embarking on a strange journey in what Alanna Thain identifies as a heterotopic space.[30] As the couple walk through the bleak but beautiful landscape, Philippe admits his existential angst: 'The more I know things, the more I doubt. I manage less and less to understand the world around. It's crumbling.'[31] The film's sense of unreality is heightened by references to extra-terrestrials associated with the US Southwest, and it concludes enigmatically, leaving the

Figure 1.1 Morille (David La Haye) in 'Le Technétium', Villeneuve's contribution to the omnibus *Cosmos* (1997), before his make-over by Tekno.

Figure 1.2 Morille after his make-over by Tekno.

viewer, like its protagonists, without clear answers, suggesting alternately the futility of leaving home behind or the impossibility of returning unchanged.

Whereas Simone and Philippe experience a literal deterritorialisation, the protagonist of *Maelström* remains physically in Montreal throughout all but the final sequence of the film; instead, Villeneuve effectuates a metaphorical deterritorialisation through a compounded series of references to Norwegian culture.[32] Also focused on the formation of the heterosexual couple, it begins not with a conception but rather with an abortion. Rather than practicing responsible sex, Bibiane Champagne (Marie-Josée Croze) signals Generation Xers' perceived lack of concern for the consequences of their actions, as well as contemporary Quebec's break with its historically conservative Catholic morality; critiques of using abortion as a form of birth control have become almost a leitmotif in Quebec film since 2000. A female counterpart to Villeneuve's anguished men, the self-absorbed and rootless Bibi represents for the filmmaker a generation of privileged young Montrealers living off their parents' success, purportedly taking for granted the economic and cultural gains that baby boomers had won for francophones during the nationalist battles of the 1960s and 1970s.[33] As in *Un 32 août*, a car accident triggers a crisis when a drunken Bibi kills a middle-aged working-class Norwegian fish processor in a hit-and-run; haunted (although rather humorously) by the evidence of her own crime, Bibi fails even her own suicide. A first step toward atonement brings her face-to-face with her victim's son, Évian (Jean-Nicolas Verreault), to eventually find love and redemption with him; the film ends as the young lovers pour the ashes of the previous generation into the sea. Thus summarised, accusations of moral glibness appear justified, but *Maelström* must be understood through the lens of magical realism, as it transports its viewers from a relatively social realist – although always aestheticised through cinematographer André Turpin's lens – vision of contemporary Montreal into the fairy tale world of Bibiane's reality,[34] an estrangement further underscored by *Maelström*'s narrator, an animatronic fish (Pierre Lebeau). Villeneuve's most unambiguously happy ending suggests that Bibi has been successfully transformed by her figurative journey: '[T]he film succeeds in its primary goal of imposing a new vision, a new point of view on the world and on people' (Mandolini 35).[35]

Villeneuve's Generation X love stories might simply be written off as male fantasies; in *Un 32 août*, the dorky intellectual Philippe joins with the icily beautiful Simone, and *Maelström*'s stunning Bibi falls for the lanky, uncultivated Évian. But his most deeply rooted Québécois film memorialises the victims of an explicitly anti-feminist massacre at Montreal's École Polytechnique on December 16, 1989, valid criticism by feminist scholars notwithstanding.[36] Soberly filmed in black and white, devoid of a musical score, *Polytechnique* nonetheless fictionalises the events by refusing to name the killer (Maxim Gaudette) who, believing himself on a purging mission, targets female students admitted into a bastion of male

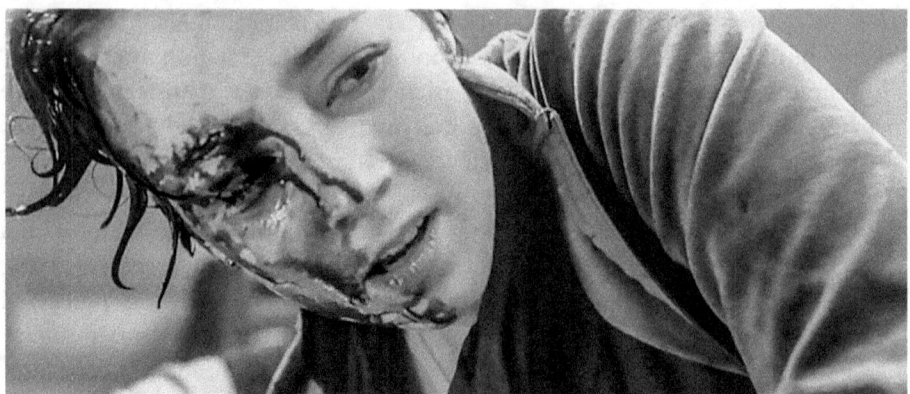

Figure 1.3 Val (Karine Vanasse), a survivor of the shooting in Villeneuve's *Polytechnique* (2009), returns to consciousness after the attack.

privilege, the science and technical college meant to prepare future technocrats to lead the nation into the modern era. Despite its undeniable *québécitude*, Villeneuve's only obvious engagement with the nation's sometimes overbearing historical memory left critics divided. Stephane Defoy nonetheless describes it as a contribution toward collective healing through memory, 'a collective outlet, an obligatory passage in order to finally begin the necessary process of healing' ('Exorciser' 22)[37].

Although it is Villeneuve's only film in black and white since 'Le technétium', *Polytechnique* nonetheless stands aesthetically with the rest of his œuvre due, in part, to its carefully planned imagery, including many close-ups, such as this image (Figure 1.3) of shooter victim, Val (Karine Vanasse). It also marks his first foray into the graphic, yet somehow aestheticised, portrayal of violence further developed in *Incendies*, *Prisoners*, and *Sicario*. Thematically, it joins his other works with its preoccupation with life and death, survival after violent tragedy, definitions of humanity and monstrosity, and even human reproduction, as it ends on a hopeful note with its female survivor, Val, learning that she is pregnant. In contrast with its female protagonist's ultimate resilience, *Polytechnique* depicts the Québécois male as powerless. Indeed, following the path of its anonymous killer, its partial hero, a fictionalised male survivor of the massacre emblematically named Jean-François[38] (Sébastien Huberdeau), eventually commits suicide. Villeneuve elides, in the post-9/11 anti-Muslim climate, a significant aspect of real-life perpetrator Marc Lépine's alienation, the child of a Québécoise and an Algerian. Despite the fact that he adopted his mother's French-Canadian name ostensibly to erase his own foreignness in Quebec, Lépine's suicide note attributed his actions to a personal war on feminism, implying his rejection of Quebec's official ideology of gender equality. *Polytechnique*'s refusal to explore the shooter's identity sets aside the question of deterritorialisation, but Villeneuve's next film approaches the question from a slightly different angle, exploring the problem of migrant identities in Quebec.

Set partially during the sectarian border conflict of the Lebanese Civil War (1975–90), among Villeneuve's Quebec-made films, *Incendies* most obviously signals his engagement with world citizenship. Its nomination for an Academy Award for Best Foreign Language Film also launched his international career. But *Incendies*, too, makes a distinct statement about Quebec as an evolving, multicultural society, adapting the work of an internationally acclaimed playwright. The Lebanese-born Québécois Wajdi Mouawad's œuvre explores trauma and hybridity in migrant identities; reflecting aspects of epic tragedy, his play *Incendies* (2003), exceeds the limits of social realism in its chronology and Œdipal plotline, revealing an affinity with Villeneuve's supra-realist storytelling.[39] The film's primary focal character, Nawal Marwan (Lubna Azabal), is a direct victim of the Lebanese Civil War and its violence; imprisoned and raped, she finally finds refuge in Quebec. Born in prison but raised entirely in Quebec, her children, Jeanne (Mélissa Désormeaux-Poulin) and Simon (Maxim Gaudette), however, are pulled into an identity quest after her death, triggered by the resurgence of her Lebanese torturer in the territory of Quebec. Franco-Québécois actors were cast in the roles of Jeanne and Simon,[40] a decision that may be viewed as a political statement about the necessity to reformulate Québécois identity to include diversity. By 'naturalising' Nawal's children as fully Québécois subjects, *Incendies* blurs boundaries between the territorialised Franco-Québécois 'Self' and its migrant 'Others'. Villeneuve describes it, though, as moving from the specific toward the universal:

> Neurotic anger transmitted from generation to generation is a theme that particularly touches me. To free oneself from childhood anger remains the ultimate step toward adulthood. The text's force is in carrying this idea beyond individuals and into the spiral of History. (Villeneuve quoted in Bertin 68)[41]

This propensity to find global meaning in the local, and vice versa, undoubtedly fuelled Villeneuve's transition from Montreal to Toronto and Hollywood.

VILLENEUVE, CITIZEN OF THE WORLD

After only two features, André Lavoie observes that 'Villeneuve has a traveling soul and his characters seem only in transit in Montreal, waiting for a departure to a more exotic elsewhere, or at least one unique enough to make them forget what they left behind' (61).[42] Like his protagonists, Villeneuve leaves home to achieve fuller self-realisation, but his decision to film in Hollywood was not uncontroversial.[43] Patricia Robin, however, expresses national pride in his success, defending Villeneuve and other talents like Jean-Marc Vallée (1963–2021) and Philippe Falardeau (b. 1968) for heading 'South':

> Obviously, playing with the big boys is part of the most secret dreams of most directors from here. They want to leave a system of subventions, gaining elbow room for productions of less constraining dimensions [. . .]. And, above all, they want to find a larger audience. (5)[44]

Ultimately, his defenders insist that 'even in Hollywood, Villeneuve is Villeneuve' (Perez-Delouya 55).[45]

Villeneuve's English-language corpus explores an array of realities beyond Quebec's borders, from the Canadian metropolis of Toronto (*Enemy*) to the suburban United States (*Prisoners*) and a fully globalised future North America (*Blade Runner 2049*), into an alien spaceship (*Arrival*) and out into the cosmos (*Dune*). That said, N. Christine Brookes argues that even his US/Mexico border thriller *Sicario* (2015) reflects Villeneuve's particular sensibility as a Québécois.[46] Although to a lesser extent – due to production conditions, including Anglo-American investments and screenplays written by others – Villeneuve's films in English reflect his home territory's preoccupations with language, technology, globalisation, and human connection. Furthermore, they engage the problem of identity linked to genealogy and reproduction, developing a problematic deeply rooted in Quebec's obsession with definitions of national and individual identity. He simply expands his development of this problematic to more literally universal stories, particularly in his Hollywood science-fiction films.

As a director for hire, Villeneuve loses, of course, some creative control and auteur clout established in Quebec. He is also forced to abide by the Hollywood genre system, beginning with the thriller, *Prisoners* (2013). On the other hand, he has the opportunity to work with an internationally reputed cast, including Hugh Jackman, Jake Gyllenhaal, and Terrence Howard, and a budget significantly larger than any of his previous films.[47] Based on an original screenplay by relative newcomer Aaron Guzikowski, *Prisoners* offers a conventional tale of vigilantism and sequestration as a suburban father (Jackman) holds prisoner a man (Paul Dano) suspected of kidnaping his daughter (Erin Gerasimovich). Although there is nothing overtly Québécois about *Prisoners*, its North American suburban setting and crime-linked plot resonate with recent trends in Quebec national cinema. Its suggestion that forces of deviance threaten the twenty-first-century family, and that, faced with a failed justice system, it must defend itself, appears in *Que Dieu bénisse l'Amérique* (Robert Morin, 2006) and *Les 7 jours du Talion* (Daniel Grou aka Podz, 2010), among others.

The former depicts a suburban community's paranoid reaction to the possibility that a child sexual predator lurks among them, and the latter explores more directly *Prisoners*' narrative of a father meeting out the eye-for-an-eye justice of Talion law. Adapted from a 2002 novel by Patrick Senécal, a writer frequently referred to as Quebec's Stephen King, *Les 7 jours du Talion* explores a father's grief and rage after his daughter's murder by a child predator. Furthermore, in the Quebec context, dramatisations of sequestration inevitably invoke a signal historical event: the October 1970 kidnaping of two government figures by the sovereigntist terrorist organisation, the Front de Libération du Québec (FLQ). Pierre Falardeau's claustrophobic *Octobre* (1994), released at the dawn of Villeneuve's career, dramatically recounts the internal struggles faced by the FLQ's Chénier Cell leading up to the death of provincial minister Pierre Laporte, and since 2010 several other films deal, more or less directly, with the October 1970 crisis.[48] Reading Villeneuve's American films through the lens of Quebec national cinema provides another layer of understanding[49] and, conversely, links film in Quebec to broader North American trends.

Villeneuve carries his deeply Québécois predilection for the male protagonist experiencing an identity crisis over to his second English-language release, *Enemy* (2013).[50] Although Charles-Henri Ramond notes a stylistic break with his previous works,[51] Villeneuve situates his first international co-production in relation to Quebec's canon, describing it as '[Denys] Arcand on acid' (Villeneuve quoted in Ramond 'Entrevue').[52] Despite its cosmopolitan origins, based on a novel by Portuguese Nobel laureate José Saramago, *Enemy* transposes familiar Québécois themes onto the English-Canadian landscape of Toronto. Adapted for the screen by Spain's Javier Gullón, it depicts identity troubles triggered by its protagonist's discovery of a living double, both played by Jake Gyllenhaal. Drawing on the Gothic *doppelgänger*, as a psychological thriller *Enemy* externalises Adam's mental anguish, blurring the lines between the subjective and the real, as he is haunted by a second self. Simon Harel's description of *Cosmos*, including 'Le technétium', as 'a fabulation, rather similar to Freudian discourse's primary process' (69)[53] applies equally well to Villeneuve's tentative early foray outside Quebec's filmmaking institutions.

Despite its European literary origins, *Enemy*'s tale resonates as specifically Canadian. Invoking tensions between Quebec and the Rest of Canada, described alternately through the metaphors of 'two solitudes'[54] – two entities cohabiting the same nation in isolation from each other – and 'Siamese twins',[55] the notion of the double allegorises the troubling national relationship between Canada's two so-called founding nations. From an Anglo-Canadian perspective, Quebec represents its disturbing other half, a destabilising double that, in some ways, defines its difference from that of the United States. From Quebec's point of view, the English presence represents one twin's conquest of the other, forcing it to become a repressed, less dominant ego. Read within the context of his œuvre, Villeneuve territorialises Saramago's universal theme as a specifically Québécois/Canadian parable.

After tackling the Canada/Quebec binary, Villeneuve's next film turns south: to the US, Quebec's 'South,' and Mexico, the US's 'South.' Dealing with border crossings and US/Mexico relations, *Sicario* indirectly concerns Canada and Quebec, particularly in the post-9/11 era.[56] Reviewing its aesthetic and thematic relationship to earlier border films, such as Steven Soderbergh's *Traffic* (2000) and the Coen Brothers' *No Country for Old Men* (2007), Brookes argues that 'Villeneuve is in dialogue with his director peers', but that he also articulates 'a postnational Canadian vision of a changing world to counter the dominant American narrative' (149). Written by actor Taylor Sheridan, *Sicario* is also a tale of lost innocence for DEA agent Kate Macer (Emily Blunt), as she is initiated into the realities of twenty-first-century law enforcement, constructing parallels between the war on drugs and the war on terror. Like other Villeneuve heroines, Macer undergoes a deterritorialising journey that leads to new (but troubling) understanding. *Sicario*'s engagement with globalisation is more than thematic; its production team including a Québécois director, a Puerto Rican-born star (Benicio del Toro), and two key players from the UK: director of photography Roger Deakins and lead actress Emily Blunt. Villeneuve first collaborated with Deakins on *Prisoners*, clearly developing – as he had for his Québécois films with André Turpin – a productive relationship that continued after *Sicario* to the more ambitious *BR 2049*. Both cinematographers contribute to Villeneuve's reputation for an affinity for vast desert-scapes that visually link *Un 32 août sur terre* and *Incendies* to *Sicario* and *BR 2049*. In both *Sicario* and *Incendies*, Villeneuve refuses to shy away from the spectacularisation of the violence, brutally revealing the human toll taken by state-mandated efforts to protect territorial boundaries. 'Faithful to his themes and reflections' (Robin 4),[57] *Sicario* implicitly condemns the nation-state's prerogatives and questions their relevance in the contemporary era, a deterritorialising stance that remains paradoxically territorialised as it engages one of Quebec's foremost political debates.

From that project about globalisation, Villeneuve moves to another that engages the cosmos as a whole with *Arrival* (2016), based on Ted Chiang's 'Story of Your Life' (2002).[58] Language and the dire need to communicate with humanity's Others are the core themes of this brainy science-fiction film, topics also at the core of Quebec's national dilemma. *Arrival* depicts how humanity's compartmentalisation of its territory, the planet Earth, into nation-states nearly results in its demise as rival governments scramble to decode the extra-terrestrial visitors' message, their presence spreading a panic that triggers the near breakdown of global civil society. Only the non-partisan efforts of an earnest linguist, Dr Louise Banks (Amy Adams), and her physicist partner, Dr Ian Donnelly (Jeremy Renner), uncover why the alien Heptapods have come to Earth, seeking help to resolve a problem of their own. Yet another deterritorialised heroine, Banks experiences – through her growing understanding of the Heptapods' language – a new, non-linear relationship with time that aligns well with Villeneuve's affinity for the suprarealist. She uses this experience to mitigate international tensions, forcing human governments to work together instead of at cross purposes.

This message of working together across boundaries can be read as distinctly federalist in the Canadian context, but the way in which *Arrival* foregrounds language is also deeply territorialised in Quebec. Once again, Villeneuve's choice of project, despite its global, even cosmic, scope connects him back to his Québécois experience. Banks must solve the mystery of the Heptapods' unique language, finding a way to communicate across the physical barriers that separate the two species. In so doing, she discovers that language informs reality; but whereas human languages constrain us within linear time, the Heptapods' transcends its confines. This sense that only by intimately knowing an Other's language can one reach some form of mutual understanding, but also that the Other's language holds something unique and enriching, applies metaphorically to Quebec. It is precisely through the French language that Quebec has defined itself, acknowledging its colonial past but also looking toward present and future, but it also seeks recognition by its Others for its distinctiveness. Additionally, *Arrival* engages a woman's decision (or not) to become a mother, seen in *Un 32 août*, *Maelström*, and even *Polytechnique*, as Louise's experience of time forces her to make a significant decision regarding the daughter to whom she addresses the titular 'story of your life'.

Villeneuve grew up on the French science-fiction comics that partially inspired Ridley Scott's *Blade Runner* (1982);[59] by extending its narrative even farther into the future, *BR 2049* further extrapolates the effects of globalisation, seemingly erasing the nation-state as a player. As a visual feast, provoking haptic sensory overload, *BR 2049* reflects the culmination of an aesthetic Villeneuve develops across his career, paying homage to a significant French influence, the 1980s *cinéma du look*. André Caron notes that *BR 2049* shares 'nostalgia and memories of a bygone era' (23)[60] with Jean-Jacques Beineix's signal 'look' film, *Diva* (1981),[61] a trait already present in 'Le technétium'.[62] Thematically, *BR 2049* explores the problems of identity and authenticity, but also of birth and genesis found in Villeneuve's earliest Quebec films.[63] Its story of the Replicant (an artificially developed humanoid), K (Ryan Gosling), and his quest for origins and identity, including recognition as fully human, resonates with an entire canon of Québécois literature and film that explores the alienation of the French-Canadian subject as a minority in its own homeland. Its revelation that Replicants have now become capable of self-reproduction, something K learns by connecting with an underground society that resists the oppressive capitalist-human regime of the majority, further echoes French Canadians' historical struggle for recognition of the francophone presence in

North America in the face of an Anglo-American majority. Villeneuve's most recent release, *Dune* (2021), further reflects his aesthetic and thematic preoccupations, brilliantly conveying the full potential that Frank Herbert's 1965 novel held for stunning visuals.[64] As with *BR 2049*, Villeneuve had a signal film precursor, David Lynch's 1984 adaptation, as a visual intertext to draw from. However, Villeneuve admits to being 'mesmerized' (Holub 49)[65] by the novel as a teenager and explicitly states his desire to remain 'closer to the spirit of the book' (Holub 49) than Lynch, a feat he accomplishes neatly with key film sequences built around the novel's most memorable moments. As a science-fiction saga, *Dune* engages with empire and colony, hidden genealogies, and messianic prophecy in ways that clearly resonate with dominant Québécois *topoï*,[66] so that, once again, Villeneuve brings his sensibility as a Québécois, a marginal, minority positionality, to a stunning visual retelling of an oppressed group's struggle to overcome adversity and not just survive, but eventually to conquer the universe.

CONCLUSION

This survey demonstrates a clear continuity between Villeneuve's Quebec-made films and those made in Hollywood, informed by his dual identity as both a Québécois and a citizen of the world. His career has unfolded out of a larger context in Quebec cinema's development from a small nation film preoccupied with local concerns into an industry exploring the full array of film genre expression. On the forefront of the so-called 'nouvelle génération' of filmmakers, Villeneuve developed a hybrid aesthetic that maintains aspects of independent, auteur film while exploiting the popular accessibility that genre film conventions allow, leading to the development of an 'auteur genre film'. His entire body of work reveals a common set of aesthetic and thematic preoccupations, and as Villeneuve insists: 'I don't feel exiled, but I feel that I continue to make films in a different way' (Villeneuve quoted in Vaillancourt 6).[67]

Within the national context, Villeneuve's career unfolded after the 1995 failure of Quebec's second referendum on sovereignty. As sovereigntist fervour appears to have waned, his career also played out in a so-called post-nationalist context of globalisation. Through its staging of protagonists' deterritorialisation, Villeneuve's work aspires to a form of universalism but nonetheless consistently loops back to his roots as a Québécois. Critics in Quebec frequently perceived his early work as in rupture with the timeworn traditions of Quebec national cinema. Instead, his early films depict characters that partake in that tradition's obsession with alienated local figures reflective of a national existential angst, but as his cinema evolves, Villeneuve represents through them (and in his own career trajectory) a *new* type of Québécois subject ready for the twenty-first century. Jolted out of their zone of (dis)comfort, they lift their gaze up and out, leaving behind their self-absorption to survive the crisis and reveal themselves as ready to take on the world.

NOTES

1. Chartier, Daniel, 'Le Cinéma du pays de la neige devient pluriculturel', *Études romanes*, vol. 59, 2009, pp. 141–53; Poirier, Christian, 'Le Cinéma québécois et la question identitaire. La Confrontation entre les récits de l'empêchement et de l'enchantement', *Recherches sociographiques*, vol. 45, no. 1, January–April 2004, pp. 11–38.
2. *Québécitude* is defined as 'the cultural specificity of the Quebec character' (Fournier 333), Fournier, Marcel, 'Quebec Sociology and Quebec Society: The Construction of a Collective Identity', *The Canadian Journal of Sociology*, vol. 26, no. 3, 2001, pp. 333–7.
3. Privet, Georges, 'Universalisme', *24 images*, vol. 105, 2001, p. 15.
4. This chapter builds on their application to *Maelström* in Ransom, Amy J., 'Deterritorialization and the Crisis of Recognition in Turn of the Millennium Québec Film', *American Review of Canadian Studies*, vol. 43, no. 2, June 2013, pp. 176–89.
5. Hjort, Mette and Duncan Petrie, 'Introduction', *The Cinema of Small Nations*, edited by Mette Hjort and Duncan Petrie, Indiana University Press, 2007, pp. 1–19.
6. Marshall, Bill, *Quebec National Cinema*, McGill-Queen's University Press, 2001.
7. For example, pioneering entrepreneur Léo-Ernest Ouimet opened one of North America's first film palaces in Montreal; see MacKenzie, Scott, *Screening Quebec: Québécois Moving Images, National Identity, and the Public Sphere*, Manchester University Press, 2004, pp. 72–3.
8. Marsolais, Gilles, *Cinéma québécois: De l'artisanat à l'industrie*, Montreal, Triptyque, 2011. For reasons of space, I have not been able to develop in detail much of the historical and cultural background of Quebec's development; see instead the essays collected in Gervais, Stéphan, Christopher Kirkey, and Jarrett Rudy (eds), *Quebec Questions: Quebec Studies for the Twenty-first Century*, 2nd edition, Oxford University Press Canada, 2016.
9. '"[D]irect cinema" refers first and foremost to a technique of simultaneous sound and image recording' (Loiselle 41), Loiselle, André, *Cinema as History: Michel Brault and Modern Quebec*, Toronto International Film Festival Group, 2007.
10. Ironically, Quebec national cinema developed out of the French-language branch of Canada's National Film Board/Office National du Film; see Zéau, Caroline, *L'Office national du film: Éloge de la frugalité*, Peter Lang, 2006.
11. Czach, Liz, 'The Quebec Heritage Film', *Cinema of Pain: On Quebec's Nostalgic Screen*, edited by Liz Czach and André Loiselle, Wilfrid Laurier University Press, 2020, pp. 41–60.
12. Melnyk, George, 'Quebec's Next Génération: From Lauzon to Turpin', *Ciné-Action*, vol. 61, 2003, pp. 10–17.
13. 'Actuellement, chez la plupart des jeunes cinéastes québécois, il y a un désir urgent de raconter des histoires avec des images et non seulement par le biais du récit. Il est grand temps que le cinéma reprenne sa véritable vocation.' Castiel, Élie, '*Cosmos*: les risques du métier', *Séquences*, vol. 188, January–February 1997, pp. 22–4; all translations mine.
14. Alioff, Maurie, 'The World According to Frappier', *Take One*, Fall 1997, pp. 24–33.
15. Coulombe, Michel. 'De quelques histoires inventées, ou le cinéma québécois des années 90', *Ciné-Bulles*, vol. 16, no. 2, 1997, pp. 30–5.
16. See note 1.

17. E.g. Loiselle, Marie-Claude, 'Au-delà des apparences: *Maelström* de Denis Villeneuve', *24 images*, vol. 105, 2001, p. 49.
18. Beaulieu, Simon, '*Ma voisine danse le ska*' (Review), *Séquences*, vol. 229, January–February 2004, p. 54.
19. Stylistically and thematically, their work aligns with successful arty films such as *Como agua para chocolate* (Alfonso Arau, 1992), *Magnolia* (Paul Thomas Anderson, 1999), and *Le fabuleux destin d'Amélie Poulin* (Jean-Pierre Jeunet, 2001), to name a few.
20. E.g. Barrette, Pierre, 'Le désert de l'âme: *Un 32 août sur terre* de Denis Villeneuve', *24 images*, no. 95, Winter 1998–9, p. 51; Lavoie, André, '*Maelström* de Denis Villeneuve', *Ciné-Bulles, Le cinéma d'auteur avant tout*, vol. 19, no. 1, Fall 2000, pp. 61–2.
21. Dequen, Bruno, 'Au mauvais endroit: *Incendies* de Denis Villeneuve', *24 images*, 148, 2010, p. 62.
22. Albrecht-Crane, Christa, 'Style/Stutter', *Deleuze: Key Concepts*, edited by Charles J. Stivale, McGill-Queen's University Press, 2005. It should also be noted that Deleuze rejects reterritorialisation as a reactionary move, privileging a lifelong 'becoming' over a more rooted sense of 'being' or identity.
23. Monk, Katherine, *Weird Sex and Snowshoes, and Other Canadian Film Phenomena*, Vancouver, Raincoast Books, 2001.
24. '[U]n personnage qui écrit le scénario d'une vie bancale, comme si Montréal, dans l'après-référendum de 1995, tentait, une nouvelle fois, de proposer des points de repère et une manière de vivre qui ne fassent pas d'elle une capitale provinciale.' Harel, Simon, 'Sur la banquette arrière d'un taxi montréalais: à propos de *Cosmos* (1996)', *Études littéraires*, vol. 45, no. 2, 2014, pp. 63–72.
25. '[I]l est arrivé quelque chose comme ça avec mon ex'.
26. 'Le technétium' paints a society in which 'apparences annihilent tout contenu, où le "look" a supplanté toute réflexion philosophique ou politique' (Lahaie 99), Lahaie, Christiane, '*Cosmos*: une drôle de promenade en taxi,' *Québec français*, no. 105, 1997, pp. 98–9.
27. 'La fragilité, la peur et . . . le temps qui s'étire'.
28. This sequence plays clear homage to Truffaut's *Les 400 coups* (1959); space prevents me from discussing the critical alignment of Quebec's 'nouvelle génération' with the French Nouvelle Vague.
29. I apply the term 'postfeminist' here following its application to Québécois theatre: 'The authors of these postfeminist plays no longer feel obliged to denounce patriarchal oppression, lament victimization, or make political demands. Having achieved material comfort, reconciled with their mothers, redefined their roles within the family, and reinvented motherhood on their own terms, postfeminist playwrights are free to work on issues of emotional and sensual satisfaction' (Moss 109–10). Moss, Jane, 'Passionate Postmortems: Couples Plays by Women Dramatists', *Doing Gender: Franco-Canadian Women Writers of the 1990s*, edited by Paula Ruth Gilbert and Roseanna Dufault, Fairleigh Dickinson University Press, 2001.
30. Thain, Alanna, 'A Texture in the Fold of the Real: The Heterotopic Fold of Denis Villeneuve's *Un 32 août sur terre*', *Nouvelles 'vues' sur le cinéma québécois*, no. 11, Fall 2010. See also Kester Dyer's chapter in this volume.
31. 'Plus je sais des choses, plus je doute. J'arrive de moins en moins à comprendre le monde autour. Ça s'effrite.'
32. See Ransom 'Deterritorialization'; see also Terrance McDonald's chapter in the present volume.
33. Generational tensions between baby boomers and their Gen X children have become a leitmotif in Quebec comedy, as seen particularly well in the *De père en flic* films.
34. Marie-Claude Loiselle describes the film's 'rapport paradoxal et inquiétant à la réalité' (49).

35. '[L]e film réussit son objectif premier, celui d'imposer une nouvelle vision, un nouveau point de vue sur le monde et les gens.' Mandolini Carlo, 'Beauté glacée: *Maelström* de Denis Villeneuve', *Séquences*, no. 211, 2000, p. 35.
36. See various essays in Blais, Mélissa, Francis Dupuis-Déri, Lyne Kurtzman and Dominique Payette (eds), *Retour sur un attentat antiféministe: École Polytechnique de Montréal, 6 décembre 1989,* Montreal: Remue-ménage, 2010.
37. '[Un] exutoire collectif, de passage obligé afin d'entamer un nécessaire processus de guérison' (Defoy 22). Defoy, Stéphane, 'Exorciser le mal: *Polytechnique* de Denis Villeneuve', *Ciné-Bulles*, vol. 27, no. 2, 2009, pp. 22–3.
38. Translated, the name comes out something like John-English; François derives from an outdated spelling of *Français*, Frenchman. The mirroring of these two male characters suggests another example of Jeri English's exploration of doubling in *Incendies, Enemy* and *Blade Runner 2049* in this volume.
39. 'Il s'agit en fait d'une transposition de la réalité dans un lieu imaginaire, comme Mouawad l'a faite au théâtre' (Villeneuve quoted in Defoy 'Denis' 43); 'in fact, it's about a transposition of reality into an imaginary site, like Mouawad did in the theatre'. Defoy, Stéphane, 'Denis Villeneuve, scénariste et réalisateur d'*Incendies*', *Ciné-Bulles*, vol. 28, no. 4, 2010, pp. 42–7.
40. Villeneuve explains the casting choice as resulting from practicalities but also a desire for authenticity; originally seeking 'de jeunes acteurs arabes' living in Quebec to reflect his characters' hybrid background, but unable to do so, he chose ethnic French-Canadians who resembled individuals seen in Lebanon (Defoy 'Denis' 44).
41. 'La colère névrotique qui se transmet de génération en génération est un thème qui me touche tout particulièrement. Se libérer de ses colères d'enfant demeure l'ultime passage à l'âtge adulte. La force du texte est de porter cette idée au-delà des individus mêmes, dans la spirale de l'Histoire' (Bertin 68). Bertin, Raymond, 'Prendre une pièce pour un scénario: entretiens avec Philippe Falardeau et Denis Villeneuve', *Jeu*, vol. 134, 2010, pp. 65–72.
42. 'Denis Villeneuve a l'âme voyageuse et ses personnages ne semblent à Montréal qu'uniquement en transit, en attente du départ pour un ailleurs plus exotique ou du moins assez singulier pour faire oublier ce qu'ils ont laissé derrière.'
43. Quebec's institutional film critics are generally hostile to Hollywood, viewed as an oppressive hegemonic force primarily interested in producing commercial junk; e.g. Barrette, Pierre, 'Made in Québec: Le cinéma Québécois, entre imitation et critique du modèle hollywoodien', *24 images*, no. 128, 2006, pp. 17–18; Loiselle, Marie-Claude, 'Téléfilm Canada ou le règne de la bêtise', *24 images*, no. 88–9, 1997, p. 3; and Loiselle, Marie-Claude, 'Éditorial', *24 images*, no. 121, 2005, p. 3.
44. 'Évidemment, jouer dans la cour des grands fait partie des rêves les plus secrets de la plupart des réalisateurs d'ici. Ils souhaitent sortir d'un système subventionnaire pour s'offrir des coudées plus larges et plus franches sur des productions aux dimensions moins contraignantes [. . .]. Et surtout, ils désirent s'adresser au plus grand nombre' (Robin 5). Robin, Patricia, 'La force tranquille: *Sicario* de Denis Villeneuve', *Séquences*, no. 298, 2015, pp. 4–5.
45. '[M]ême à Hollywood, Villeneuve est Villeneuve', Perez-Delouya, Asher, 'L'aboutissement d'une nouvelle démarche: *Prisoners*', *Séquences*, no. 287, 2013, p. 55.
46. Brookes, N. Christine, 'South of the 49th Parallel: Denis Villeneuve's *Sicario* (2015)', *Québec Studies*, vol. 65, no. 1, 2018, pp. 149–67.
47. Even *Incendies*, spectacularly filmed on two continents, came in at $6.8 million, in contrast with this relatively modest thriller's $46 million budget; imdb.com.
48. These include Alain Chartrand's *La Maison du pêcheur* (2013), Simon Lavoie and Mathieu Denis's *Corbo* (2014), and Luc Picard's *Les rois mongols* (2017).

49. Indeed, Alex Frohlick's paired analysis of *Prisoners* and *Sicario* in the present volume suggests the possibility of reading *Prisoners* as a national allegory: Villeneuve's statement about the illegitimacy of terrorism and the FLQ.
50. A topic developed by Jeri English in her contribution to the present volume.
51. Ramond, Charles-Henri, 'Méandres identitaires: *Enemy* de Denis Villeneuve', *Séquences*, no. 290, 2014, p. 53.
52. Ramond, Charles-Henri, 'Entrevue avec Odile Tremblay', *Le Devoir*, 8 March, 2014.
53. '[U]ne fabulation, assez semblable au processus primaire du discours freudien.' Tentative because *Enemy* was subsidised not only by Telefilm Canada but also by Société de Développement des Entreprises culturelles (SODEC).
54. Drawn from Hugh MacLennan's Montreal-set novel *Two Solitudes* (1945).
55. Drawn from John Ralston Saul's essay *Reflections of a Siamese Twin* (1998).
56. The action comedy *Bon cop, bad cop 2* provides a comic twist on Canadian perceptions of post-9/11 relations between the US and Canada.
57. 'Fidèle à ses thèmes et à ses réflexions.'
58. Chiang, Ted, 'Story of Your Life' (1998), in *Stories of Your Life and Others*, Vintage, 2016, pp. 91–146.
59. Scott was influenced by Moebius's *Métal hurlant* (1974–87); Bukatman, Scott, *Blade Runner*, BFI, 1997, p. 17.
60. '[L]a nostalgie et les souvenirs d'une époque révolue' (Caron 23). Caron, André, '*Blade Runner 2049*: Si seulement tu voyais le même film que j'ai vu', *Séquences*, no. 311, 2017, p. 23.
61. See Ransom, Amy J., 'The Director's Cut: Denis Villeneuve before *Blade Runner 2049*', *Science Fiction Film and Television*, vol. 13, no. 1, 2020, pp. 119–27.
62. Gendron, Thierry, '*Cosmos*' (Review), *Ciné-Bulles*, vol. 15, no. 4, 1997, pp. 57–8.
63. See Christophe Gelly and David Roche, and Kinsgley Marshall's chapters in the present volume; see also essays collected in a special issue of *Science Fiction Film and Television*, vol. 13, no. 1, 2020, dedicated to *BR 2049*.
64. Herbert, Frank, *Dune*, New York, Ace Books (1965), 2005. See Trip McCrossin's chapter included here.
65. Holub, Christian, '*Dune*', *Entertainment Weekly*, November 2021, p. 49.
66. See Ransom, Amy J., *Science Fiction from Quebec: A Postcolonial Study*, McFarland, 2009.
67. 'Je ne me sens pas exilé, mais je sens que je continue à faire du cinéma d'une manière différente.' Vaillancourt, Julie, 'Entretien: Denis Villeneuve', *Séquences*, no. 298, 2015, p. 6.

CHAPTER 2

Science Fiction, National Rebirth and Messianism in *Un 32 août sur terre*

Kester Dyer

INTRODUCTION

Two years after the successful anthology film *Cosmos* (Jennifer Alleyn, Manon Briand, Marie-Julie Dallaire, Arto Paragamian, André Turpin, Denis Villeneuve, 1996), Denis Villeneuve's debut solo feature, *Un 32 août sur terre* (1998) consolidated his status as the leading figure of a new generation of Quebec filmmakers. The so-called '*Cosmos* generation' reacted to established predecessors such as Denys Arcand, whom Villeneuve regarded as talented, but lacking in visual inventiveness (Alioff 31).[1] In turn, Villeneuve and others have, since 2005, become the object of an analogous response from the *renouveau* (Quebec New Wave) generation filmmakers, who display an aversion to the 'TV-commercial affectations' of the 1990s (Sirois-Trahan).[2] Indeed, at the time of its release, *Un 32 août* was criticised for privileging form over content, for having 'no clear vision of cinema or of life', and for attempting to mask a superficial storyline with beautiful images (Barrette 51).[3] Yet, the clashes that accompany such generational shifts also reveal telling continuities. The persistence of motifs alluding to Quebec's Catholic legacy and to mutating forms of nationalism, for example, significantly elucidate this geopolitical context. As such, *Un 32 août*, directed by an emergent filmmaker just a few years after Quebec's second failed referendum on political independence, proves especially indicative of the history of Quebec cinema and society.[4]

Premised on the miraculous 'rebirth' of the film's protagonist, Simone Prévost (Pascale Bussières), who walks away uninjured from a horrific car crash at the beginning of the film, and her consequent decision to reorient her life by having a baby, *Un 32 août* brings together two striking thematic elements. Firstly, the film exhibits persistent signs of Quebec's Catholic tradition through a counter-realist expression of the miraculous, versions of which occur in antecedent films like *La vraie nature de Bernadette* (Gilles Carle, 1972) and *Les dernières fiançailles* (Jean-Pierre Lefebvre, 1973), as well as in more recent productions like *Miraculum* (Podz, 2014) and *Il pleuvait des oiseaux* (Louise Archambault, 2019). Unlike the films mentioned above, however, *Un 32 août* draws on elements of science fiction, which emphasises the film's engagement with futurity, otherness, and knowledge. Secondly, by associating childbirth with the miraculous and with a reconceptualised temporal framework, *Un 32 août* links Quebec's religious tradition with the theme of rebirth, a premise which, in the years following the 1995 referendum's failed attempt at political genesis, proves particularly resonant.

Considering this, the following chapter focuses on *Un 32 août*'s historical and political context. Drawing on the concept of decoloniality developed by Walter Mignolo, I assess how *Un 32 août* foregrounds Quebec's failure to achieve nation-statehood and interrogate whether this film undermines the nation-state paradigm by pointing to genuinely different options, or simply refreshes a linear and Eurocentric 'discursive rhetoric of modernity' through its aesthetic innovations (Mignolo 'Decolonial' 110).[5] As part of this investigation, I consider whether Villeneuve's film echoes a vacuum in contemporaneous Quebec nationalism, which drifted away from its anticolonial and egalitarian objectives after the Quiet Revolution.[6] I thus seek to determine whether *Un 32 août* can be read as a symptom of Quebec's underlying dissatisfaction at the relegation of meaningful social and economic change by an ossified form of nationalism, and whether it harbours an implicit desire for forms of collective association distinct from the model offered by capitalist, liberal-democratic settler colonial states. Overall, this chapter argues that *Un 32 août*, although not a science-fiction film *per se*, aligns itself with this genre to resist entrenched links established between realism and nationalist politics in Quebec cinema, and that the film ultimately reinforces continuities by drawing upon the trope of childbirth to allegorise the reinvention of nationhood while buttressing Eurocentric assumptions about historical progress. As such, *Un 32 août* captures a postmodern period in Quebec cinema reflected in the work of the *Cosmos* generation filmmakers and beyond, following predictably from the emergence into modernity emblematised by Quiet Revolution filmmakers, who were themselves preceded by the 'premodern' films of Quebec's postwar era. Thus, while *Un 32 août* may destabilise Quebec's historical investment in religious and analogous forms of authoritarianism, the film's inability to radically break from conceptions of nationhood underpinned by linear Eurocentric worldviews extends this hegemonic perspective and, in fact, converges with the aims and patterns of contemporary Western secularism.

UN 32 AOÛT SUR TERRE AS SCIENCE FICTION

In *Un 32 août*, Simone experiences an epiphany after falling asleep at the wheel of her car and waking up inside the overturned wreck of her vehicle. Almost entirely uninjured after an accident that clearly should have been fatal, Simone gets picked up on the roadside by a passing motorist (Serge Thériault) and taken to a nearby clinic. She learns that it is the next day, August 32nd, the peculiar timeline confirming the counter-realist mode foreshadowed by her miraculous survival. After wandering on foot from the clinic, Simone finds a motel room for the night and, the next day, rejects the superficial life she had been leading up to that point as a jet-setting model. She cancels her trip to Italy, quits her modelling job, and summons her closest male friend, Philippe Despins (Alexis Martin), to conceive a baby with her. Philippe, who has been carrying a torch for Simone for years, buys time by accepting her request on condition that they make love in a desert, a suggestion that Simone readily accepts, declaring this kind of whim to be precisely what she loves about Philippe.

Although *Un 32 août* comes across as a romantic drama or dramatic comedy, several factors, including Villeneuve's subsequent career trajectory and recognition as a major science fiction auteur, indicate the plausibility of reading this film as science fiction. However, in contrast with Villeneuve's later films, *Un 32 août* only timidly asserts this generic identity. Of course, such hesitancy reflects the necessarily limited budget a debut solo feature implies. Villeneuve's deliberate restraint at the writing stage confirms his mindfulness of budgetary limitations ('Lorsque Pascale' G5),[7] which, coupled with longstanding resistance in Quebec to overtly non-realist films,[8] undoubtedly inhibited any latent ambition to realise a credible science-fiction film deploying all the spectacular potentialities of the genre. Nevertheless, several markers embedded in *Un 32 août* allude to specific aspects of science fiction. Among these, three generic conventions prove especially significant and indicate the value of this approach: the manipulation of time, a tendency to convey political allegory, and an overlap with religious experience via the figure of the alien messiah.

The unusual timeline of *Un 32 août* not only likens this film to science fiction, but also illuminates the extent to which it challenges Eurocentric pretentions to universalism. Indeed, *Un 32 août*'s strange temporality resembles a subset of science fiction labelled 'slipstream', a narrative style comprising a formal or narrative component that is 'estranging and anti-realist' (De Zwann 501).[9] Accordingly, Simone's unlikely survival of a car accident that would have proven fatal in any resolutely realist context (Figure 2.1) and the surreal extension of the month of August beyond its conventional thirty-one days immediately dissociate *Un 32 août* from realism. Moreover, according to Bruce Sterling, who coined the term in 1989, the strangeness generated by

Figure 2.1 Simone (Pascale Bussières) awakens on August 32nd, and miraculously walks away uninjured from the wreck of her car in *Un 32 août sur terre*.

slipstream narratives echoes that felt by living in the late twentieth century and applies especially to individuals described as sensitive,[10] an attribute that captures Philippe's quirky introspection, lack of assurance, and vulnerable emotional attachment particularly well. As such, following slipstream's opposition to 'consensus reality' (Sterling 78), *Un 32 août*'s slipstream temporality enables it to challenge universalism within the limits of the postmodern paradigm.

However, as Mignolo explains, postmodernity emerges as a logical extension of European modernity, which presupposes universalism. Postmodernity, for Mignolo, inevitably incorporates this Eurocentric logic by applying its own critique of modernity across the globe.[11] In contrast, decoloniality constitutes a paradigm that originates outside of European tradition and assumes that knowledge emerges from multiple de-centred regional perspectives (Mignolo *Darker* xvi). Consequently, decoloniality foregrounds temporalities that don't subscribe to the linear thinking of modernity as implied in Hegel's claim of a 'chronological and ascending unfolding of a universal human history' (Mignolo 'Decolonial' 110). The narrative of *Un 32 août* stresses its Québécois specificity, and its temporarily adopts an alternative or delayed chronology, which reflects this difference, but time continues to progress in a linear fashion in this film. Admittedly, the film's timeline allows for the simultaneous coexistence of at least two different narrative outcomes. The first takes the story at face value and follows Simone from her survival of the car crash, through her travels with Philippe to the Salt Lake desert of Utah where they fail to make love on two occasions (first in the desert itself, then in an airport capsule hotel room), and to the pair's eventual return to Montreal to their respective apartments. This plotline culminates with Simone reading a confessional love letter from Philippe and then reaching out to him, but before Philippe can join her, he is randomly attacked by a group of joyriders in Montreal's business district and rendered comatose. With Philippe left suspended between life and death in a hospital room, Simone locks the door and prepares to make love to him despite his unconscious state. In parallel, another plausible reading posits the whole film and its extended month of August as a figment of Simone's hallucinating imagination after her car accident places her, not Philippe, in a coma (Thain 22).[12] Regardless of the coexistence of multiple narrative possibilities, or of the unsettling effects generated by these alternatives, *Un 32 août* remains founded on linear (if somewhat unusual and destabilising) Eurocentric conceptions of temporality. Ultimately, after the attack on Philippe near the end of the film, dates stop extending endlessly into the month of August and the calendar catches up on days missed in early September, thereby restoring the film to a conventional calendar. Thus, by the end of the film, Villeneuve's protagonists have 'caught up' to the linear Western temporal axis and base their future on an acceptance of these dominant epistemological and universalising principles.

This 'catching up' evokes the promise of *rattrapage* guiding the rapid modernisation of the Quiet Revolution. Indeed, according to Mignolo, after the Renaissance and the Enlightenment, 'the postmodern invention of the acceleration of time' comprises the third key moment in 'the colonization of time'. Mignolo stresses that in the postmodern era 'to *fall behind* is to lose' and 'to go faster is to win' (*Darker* 177). These principles are foreshadowed and perhaps critiqued in the film via Simone, whose accident occurs precisely because she falls asleep at the wheel of a speeding car as she hurries to an important international assignment. Though Simone subsequently rejects this life, she upholds the linearity and urgency of its temporal framework in her plans to conceive a child, which forms the core focus of her new existence. Thus, she boasts to Philippe about her menstrual cycle's Swiss watch regularity, speedily locates the nearest desert to expediate the conception process and manifests palpable impatience at the slow awkwardness of the desert space itself, which is underlined by uncomfortably long takes. Arguably, the film suggests that it is precisely these reflexes that Simone must overcome, but the narrative's return to a conventional calendar at the end of *Un 32 août* and her impatient decision not to wait for Philippe to emerge from his coma seemingly yields to dominant temporal parameters.

Like the film's treatment of time, space in *Un 32 août* evokes a science fiction setting that potentially unsettles commonplace understandings of geography, but ultimately offers a competing Eurocentric vision rather than a fundamental challenge to such ideas. It thus also remains tied to Western conceptions of postmodernity. For instance, the desert (an iconographic element that reoccurs in Villeneuve's body of work), by recalling the whiteness of the wintery Quebec landscape (Thain 6), enables the film to blur national boundaries and emphasise analogical interconnections between Quebec and other areas of the North American continent. Similarly, a sequence that takes place in a futuristic space-pod-like Japanese capsule hotel at Salt Lake City International Airport where Simone and Philippe fail to make love for a second time, while an apparently random diversion from the central plotline, connects this claustrophobic setting to Québécois cultural and historical markers via the soundtrack. This sequence deploys the opening sounds of the classic Québécois psychedelic rock song *Lindberg* (1968) composed by Robert Charlebois and Claude Péloquin and performed by Charlebois with Louise Forestier. The use of this song underscores the hotel room's similarity to a spacecraft, which is further emphasised by Philippe's comical mimicking of the effects of weightlessness (Figure 2.2). Villeneuve limits himself to the song's opening sound effects, which creates a mood reminiscent of David Bowie's celebrated opening to *Space Oddity* (1969)

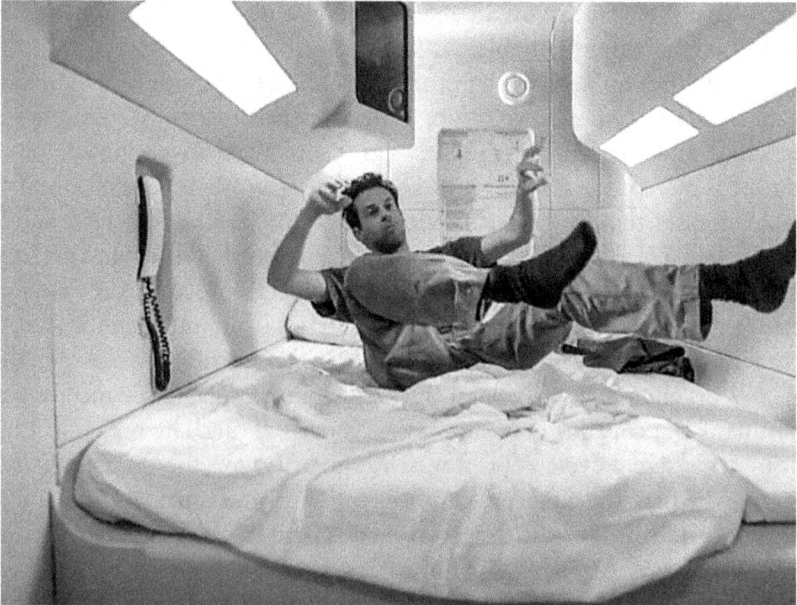

Figure 2.2 Philippe (Alexis Martin) mimicking the effects of weightlessness inside the Japanese capsule hotel room in *Un 32 août sur terre*.

and evokes, for anyone familiar with the chorus of *Lindberg*, a litany of references to airline companies that also drifts off surreally into orientalist clichés about modes of transportation like camels and magic carpets. Reflecting contemporaneous media preoccupation with the space race, the song's combination of allusions to aircraft, airline companies (including the local Québecair), as well as exoticised forms of travel, insists on global connections, but also evokes Western assumptions about science, exploration, evolution and progress frequently intertwined within science fiction narratives. Thus, the sequence satirically interrogates Quebec's spatiotemporal position in an imagined hierarchy of cultures. The reference to *Lindberg* enhances the film's attempt to complicate borders between Quebec, the United States, and the rest of the globe from Quebec's perspective as a historically marginalised minority culture. However, for Mignolo, border thinking implies different epistemological foundations. The question remains then, to what extent does the portrayal, in *Un 32 août*, of one historically marginalised European settler culture rubbing against another unquestionably more hegemonic counterpart generate subversive possibilities that fundamentally challenge dominant geopolitical paradigms?

POST-REFERENDUM REBIRTH

As Vivian Sobchak points out, science fiction tends to tackle problems on a social rather than individual scale, with issues that affect arenas such as 'the large city, the planet Earth itself' (30).[13] As such, thinking of *Un 32 août* as science fiction meaningfully extends the portrayal of its protagonists to their broader national group and enables us to explore the relationship Quebec continues to elaborate with the North American continent. Accordingly, the current chapter builds on ideas put forward in a thought-provoking article by Alanna Thain, and insists on their applicability to the historical, sociopolitical and cultural context of Quebec. For Thain, the desert in *Un 32 août* functions as 'what Michel Foucault calls a heterotopia, a counter-site of as-yet unactualized potential' (2), a site of transformation (7), and 'an ethical encounter' (13). Thain observes that the bodies of the film's central couple are staged in such a way as to be 'overwhelmed by their environment', where their relation is not limited to themselves, but also includes their milieu (13), and specifies that, for Foucault, heterotopia relates to the 'uncertain geography of the body itself', which notably includes pregnancy as a physical condition (15). *Un 32 août* displays this insofar as 'the desire for a child is almost exclusively imagined through the mutability of pregnancy itself' and the physical changes this will bring to Simone (Thain 15). By extension, the mutability of the body and its potential to generate new life echoes the political geography of Quebec, as well as the mutability of the coveted nation-state and its borders. Indeed, in the wake of the 1995 referendum, opponents to Quebec sovereignty undermined this option precisely by suggesting the divisibility and mutability of the territory known today as Quebec. This example highlights the transformative importance of the heterotopic space, the effectiveness of which also suggests that in the post-referendum context of the film where Canadian and Québécois borders have been reaffirmed, heterotopia may yet offer the possibility of the nation mutating into other forms of collectivity, and thereby circumvent the frame imposed by borders to move beyond the Eurocentric nation-state paradigm.

In this respect, *Un 32 août* capitalises on the deployment of the trope of rebirth to re-conceptualise national foundations inscribed memorably in the history of Quebec cinema by Anne Claire Poirier's seminal feminist documentary *Les filles du Roy* (1974). In contrast with Poirier's work, Villeneuve's film displays no explicit commitment to ideological shifts, but nonetheless mirrors a contemporaneous movement to embrace *américanité* (Americanness), which, during the 1980s, became the dominant paradigm for Québécois to ground themselves in North America (Dupont 27).[4] Distancing Quebec from French colonial history (Dupont 43), *américanité* posits 'Americanness' as a positive aspect of Québécois identity and views the American continent as 'an opportunity' (Dupont 45). In *Un 32 août*, Simone's decision to reinvent herself by conceiving a child in the heart of North America reframes Québécois identity in terms of *américanité*. However, Villeneuve's reuse of the trope of national rebirth mobilised more radically by Poirier a generation earlier paradoxically mitigates his film's departure from tradition. Moreover, the influence of the French new wave on both *cinéma direct* and *Un 32 août*, which pays homage to this film movement in several scenes, precludes any emphatic ideological shift, manifest iconoclasm, or break with Europeanness, maintaining what Mignolo describes as the logic of modernity, and largely extending fundamental viewpoints promulgated by the Quiet Revolution into a postmodern era.

The nominal nature of *Un 32 août*'s break with tradition coupled with the constancy of its epistemological principles, framed within a discourse of freshness characteristic of emerging artistic movements, converges with its engagement with the themes of hypocrisy and betrayal. Drawing an astute connection between the white decor of a motel room near Montreal where Simone spends the night after her life-changing accident and the whiteness of the Salt Lake desert, as well as the capsule hotel where she and Philippe attempt to make love a second time, Thain observes that *Un 32 août* 'inverts the managed heterotopia of the motel' proposed by Foucault 'to ask how, and where, such infidelity could happen otherwise, and what that infidelity could be' (8). For Thain, the infidelity these actions imply for Philippe's girlfriend Juliette (Évelyne Rompré) becomes 'an infidelity to the self' (9). Reading the film more broadly, this extends to the betrayal of an imagined national self or ideal and hints at how nationhood should be reconceived, on what foundations such a re-genesis can happen. As Thain states, 'The struggle in *Un 32 août sur terre* is about how to live an impossible present and how to imagine another future into existence' (13). The impossible present alluded to here is redolent of the humiliating post-referendum period through which Québécois must painfully trudge for a second time, mirrored in Simone and Philippe's two failed attempts to make love, while the other future invokes a reconceptualised collective project based on fresh (and more viable) ideological grounds. The difficulty of concretely imagining such a project so soon after the devastating failure of the 1995 referendum and the recentness of this hurt further justifies the pertinence of Villeneuve's recourse to non-realist modal and generic options. The desert's whiteness is significant, not only for its sensorial connection to the motel room, but also because it invokes the totalising perspective of the film title's reference to the whole Earth. As a stand-in for the entire planet, and as the site of re-genesis enacted by a heterosexual white settler couple, the desert's emptiness recalls the iconographic landscapes of that other Hollywood genre closely associated with colonial representations: the Western. Consequently, it evokes the colonial concept of *terra nullius* embedded in both mainstream Western and science fiction narratives, which presume the inherent benevolence of 'New World' re-geneses carried out without the consultation of Indigenous peoples (or their alien stand-ins). For Quebec more specifically, this implies that the reinvention of its collective identity is again being elaborated without any kind of Indigenous partnership or participation, following what Mignolo describes as the logic of modernity/coloniality, which evacuates, not only other (living) human presences, but also epistemological conceptions of humanity that are distinct from Western ones. For Thain, Simone and Philippe's adultery proves unethical, not because they are betraying Juliette, 'but because they resist the idea that anything will truly change as a result of their encounter' (13). On a wider level, the moral dimension that Thain attaches to the refusal of meaningful change suggests a lack of transformation in the conception of Quebec nationhood and the betrayal that such inertia implies to all populations living on this territory.

By highlighting self-betrayal in *Un 32 août*, Thain makes visible the correlation between this theme in Villeneuve's film and Ernest Renan's famous formulation of nationhood, which rationalises self-deception, positing that to ensure the nation's existence one must selectively forget negative aspects of its history. Indeed, Thain observes that Simone and Philippe 'ignore or selectively sample their own past' to carry out their plan to conceive a child (13). More precisely, she argues that to construct the future embodied by the generative act, Philippe must 'resist a present' determined by his 'memory of the pain caused by his love for Simone' while Simone must also resist a present determined by her 'dissatisfaction with her shallow existence' (13). Allegorically speaking, the recentness of Philippe's painful memory associates his love for Simone with the emotional heartbreak felt by sovereigntist Québécois in the wake of the second failed referendum. On the other hand, Simone's sudden dissatisfaction with her shallowness and sharp turn away from this lifestyle suggests a parallel attraction to a more utopian national ideal. This echoes disappointment in the kind of nationalism justified by and promoted with practical economic motives and strategies over one based on an egalitarian and anti-colonial social project. The former approach, adopted more overtly by the 1995 yes campaign, renders the sovereignty project a redundant copy of other settler colonial states, including Canada, and therefore morally unattractive. However, even in its less transparently oppressive manifestations, the Western nation-state model conceals ethical contradictions. In *Un 32 août*, even though Simone rebuilds her life on purportedly new foundations, the determining influence of a flawed structure lingers and continues to determine her actions, which are characterised as directionless and fickle.

Because of its persistent underlying flaws, the revised national model conjured by spontaneous life-changing decisions in *Un 32 août* leads to the repetition of past failures. For instance, in his confession letter to Simone explaining that he cannot have sex with her nor see her again because he truly loves her, Philippe assigns different local and global territories to each of them so that they may avoid awkward encounters in the future. This partition of the world constitutes a colonial gesture evocative of French and British imperialisms, which in turn points to Quebec as a specific site of conflict between these two major powers in North America as well as the ongoing exclusion of Indigenous and other minority perspectives overshadowed by the preservation of Canada's 'two solitudes' dichotomy. Notably, Philippe reserves the area east of Saint-Laurent Boulevard in Montreal, which is traditionally associated with the city's francophones in opposition to the predominantly English-speaking western section of the city. Near the end of the film, Simone whispers tenderly to Philippe as he lies in a coma, jokingly communicating her intention to negotiate the specific terms of world partition and stressing her desire to keep India for herself. Simone thus accepts the colonial parameters proposed by Philippe. Temporarily setting this negotiation aside though, she highlights procreation as the immediate priority and looks to have sex with Philippe unimpeded, thereby emphasising reproduction and simultaneously evoking the legendary *revanche des berceaux* of Quebec's era of *survivance*,[15] a period that peaked during the late nineteenth and early twentieth centuries characterised by self-preserving insularity and centred on traditional values, most notably the Catholic Church, the French language, and rural life. Insofar as they merely react to the threat of personal (and by extension cultural) disappearance, Simone's bases for a new collectivity are similarly defensive and lack utopian vision. Furthermore, Simone's desire to procreate first and ask questions about territorial boundaries later, while acknowledging and maintaining borders as an organising principle, exposes Quebec's corollary anxiety surrounding immigration. Indeed, soon after her car accident, Simone is warned by a doctor (Ivan Smith) whose background is Indian that she may experience short-term memory loss, a prediction the film never explicitly follows through on. Only at the very moment the doctor announces this symptom as a possible consequence of her accident do we see its clear manifestation when he tests her memory using his own name and origins as an illustration. Tellingly, Simone's memory appears to block out (or selectively forget) information about his 'foreignness' (India strangely being the very country she later covets), and it is shortly after this experience that she urgently decides to conceive a child with her white francophone friend. As with previous iterations of Quebec's nation-state project then, the re-genesis proposed by Simone and Philippe remains marred by colonial principles and the exclusion of difference, its purported shift to a new paradigm of *américanité* ultimately revealing itself to be directed by values that overlap with and extend those of *survivance*.

MESSIANISM AND RELIGIOUS CONTINUITY

The continuities observed above correlate with similar threads linking religiosity, secularism and Western science and are embodied by the counter-realist cinematic tropes deployed in *Un 32 août*. In an essay focusing on a film by another *Cosmos*-generation filmmaker, *La turbulence des fluides* (Manon Briand, 2002), Erin Manning argues compellingly that this film exposes analogies between Quebec's Catholic tradition and what she describes oxymoronically as 'spiritual nationalism' and 'religious atheism' (1).[16] Manning provocatively suggests that 'the secular and the scientific call forth a certain religiosity that, despite secularization in Quebec – or perhaps even because of it – continues to be at play within Quebec cinema' (3). Paradoxically, contemporary antagonism to conspicuous religious expression in Quebec is reminiscent of the very fundamentalism that secularism seeks to denounce, a contradictory uniformity consistent with the cyclical and somewhat hollow reformulation of both film movements and Eurocentric worldviews under the respective guises of innovation and progress, which are underpinned by steadfastly linear constants. Moreover, collusion between religious fervour and unshakeable faith in the objectivity of Western science, largely disavowed in mainstream contexts, becomes foregrounded in the science-fiction trope of the 'alien messiah' identified by Hugh Ruppersberg. In accordance with its subtle assertion of science fiction tropes, *Un 32 août* relies on the absent presence of the alien messiah rather than its explicit manifestation, partially announcing such a figure via Philippe and the dynamics of his relationship with Simone. According to Ruppersberg, the alien messiah is 'an overtly or covertly religious personage, whose numinous, supra-human qualities offer solace and inspiration to a humanity threatened by technology and the banality of modern life' (33).[17] While Simone's story stems from a disaffection that

Ruppersberg describes as 'feel[ing] trapped in a meaningless, trivial existence' (33), Philippe is far from possessing 'supra-human qualities'. Rather, he recalls Quebec cinema's typical unassertive male protagonist and echoes the disparaging self-derision of Québécois regarding their failure to seize their own political destiny. Nevertheless, his affective idealism works to inspire (or evangelise) Simone following the car accident that instigates a change in her viewpoint on life. Philippe's love for Simone and refusal to participate in her project because it adulterates this idealism extends to Quebec's relationship with its own national project.[18] Indeed, by sabotaging their plans to make love, Philippe refuses 'what should have been the most beautiful moment of [his] life'. Strongly attracted to Simone's proposal, he yet hesitates to carry it through. When she takes his indecision as a green light to go ahead with the plan, he exclaims, 'Wait! I didn't say yes', adding that he will say yes, but 'on one condition'. Philippe's hesitation to embrace what he desires most, his clinging to an unsatisfying alternative, and the ludicrous condition that he imposes on Simone, echo the absurdly roundabout first referendum question on sovereignty-association, as well as Quebec's persistent reluctance to boldly seize political independence, all the while remaining unattracted and unable to adhere earnestly to Canadian federalism or identity.

Villeneuve's subtle deployment of the alien messiah trope in *Un 32 août* also allows the film to explore Quebec's ambiguous relationship with the United States as a more dominant settler colonial nation. Ruppersberg makes clear how the alien messiah mirrors, through inversion, colonisers cast as superior, godlike, benevolent civilisations seeking to redeem the 'uncivilised' (34–5). Such fantasies of being saved by superior beings, which disavow settler colonial aggression, become doubly pertinent in Quebec where white francophone settler culture has historically experienced devaluing patterns characteristic of colonial relationships (Memmi 138–41),[19] and where ambiguity persists in Quebec's self-perception as both coloniser and colonised. In *Un 32 août*, a significant close-up emphasises a book read by a taxi driver (Richard S. Hamilton) at Salt Lake City International Airport, whom Simone and Philippe hire to take them to the Great Salt Lake desert where they plan to conceive their child. Tellingly, the shot reveals the book's title as *How to Develop Friendship with Extraterrestrials*, ironically coding the Québécois couple as 'alien' visitors, but also indicating the taxi driver's desire for an encounter with literal extraterrestrials, a desire seemingly shared by Simone who later excitedly points to a UFO as she sits in the desert with Philippe. Complementing the film's title which stresses the whole Earth as a setting for the narrative, these longings to befriend extraterrestrials and the tense encounter that ensues between the taxi driver and the Québécois visitors recall commonly conflictual first contact tropes between humans and aliens in science fiction films as well as the alien messiah pattern epitomised in Villeneuve's later Hollywood film *Arrival* (2016).

Clearly though, Simone and Philippe do not correspond to the kind of 'superior' aliens the taxi driver hopes to befriend. Indeed, he displays only contempt for these odd foreigners and does not hesitate to exploit their vulnerability. On the other hand, the Québécois pair are presented as intellectually and morally more complex than the crass, opportunistic and ultimately violent taxi driver who extorts money from them, remains unimpressed by the astounding beauty of the desert, and finally injures Simone before abandoning them in the desert. Yet, insofar as Simone and Philippe's purpose is one of resurrection and rebirth, their encounter with the taxi driver, as well as their later discovery of the charred and handcuffed body of a murdered man in the desert, insinuates the challenges sophisticated aliens face in communicating with brutal Earthlings. Indeed, consistent with several of Amy Ransom's observations on Quebec science-fiction cinema (8–9, 16),[20] *Un 32 août* de-centres the United States from the narrative by privileging a self-derisive tongue-in-cheek tone that also satirises United States and Hollywood hegemony. In this respect, *Un 32 août* adopts the perspective of two Québécois who, as knowing but somewhat astonished and bumbling outsiders, look down on the shortcomings of US power from the margins, thereby aligning themselves with messianic aliens.

By irreverently intimating the evangelistic potential of French-Canadian culture via the figure of the alien messiah, and by situating a narrative founded on anxieties of *survivance* in a context that accentuates *américanité*, Villeneuve exposes the compatibility between these two paradigms generally contrasted and associated with different eras of Quebec history. Of necessity preoccupied with ensuring continuity, *survivance* is associated with the dominance of clerical elites hostile to emigration to English-speaking areas of North America and who fear the attrition of French-Canadian culture. Appropriately, the premise of *Un 32 août* encapsulates Québécois' contradictory attraction to America. The perceived precarity of Simone and Philippe's lineage mirrors Quebec's own cultural-linguistic and demographic anxieties. Simone's accident and realisation of her own mortality explicitly trigger her decision to become pregnant, as evidenced by her declaration to Philippe that '[she] could die anytime' if she doesn't have a child, and her toasting of the baby they plan to have as their '*descendance*'. Filmed in the Great Salt Lake desert where the procreative act is intended to take place, the couple are often framed in extreme wide shots that render them tiny specs in a massively imposing landscape and invoke Québécois' longstanding fears of being a small francophone enclave overwhelmed by a whole continent of anglophone culture.

However, certain inflections of the ideology of *survivance* expound the view that French Canadians hold a missionary purpose to Catholicise North America in opposition to the Protestant influence on the continent (Dumont 30–31). *Un 32 août* reformulates this exalted role as an evangelistic version of *américanité*, thereby stressing a correspondence between the two concepts. Although the taxi driver's dismissive attitude and the anonymousness of Philippe's call to the police about the dead body that he and Simone find in the desert signal the imperceptibility of Quebec's impact on America, its discreet evangelism nonetheless coheres with Villeneuve's own professional ambition to make incursions as a Québécois filmmaker in Hollywood. Even as a prominent director, Villeneuve's power to globally disseminate profound aspects of Québécois culture through Hollywood films remains admittedly limited. Yet, preoccupations characteristic of his own cultural background implicitly underpin the main theme of *Arrival,* which focuses centrally on how knowledge and civilisation are shaped by language, undoubtedly one of the most significant markers of Québécois identity. Indeed, this later film shares with *Un 32 août* a contempt for aggressive US power and violence and expresses more explicitly and ambitiously the alien messiah trope explored by Villeneuve in his debut feature.

Through the figure of the alien messiah then, Villeneuve's film links miraculous survival and procreation, as well as Quebec's *survivance*, underpinned by religious doctrine and transposed into a secular religiosity compatible with the concept of *américanité*, which is conceived here not only as Quebec partaking in and embracing the American continent, but didactically attempting to shape the cultural hegemony of the United States. As Ruppersberg observes, '[u]nderlying the motif of the alien messiah is the mythos of the Christian messiah, begotten by the divine Jehovah on a mortal woman, sent to redeem a sin-ridden humanity and offer immortality' (34). Although Philippe seemingly bears no divine characteristics, his role in *Un 32 août* as Simone's designated impregnator reveals a secularised desire to redeem Quebec from its previous failed national incarnations and ensure the ongoing viability and influence of this culture according to the logic of *survivance*. Philippe and Simone also display the understated evangelistic dynamic of *Un 32 août* and the convergence of Quebec's religious past and secular present via biblical namesakes, and through Philippe's repeated use of a particular Québécois ecclesiastical curse, the somewhat outdated and mild 'simonac'. As with many Québécois curses, this word invokes Quebec's fraught relationship with the Catholic Church and abrupt severing from its dominance, a historical transition paradoxically highlighted as absolute even as its continuities are audibly manifested by such expressions. Given the similarity of this exclamation to Simone's name, it cannot fail to also evoke Philippe's personal frustration with her. Interestingly, the etymological origin of the word refers to the religious crime of simony perpetrated by Simon Magus, famously converted to Christianity by none other than Philip the Evangelist (Glazier 130).[21] The biblical namesakes of the main protagonists may seem coincidental, yet they underscore *Un 32 août*'s invocation of the religious dimensions that underpin Quebec history and society, which correspond to what Mignolo describes as the salvational aspect of 'the rhetoric of modernity', whether manifested through religious conversion or adherence to economic doctrines of 'progress' or 'development' (*Darker*, xxiv).

When considered in the context of national allegory, Simone and Philippe's biblical namesakes inform specific tensions at play in *Un 32 août*'s vision of a reconceptualised Quebec nationhood. The ecclesiastical crime of simony refers to the trafficking of the spiritual through material means. Originating with Simon Magus who attempted to purchase the miraculous power of laying on hands (Glazier 131), this crime has since become associated with Simon's name and consequently with the curse 'simonac', of which Philippe is so fond. Meanwhile, Simone's backstory depicts her as superficially capitalising on her image for profit. Although the miraculous car crash initiates her conversion to an apparently more meaningful existence, she continues to haggle to achieve loftier goals. A prior 'deal' with Philippe draws him into her plan to have a baby. It is Simone who negotiates with the taxi driver for access to the desert and who comments upon the cost of the Japanese capsule hotel. Moreover, she admits the ideological vacuousness of her project from the outset when Philippe asks her what she will do after quitting her job. 'Nothing', she responds, adding: 'It's not easy to do nothing. Have you tried? [. . .] Want to do nothing with me?' Only Philippe's confessional letter eventually 'converts' Simone to a fuller commitment to love as an ideal upon which to base their offspring's future. The 'miraculous' act of perpetuating human life on Earth or by extension of perpetuating a collective identity cannot be negotiated with money, the film suggests: it must be conceived idealistically. And although Philippe's letter is ostensibly successful in evangelising Simone, the film forecloses on his own active participation in the execution of her venture. In fact, Philippe's behaviour seems to anticipate or wish for the arrival of an alien messiah, *deus ex machina*, an arbitrary mechanism embodied in the film's deceptively random violent events, a car accident and a beating that reorient the two protagonists' narratives and transform them.

CONCLUSION

Albeit a film emblematic of the *Cosmos* generation emerging in the late 1990s and displaying a willingness to depart from the dominant realism of the Quebec corpus, *Un 32 août* owes a debt to NFB filmmakers of the 1960s, especially, but not overtly, Anne Claire Poirier, whose memorable deployment of the trope of national rebirth Villeneuve's film repurposes. Furthermore, comparisons between *cinéma direct* and the more recent *renouveau* generation, and debates about how to clearly distinguish Villeneuve's work from the latter movement,[22] underscore the partly arbitrary nature of such trends. More importantly, an epistemological continuity is reflected in counter-intuitive overlaps between religiosity and secularism/science, *survivance* and *américanité*, as well as (post)modernity and coloniality, which *Un 32 août* exposes as false dichotomies via the figure of the alien messiah. Thus, Villeneuve's film exhibits an ironically self-deprecating portrayal of the central male character as either alien messiah or as announcing this figure, a role and a sardonic posture that extends to Quebec and arguably to Villeneuve's own status as auteur.

Although *Un 32 août* ostensibly centres on a female protagonist, the male protagonist's emotional perspective dominates. The viewer shares Philippe's secret feelings about Simone, while the reverse does not occur. Indeed, the film's central suspense hangs on the delayed revelation of Philippe's affection for Simone. These feelings are disclosed to the viewer early on, but remain withheld from Simone until the film's *dénouement*, thereby encouraging stronger empathy for Philippe, an investment most keenly felt when Jean Leloup's hit song *Isabelle* (1990) communicates Philippe's heartbreak as he listens to it alone in his apartment after his confession. As Thain aptly points out, most Québécois will associate this song with romantic betrayal and fickleness (5–6). Its inclusion in the diegesis therefore not only privileges Philippe, but also discredits Simone's character. Indeed, Simone's active role in driving change is hampered by the film's characterisation of her project as vacuous and flawed, and ultimately requiring inspiration from Philippe. The film directs the viewer to the possible, but by no means certain, re-emergence of Philippe himself as the messianic figure when the hospital doctor (Paule Baillargeon) explains that she cannot predict whether, when or 'in what state' he might ever return. Thus, *Un 32 août*'s closing moments suggest that the fundamental reimagining of nationhood will eventually arise from the male protagonist's resurrection and renewal, but simply burden the miraculously surviving and transformed but still marginalised female protagonist with the task of sustaining continuity until that moment occurs.

In the end, by camouflaging Simone's relegation within a narrative that outwardly exhibits gender balance, *Un 32 août* underplays concrete struggles to meaningfully reforge Québécois nationhood. Instead, Villeneuve's film points to 'love' as a vague placeholder for the theoretical principle(s) the nation lacks for successful refoundation and tends to reduce procreative experience to mere symbols or abstractions. Despite this, Simone's search for solutions through action rather than abstraction provides hope for moving beyond the mind-body dichotomy of Western epistemological tradition and contests its exclusion of subjective experience from knowledge production. Equally, although *Un 32 août* perpetuates the very status quo that it critiques, by deferring its pronouncement on the form of nationhood to a future messianic figure, the film acknowledges its inability to imagine a radical challenge to the hegemony of the nation-state paradigm, and thus displays a degree of humility that offers a faint openness to other ways of bringing collective human futures into being.

NOTES

1. Alioff, Maurie, 'Denis Villeneuve's *Un 32 aout sur terre*: Lost in the Desert', *Take One: Film & Television in Canada*, vol. 7, no. 21, 1998, pp. 29–31.
2. Unless otherwise indicated, all translations from French-language sources are my own. Sirois-Trahan, Jean-Pierre, 'Introduction: Du renouveau en terrains connus', *Nouvelles vues: revue sur les pratiques et les théories du cinéma au Québec*, edited by Jean-Pierre Sirois-Trahan and Thomas Carrier-Lafleur, no. 12, Spring–Summer 2011.
3. Barrette, Pierre, 'Le désert de l'âme/ *Un 32 août sur Terre* de Denis Villeneuve', *24 images*, no. 95, 1998, p. 51.
4. Quebec has held two referenda on political sovereignty, both unsuccessful. The first, in 1980, on sovereignty-association, obtained 40.44% of the affirmative votes, while the second, in 1995, on Quebec independence, obtained 49.42%.
5. Mignolo, Walter D., 'The Decolonial Option', *On Decoloniality: Concepts, Analytics, Praxis*, edited by Walter D. Mignolo and Catherine E. Walsh, Duke University Press, 2018, pp. 103–244.
6. The period of modernisation, secularisation, renewed nationalism, and reform in 1960s Quebec is popularly known as the Quiet Revolution. It is generally understood to coincide with the election of Jean Lesage's Liberal Party in 1960 following the death of ultra-conservative *Union nationale* Premier Maurice Duplessis in 1959.
7. 'Lorsque Pascale est arrivée aux auditions, ça m'a fait chavirer', *La tribune*, 31 October 1998, p. G5, Collections de BAnQ, https://numerique.banq.qc.ca/patrimoine/details/52327/3887195 (last accessed 1 June 2021).
8. Pierre Véronneau notes that attempts to deploy supernatural tropes in the 1970s were poorly received. He speculates that contemporary critics' misunderstanding of genre and the dominant influence of the National Film Board of Canada (NFB) may explain this, adding that some commentators perceived counter-realist approaches as a betrayal of Quebec nationalism (108–109), and of Quebec's documentary tradition (118). Véronneau, Pierre, 'Genres and Variations: The Audiences of Quebec Cinema', *Self Portraits: The Cinemas of Canada Since Telefilm*, edited by André Loiselle and Tom McSorley, The Canadian Film Institute, 2006, pp. 93–128.
9. De Zwann, Victoria, 'Slipstream', *The Routledge Companion to Science Fiction*, edited by Mark Bould, Routledge, 2009, pp. 500–4.
10. Sterling, Bruce, 'Slipstream', *Science Fiction Eye*, no. 5, 1989, pp. 77–80 (p. 78).
11. Mignolo, Walter D., *The Darker Side of Western Modernity*, Duke University Press, 2011, p. 105 and p. 138.
12. Thain, Alanna, 'A Texture in the Desert of the Real: The Heterotopic Fold of Denis Villeneuve's *Un 32 août sur terre*', *Nouvelles Vues: revue sur les pratiques et les théories du cinéma au Québec*, no. 11, Fall 2010.
13. Sobchack, Vivian Carol, *Screening Space: The American Science Fiction Film*, 2nd, enl. ed., Ungar, 1987.
14. Dupont, Louis, '*L'américanité* in Quebec in the 1980s: Political and Cultural Considerations of an Emerging Discourse', *American Review of Canadian Studies*, vol. 25, no. 1, 1995, pp. 27–52.
15. *La revanche des berceaux (The Revenge of the Cradles)* refers to the unusually high levels of fertility experienced in Quebec from the 17th century to the middle of the 20th century. Bouchard, Gérard, 'L'imaginaire de la grande noirceur et de la révolution tranquille: fictions identitaires et jeux de mémoire au Québec', *Recherches sociographiques*, vol. 46, no. 3, 2005, pp. 411–36 ; Bouchard, Gérard, and Richard Lalou, 'La surfécondité

des couples québécois depuis le XVIIe siècle, essai de mesure d'interprétation', *Recherches sociographiques*, vol. 34, no. 1, 1993, pp. 9–44; Fournier, Daniel, 'Pourquoi la revanche des berceaux? L'hypothèse de la sociabilité', *Recherches sociographiques*, vol. 30, no. 2, 1989, pp. 171–98.

16. Manning, Erin, 'Fluid Relations: Quebec Cinema and the Church', *Nouvelles Vues: revue sur les pratiques et les théories du cinéma au Québec*, no. 4, Fall 2005.
17. Ruppersberg, Hugh, 'The Alien Messiah', *Alien Zone: Cultural Theory and Contemporary Science Fiction Cinema*, edited by Annette Kuhn, vol. 1, Verso, 1990, pp. 32–8.
18. It is worth noting that Quebec's unofficial national anthem *Gens du pays* (1975), composed by Gilles Vigneault, is framed as a declaration of love. McLeish, Megan, *Les thèmes nationalistes dans la chanson folk et la chanson québécoise pendant les années 1960 et 1980 au Canada: Une étude de Stan Rogers et de Gilles Vigneault*, 2014, University of Waterloo, MS thesis, pp. 83–4.
19. Memmi, Albert, *Portrait du colonisé, précédé du Portrait du colonisateur et d'une préf. de Jean-Paul Sartre, Suivi Les Canadiens français sont-ils des colonisés?* Montreal, L'Étincelle, 1972.
20. Ransom, Amy, 'The Future of Quebec in SF Film and Television', *Science Fiction Film & Television*, vol. 8, no. 1, 2015, pp. 1–28.
21. Glazier, Michael, and Monika Hellwig, *The Modern Catholic Encyclopedia vol. 13*, rev. and exp. ed., Liturgical Press, 2004.
22. Dequen, Bruno, 'Table ronde sur le renouveau du cinéma québécois', *Nouvelles Vues: revue sur les pratiques et les théories du cinéma au Québec*, edited by Jean-Pierre Sirois-Trahan and Thomas Carrier-Lafleur, no. 12, Spring–Summer 2011.

CHAPTER 3

Close-ups and *Gros Plans*: Denis Villeneuve the Macrophage

Marie Pascal

> I will never be able to say how much I love American close-ups. Neat. Briskly, the screen displays a face and the drama, face to face, speaks intimately to me and gains some unexpected intensities. Hypnosis. Now, tragedy becomes anatomic. The fifth act's setting is now this corner of a cheek that a smile sharply tears apart. (Epstein 93)[1]

3,330. This figure represents the number of close-ups I found in Denis Villeneuve's œuvre, from *Un 32 août sur terre* (1998) through to *Blade Runner 2049* (2017) – roughly 1,026 minutes of moving images.[2] Although several critics have focused on Villeneuve's penchant for the macro – Joanne Comte even dubs him the 'macrophage' (11)[3] – no one has as of yet endeavoured to explain the recurrence of close-ups within his films, nor spoken about their impact on the spectator. Yet, from the blatant clues disseminated in his thrillers – *Polytechnique* (2009), *Prisoners* (2013), *Enemy* (2013) and *Sicario* (2015) – to the lingering on actors' beautiful faces in *Un 32 août sur terre*, *Incendies* (2010), and *Arrival* (2016), to the recurrence of an ominous 'Entity' in *Maelström* (2000), emerge a variety and depth with regards to this cinematic technique which brings to mind Gilles Deleuze's focus on the 'image-affection'. Deleuze considers that the close-up induces an 'affective reading' (97)[4] of the film and states that as a polysemic formal choice, it can work autonomously or institute a dialogue with other shots in the movie, while linking to a deep intertextual web spanning the entire cinematic medium.

Analysing Villeneuve's perspective on this type of shot relates to both a cinematic and a historical context, as one first needs to elucidate the important terminological difference between languages, rightly highlighted by Gilles Thérien and Mary-Ann Doane:[5] whereas the French phrase *gros plan* focuses on the largeness of the filmed object, the English term 'close-up' emphasises the short distance between the latter and the camera. This discrepancy foreshadows a philosophical opposition engaging the transcendence or possession of the filmed object, and is crucial when focusing on the impact of close-ups in a specific cultural context. As a Quebec director who turned to the Hollywood market, Villeneuve promises to be the perfect example of such cultural differences.

In this chapter, I will identify two binary couples, namely largeness/nearness and transcendence/possession, creating a grid with which to analyse the many close-ups in Villeneuve's nine feature films. The purpose of this chapter, constructed as a first analysis of an omnipresent formal element in his filmography, is to give meaning to a cinematic effect sometimes labelled superfluous or superficial.[6] As a preliminary step, I will apply Deleuze's theory on 'image-affection' (as an intensive or reflexive image) to Villeneuvian close-ups. I will then offer a typology of the macro and study its impact within each film, its evolution throughout the œuvre, and some of its effects on the spectator of different genres (introspective francophone movies, Hollywood thrillers, and science fiction films).

I. A LARGE ARRAY OF CLOSE-UPS AS 'IMAGE-AFFECTION'

The close-up has been at the centre of film scholars' attention while remaining, somehow paradoxically, quite problematic. Although it is seen as 'the vehicle of the star, the privileged receptacle of affect, of passion, the guarantee of the cinema's status as a universal language, one of, if not *the most*, recognisable units of cinematic discourse, yet [it is] simultaneously extraordinarily difficult to define' (Doane 90). While studying the moving image, Deleuze first focused on the close-up – or rather the *gros plan* as it is called in French – and stated: 'Image-affection is the close-up and the close-up is the face' (125).[7] Both critics hence narrow the terminology to the impact of the face on screen, to which Deleuze would ask two questions: 'What are you thinking about?' and 'What are you feeling?' Such questions so deepen Deleuze's comprehension of this cinematic device that they will ground a conceptual dichotomy: whereas some faces are wondering – hence the question, 'What are you thinking about?' – others are moved by imperceptible changes leading to an emotional paroxysm, hence the question, 'What are you feeling?' (Deleuze 127).[8]

I will investigate Villeneuve's œuvre in order to validate the terms of such a critical opposition between the 'reflexive' features of the image-affection (the face as immutable) and its 'intensive' particularities (the features as autonomous), accordingly validating Deleuze's idea that the *gros plan* reveals feelings, connotes the whole movie, and triggers many of the public's reactions.

i. The reflexive face: What are you thinking about?

In most of Villeneuve's early movies, the face of the actor is pictured in wonder or pondering; the close-up thus summarises, in one single shot, the characters' loneliness. Although the spectator may disregard their connotation, such close-ups tangibly impact the story. Accordingly, *Maelström* opens with a complicated metanarration scene with a dying fish, which is followed by the presentation, in extreme close-up, of the main character, Bibiane (Marie-Josée Croze). Following Amy Ransom's study, such a shot 'works to bring us more deeply into the emotional life of Bibiane even though it ironically focuses on her outer beauty' (182).[9] While Bibiane's fragmented face fills the screen, her wondering face does not reveal any emotion. Hence, this numbness clashes with parallel shots where her lower body is shown as jabbed by a syringe, and her fetus disposed of. The more Bibiane is portrayed in extreme-close up, the more she appears to be the epitome of solitude, numbly passing through rough times: abortion, dangerous sex, killing, attempted suicide. Portrayed as a reflexive character – resulting in André Lavoie's labelling the film 'banal' and 'derisory' (62)[10] – Bibiane is slowly penetrated by change, and close-ups on her face then evoke Deleuze's other question, underlining a turning point in her life.

In a different though as enigmatic way, many close-ups show the Killer's expressionless face (Maxim Gaudette) in *Polytechnique*, Villeneuve's third feature-film. Some scholars, such as Janine Marchessault, explain this cinematic choice:

> The film will linger on his face in extreme close-up [. . .] as if trying to understand his thoughts – or giving us time to contemplate the extremity of his actions that we know are to come. He is framed numerous times in close-ups in his car as he sits outside of his mother's house, or outside the school as if to indicate his distance and isolation from the world. (54)[11]

Isolation is indeed stated during the time of his incomprehensible wait in his car, outside the school. This close-up lasts more than 20 seconds, but the camera doesn't only 'linger' on the face, it rather follows his hand writing a letter, charging his gun, and starting the car; then going back to the face. After a cut, the setting changes to the inside of the school, which implies the character's lack of agency as he is displaced without showing any desire to be. After a very long zoom leading to a close-up, the Killer remained still and, if not for the secretary's off-screen question, it is likely that nothing would have altered his bland behaviour. While her question ('Can I help you?') functions as a trigger, the Killer, somehow reluctantly, initiates his carnage. One can but wonder about this character's thoughts as if Villeneuve had wanted to depict the indecision at stake when one is trapped in morbid thoughts. In both aforementioned reflexive close-ups, the Killer seems so unmovable and numb that the public eventually wonders if he can credibly be the cause of the opening sequence carnage.

Last but not least of Villeneuve's debut films, *Incendies* also lingers on several images-affections of diegetically important characters, trapped in wonder. The opening sequence presents a group of child soldiers and ends on the internationally renowned face of the actor playing Nihad de mai (Hussein Sami), the son Nawal dedicates her life to finding. This sequence is punctuated by a 30-second zoom focused on young Nihad's empty face. After a cut, the next close-up pictures Nawal's vacant face (Lubna Azabal) that the camera investigates for 7 seconds. Although Villeneuve's reiteration of the same type of frame seems meaningful, these two 'reflexive faces' are only linked at the very end of the movie, answering the question 'What are you thinking about?': Nawal is in shock because she just found Nihad under the features of her torturer, Abou Tarek (Abdelghafour Elaaziz). Only the viewing of the whole movie will alleviate the initial tension of the two main characters' faces, while the answer to the initial question is endlessly postponed.

Although reflexivity is abundant in Villeneuve's French-language œuvre, it sporadically shows in his latest productions, starting with his Canadian auteur film *Enemy*. In the initial sequence, Anthony (played by Jake Gyllenhaal, who also plays his *doppelgänger*, Adam) enters a dark room where a naked woman performs an ominous show with tarantulas. While sitting in the audience, the man hides his face between his hands and seems entranced by the show. Composed of three close-ups of the still character, this scene presents Anthony from different angles: first his right side, then his front, finally his left in extreme close-up. All these reflexive frames are intertwined with close-ups of the show – either the tarantula itself, the actress's high-heel, or men in the audience. In other words, no face portrayed in this sequence shows emotion, but the rotating of the camera around Anthony foreshadows an important diegetic detail: while seeing his left side, one notices he is wearing a ring, a key detail for the movie's resolution (Figure 3.1).

Arrival too presents a protagonist, Louise Banks (Amy Adams), in a wondering state when her book on the Heptapods' language has just been published. The book-launch sequence is fragmented by six analepses relating Banks's call with the Chinese General who would have declared war on the aliens had she not convinced him otherwise. At first, only the nape of Banks's neck appears in the close-up, a technique Villeneuve sometimes uses to give non-facial emotion to his protagonists. General Shang (Tzi Ma) then enters the screen and whispers in her ear something that astonishes her, a feeling portrayed, after a cut, in a close-up. A voice-over repeats Shang's words while the analeptic sequences unravel: when she called him, Banks had managed to explain the Heptapods' harmlessness while

Figure 3.1 What are you thinking about, Anthony? (Jake Gyllenhaal in *Enemy*).

quoting his wife's last words. Her clairvoyance, inherited from learning the aliens' language, this 'tool' they had come to give humanity, saved them all. Yet, the parallel series of shots implicates that, although humanity is saved, Banks sacrificed her own peace of mind; she knows her beloved yet still unborn daughter will die, a fate she comes to realise in this very sequence of wonder.

There is finally a reflexive close-up in *BR 2049*, although K (Ryan Gosling), a little-expressive Replicant, does not share many of his emotions throughout the movie. One of the film's main debates resides in the solving of the question: can Replicants lie, disobey, or have feelings (like humans) or are they closer to being robots, deprived of any interior life?[12] The reflexive close-up I chose waves in the first direction: when K is sent to kill Deckard (Harrison Ford), father of the 'miracle' (a Replicant-human child), he is caught in his thoughts in front of the gigantic 3D reproduction of his partner, a hologram called Joi. After a few seconds of wonder, a cut presents what can be interpreted as K's memory of the scene in which he 'retired' a Replicant farmer (David Bautista), who claimed to having witnessed the miracle birth. Quite interestingly, this is the only time the spectator is given, in all of Villeneuve's œuvre, a direct and explicit answer to the question 'What are you thinking about?' K is thinking about the farmer's statement, which will lead him spare Deckard's life. While K is pondering about his two alternatives – to remain a Replicant deprived of free will, or to prove to the world that he and his kind have agency – his decision answers the question raised at the beginning of the movie.

'What are you thinking about?' This question provokes a multiplicity of answers within Villeneuve's œuvre, but always refers, more or less directly, to a state of loneliness felt by a character, that is inexpressible to the public. However, if the reading of the face will not answer the question, the movie eventually will. Such close-ups hence trigger a decision which will have consequences on other sequences, and echo undeciphered feelings and concealed ideas of great diegetic importance despite their seeming to be 'only' beautiful images.

ii. *The intensive face: What do you feel?*

The second type of 'image-affection' described by Deleuze is labelled 'intensive', and the metaphor of a clock, whose motionless shape unintentionally reflects the light while its subtly-moving hands progress to a paroxysm, convincingly represents the intensive face. Assimilated to the motor of the action, these indiscernible movements induce the second question; 'What do you feel?' Although these kinds of close-ups are less numerous, the occurrences I chose to describe are tangible enough to underline the terminological consistency.

I will begin with Villeneuve's first feature film, *Un 32 août sur terre*, which is punctuated by many expressionless faces of the main protagonist, Simone Prévost (Pascale Bussières), who falls asleep while driving, nearly dies in the accident, and eventually decides to bear a child. To this end, she asks her best friend, Philippe (Alexis Martin), to have sex with her, which he accepts as long as this happens in a desert. Upon their arrival at Salt Lake City, a succession of events thwart their plan and they soon realise, under the cynical eye of a greedy taxi driver, that their quest will fail. While they try to compose themselves, both of their faces are, in turn, filmed in long close-ups and the intensity of their minuscule facial muscle movements indicates that they have grown from their failure. Simone's face first displays disappointment, which gives way to a smile: this proud character is about to humbly express her happiness. On the other hand, Philippe's face shows shame because he so eagerly accepted his friend's proposal that his pride is shaken by their failure. The absurdity of their pact transpires in these two contiguous close-ups while they both change their minds and decide to embrace this moment together: Philippe is happy that he didn't cheat on his girlfriend; Simone realises she may be in love with Philippe. This paroxysmic sequence therefore leads to the inversion of the dynamic between the protagonists, and to the logical though cynical end of the movie.

In *Polytechnique*, although most of the Killer's close-ups are reflexive, the shot becomes inherently expressive when the victim's reactions are also pictured. Brenda Longfellow states that 'the film lingers on the faces of its innocent and wide-eyed protagonists, in a manner immediately expressive of the poignancy of their youth, their obliviousness to danger, their fresh-faced optimism about the future' (98).[13] When the Killer approaches women he is about to kill, their fear impregnates the close-up, and his off-screen presence is indicated by tenuous changes in their physiognomy – eyes widening, features swelling to express horror. What is represented in the aforementioned close-ups is mortality and fear when one faces death, a fate that reads in the multitude of movements invading several characters' faces throughout the movie.

In *Enemy*, another female face is invested by movements implying surprise and discomfort. After following a lead her husband Anthony found about Adam, who had been harassing them, Helen (Sarah Gadon) discovers her husband's *doppelgänger*, resting on a bench, at the university. This scene is a crucial turn-over in the movie, as it portrays the shocking resemblance between Adam and Anthony, seen through the lens of another protagonist. As the movie is first narrated from Adam's perspective – who could well have hallucinations – the intensity of the emotion spreading on Helen's face here gives him credit. I would argue that this shot represents the 'image-affection' *per se*, lasting some 10 seconds. When Helen meets Adam, the option of the *doppelgänger*'s existence becomes credible and, accordingly, impacts the rest of our viewing.

Therefore, the intensive face often engages a story turn-over or a change of condition, but it also guides our interpretation of the end. In the last sequence of *Prisoners*, Detective Loki (Jake Gyllenhaal) closes the case concerning the abduction of two girls by Holly Jones (Melissa Leo). As Loki is resting in front of her house, he vaguely hears an off-screen whistle – the public knows that Dover is desperately whistling in order to escape from his underground prison. The film ends on a close-up on the inspector's dubious face (Figure 3.2), and the public eagerly hopes he will push his investigation further and liberate Dover before he dies.

Figure 3.2 What do you feel, Loki? (Jake Gyllenhaal in *Prisoners*).

There is no proof that he will, but for the absence of a tiny detail, only perceptible because of the close-up: whenever Loki is misled throughout the film, an irrepressible facial tic underlines his lack of faith in his own instincts. Yet, on this very last shot, Loki's face, deprived of such uncertainty, is rather animated by two antagonist and paroxysmic desires: to find Dover, whom he will arrest for torturing Jones' nephew, or to close the case without finding Dover. Because his genuine face is altogether deprived of the facial tics that had come to characterise him, one is likely to believe that Loki will find the dying Dover, a belief that is induced by the clash between two intensive faces that make the spectator ask: 'What do you feel?'

Finally, FBI agent Kate Macer (Emily Blunt) in *Sicario* gives an excellent last example of the image-affection playing an intensive role. In the Mexican border massacre sequence, Macer is being targeted by a man determined to kill her. It is only by looking in the rear-view mirror picturing the danger that the young woman realises she will only save her life at the expense of killing her opponent – an unethical action. The next close-up shows a gun in the foreground, which greatly enhances the intensity spreading on Macer's face in the background, a character who is, for the first time, doing something illegal. The most important dichotomy in the thriller is here condensed within the minuscule movements spreading on her face; the combat between doing things by the book and saving her skin is, in this very close-up, at stake.

Functioning as motors, intensive close-ups are the place for diegetic accelerations, mirroring contradictory and intense emotions spreading on the characters' faces. This study proves that Villeneuve's use of close-ups is many things but purely cosmetic: their complexity brings to mind Marc-Emmanuel Mélon's metaphor of the 'archeological investigation' one needs to conduct in order to elucidate such infinite stratification as the one concealed in each and every one of these shots (76).[14]

Another complication when analysing Villeneuve's use of close-ups is caused by terminological differences between languages, and especially between French and English. Doane's analysis explicitly builds on this opposition: '[I]n French, the term for close-up denotes largeness or large scale [. . .]; while in English, it is nearness or proximity that is at stake. The close-up thus invokes two different binary oppositions – proximity vs distance and the large vs the small' (92). In the next steps of this analysis, my purpose is to underline a stylistic progression, directly linked to Villeneuve's use of French or English: while his French films portray 'transcendance', his English movies draw a recurrent discourse on how 'possession' can spread on the screen, following what Doane further highlights:

> As opposed to the American cinema's use of the close-up to suggest proximity, intimacy, knowledge of interiority, Eisenstein argues for a disproportion that transforms the image into a sign, an epistemological tool, undermining identification and hence empowering the spectator as analyst of, rather than vessel for, meaning. (107)

2. LARGENESS AND TRANSCENDENCE: *GROS PLANS* OR VILLENEUVE THE *MACRO*-PHAGE

In his early movies in French, Villeneuve demonstrates his understanding of the term *gros plan* as referring to transcendence: the camera presents very small objects as if willing to go beyond their surface, the intelligible side of what they represent. Within this group of four movies (*Un 32 août*, *Malestrôm*, *Polytechnique* and *Incendies*), transcendence takes several shapes, inspecting all of the films' layers, and leading one to rethink the filmic body itself.

i. Un 32 août sur terre *and dichotomies*

Villeneuve's first attempt at visiting such considerations goes back to his first feature film and takes shape as what will become the director's favourite dichotomies: nature versus technology; death versus life. When he was asked about *Un 32 août*, the young director elicited his vision in a few words: 'there's a clash between nature and technology, between the urban and desert landscape, even between creating life and aborting it' (Amsdem 24).[15] All of these clashes are highlighted at the very beginning of the movie as Simone nearly dies in a car accident provoked by her falling asleep. Her blinking eyelids are doubled four times by those of the lights of her car, as if human and machine were one single tired self. Later on, in the sequence following her stay in a hospital, Simone sits next to a road and bathes in the sun. The camera spans her universe, half natural (tree canopies and sunlight), half technological (factory and road), right before it stops on a dead rat in *gros plan*. After a cut, her lack of reaction is pictured in a *gros plan*; her hand grasps the grass right before the camera returns to her face, expressive this time, bathing in the sun. In the lapse of a minute, these four *gros plans* intercede one another in order to give a sense of harmony between the poles of the dichotomy while foreshadowing the protagonist's decision: having a baby as she's still alive and young. While this sequence happens in the first half of the movie, it dictates its whole reception because Simone appears to be cursed by the death/life dichotomy until the very end: the designated procreator, her best friend Philippe, is badly beaten by hooligans, and is left in a coma. The movie ends with her visiting Philippe's room where she eventually decides to have sex with this man, stuck between life and death.

ii. Maelström: *the Entities' metanarration*

Metanarration appears to be the most innovative use of *gros plans* in Villeneuve's œuvre, yet this technique has been overlooked by the few scholars who have studied *Maelström*. Only Ransom focuses on the first two sequences, stating that:

> [D]eath and carnality of earthly existence are heavily overdetermined in this film, a story explicitly told with the dying breaths of five different, very gory animatronic fish (voiced by Pierre Lebeau) all being hacked apart by a Viking-like figure wearing nothing but an apron, himself covered in blood. (181)

This movie is indeed punctuated by five sequences picturing the dying fish, starting with the opening scene where this atypical narrator is presented in *gros plan*, then in *très gros plan*, as if Villeneuve had wanted to portray death from different perspectives, each one gorier than the last. Many other *gros plans* reflect death throughout the movie, while Villeneuve explains that the fish-narrator is not subjected to an endless rebirth but is, instead, five *different* Entities, 'a kind of a metaphor for all the story-tellers from the beginning of mankind' (Amsdem 23). As the fish die in key moments of the movie – right after Bibiane's abortion, her killing of the fishman, her lies to the latter's son, Evian (Jean-Nicolas Verreault) – this multiplication of deaths in *gros plans* aims at transcending mortality, a mortality that ironically often addresses immortality. A cruel irony indeed spreads in the last sequence, with the last Entity's death: this fifth fish was about to tell the audience what the real purpose of life is, a secret to this day uncovered as the movie ends for shortage of narrator(s).

iii. Polytechnique: *the historical letter of the massacre*

The *gros plan* I will focus on to represent *Polytechnique* has to do with the letter the Killer left behind him, in reality, after the Polytechnique massacre. The voice-over reading of this hate-letter in the first sequence inflects the whole movie with the themes of hatred and misogyny. While a large portion of *Polytechnique* generates a menacing tone and builds on a feeling of imprisonment in this hate-cycle, the shot-sequence of the letter being written imprisons the camera in the car together with the Killer, hence making the spectator experience claustrophobia. After having pictured the motionless character, the next shot focuses on the pen hastily moving (Figure 3.3). Then, with a change of focus, the background – the hate-letter – appears in its totality. For the next 30 seconds, the Killer's hand occupies the screen to fold the letter, place it in the inside-pocket of the coat, and greedily grasp a load of cartridges, always followed by the camera. This series of *gros plan* sewn together creates an atmosphere of imprisonment and also reinforces the tragic fate that will befall the victims. Here, the historical letter left after the killing of fourteen women, in December 1989, represents the ghost of the massacre and is its only 'real' reference. The fact that Villeneuve had it read by a voice-over in the first sequence, but postponed the actual writing until right before the Killer's rampage, represents his uncertainty as to how the pre-massacre happened, such elements he didn't seem to want to carve in.

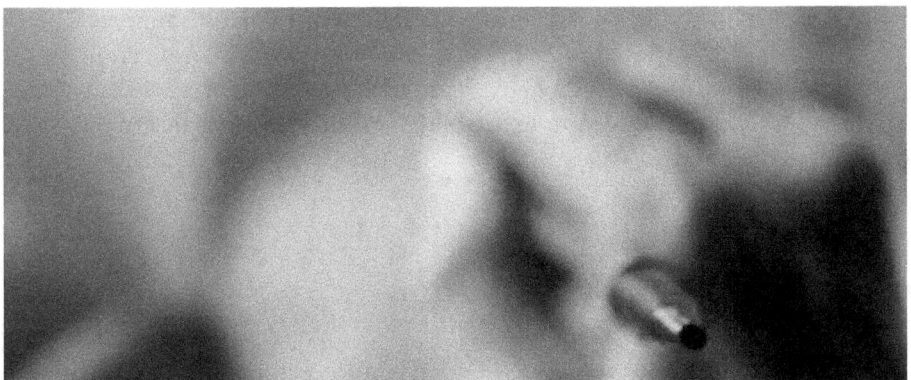

Figure 3.3 The Killer writing the hate-letter in *Polytechnique*.

iv. Incendies: *the weight of the past*

Villeneuve's adaptation of Wajdi Mouawad's eponymous play, *Incendies*, has often been referred to as an 'identity quest'. The twins Simon (Maxim Gaudette) and Jeanne (Mélissa Désormeaux-Poulin) are indeed asked, while reading their mother's will, to find their father and their brother about whom they had never been told. After retracing their deceased mother's past in her home country, they will find the two men, give them letters she left for them, and give peace to Nawal. The genre of this movie makes it somehow natural that Nawal's passport and identity picture are shown no fewer than five times, in *gros plans*, as a reference to the twin's transcendental quest. The first shot of Nawal's passport concludes the sequence when the notary gives Jeanne her mother's post-mortem instructions. Later on, Jeanne finds a photo of her mother, with Arabic inscriptions in the background. This is also shown in *gros plan*, as if it were necessary for the camera to capture the intensity in Nawal's stare: a stare that conflicts with the one, deprived of emotion, she was reduced to in her first appearance on screen. Nawal's photo, together with her passport, are often displayed during Jeanne's quest in her mother's home: it leads to her mother's village, to the prison where she was raped, and, finally, to the identity of the two men she is related to. As a testimony of Nawal's terrible past, the passport and the photo taken in prison overtly transcend time and retain their true meaning for the very instant of the plot resolution, when the twins eventually solve the unsolvable mathematical problem '$1 + 1 = 1$'.

Transcendence therefore invests different levels in Villeneuve's debut films in French: as it enlarges what is relatively small – like Nawal's stare on the picture taken in prison – the *gros plan* underpins supposedly unimportant details or transcends the opposition between fiction and reality, as is the case with the

Killer's letter in *Polytechnique*. Moreover, philosophical dichotomies – such as life vs death, illustrated in *Un 32 août sur terre* – call for a reflection on the thematic homogeneity in Villeneuve's œuvre, while instigating, like in *Maelström*, a playful relationship to his public, frustrated in their desire to be told transcendental truths.

3. NEARNESS AND POSSESSION: 'CLOSE-UPS' OR VILLENEUVE THE MACRO-*PHAGE*

While the *gros plan* draws our attention to the size of the filmed object, thereby inducing transcendence, the close-up refers to the short distance between the object and the camera, thus functioning as a metonymy of the public's desire to grasp or possess the former. In this regard, Doane underlines that 'closeness is allied with possession, possessiveness, the desire "to get hold of an object"' (92–3). This statement induces a different viewing of Villeneuve's five English-language films, leading us to apprehend the Hollywood director as a *consumer* of the macro. After having shown that the 'desire to get hold of' the object connects to the very genre of thrillers, I will illustrate that possession has more or less literal meanings, testifying that Villeneuve's latest movies' display of close-ups intrinsically deals with the understanding of the concept for English-speakers.

i. Prisoners *and pretend possession*

In his thrillers, Villeneuve has proficiently scattered clues in close-ups, but these clues are sometimes so undecipherable that they become readable only after a careful and meticulous analysis. As an example, *Prisoners* is filled with fake (or only partially reliable) hints that inevitably lead in the wrong direction. From the second sequence onwards, several close-ups on vehicle lights function as accusations: firstly, a close-up following a van's rear-light equals, for the public, to accusing its driver, namely Alex Jones (Paul Dano), of the future abduction of two girls. Together with the music, his ominous camper van is filmed from behind, lurking in the neighbourhood right before the girls disappear. The driver is then apprehended as a suspect, and the audience readily presumes he took the girls only because the filmic body explicitly pointed at him. The reiteration of misleading close-ups provokes other fast (and wrong) interpretations from the audience such as the designation of another unsavoury man, Bob Taylor (David Dastmalchian). During a ceremony organised in support of the bereaved families, a teddy bear, displayed in the middle of candles, is gently caressed by someone wearing black gloves. Imagining that we have found, at last, a clue concerning the actual pedophile, we are again baffled when Bob ends up being unveiled as another victim. And so on and so forth: blatant clues uncover such a tiny part of the truth that they inevitably give birth to invalid conclusions.

The resolution of this circumstantial puzzle is offered, at the very end, by another close-up on the tail-light of a car: Alex's uncle's. This powerful shot leads to the unravelling of the true succession of events: Alex drives the abductor's camper, not because he is guilty, but because his 'uncle' left it to him. Bob is troubled and obsessed with mazes, not because he is a psychopath, but because he was drugged and tortured for years. As a result of his poor capacity to solve the case sooner, wounded Dover (Hugh Jackman) is thrown into the hole hidden under the uncle's car. In other words, the first close-ups are but the tip of the iceberg, with the more substantial part remaining hidden until the very end, leading the spectator to opt for the simplest (and erroneous) solutions. Perverting the historical acceptation of close-ups as a technique handling clues to the public, *Prisoners* punishes their urge to take part in the investigation and only leaves a taste of guilt due to too hasty deductions and an overwhelming desire to follow quite mediocre and predictable instincts; Dover and even Loki fall prey to these same faulty impulses.

ii. Enemy: doppelgänger *and fragmentation*

The question the spectator of *Enemy* is likely to ask themselves is echoed by Deleuze's analysis of Ingmar Bergman's *Persona* (1966), a movie about *doppelgängers*: there is no point wondering if two characters look alike, started to look alike, or if they are one single person, because the close-up pushes the character's face in regions where individuation is invalidated (142).[16] This idea eloquently frames the debate concerning *Enemy*, where individuation is not only suspended by close-ups on faces, but by the fact that they rather focus on the protagonists' hands, accentuating such dis-identification. As I underlined earlier, this problem manifests itself from the first sequence onwards, where Anthony's hands veil his face, foregrounding his wedding ring. Yet Anthony is not the only side of the *doppelgänger* pair to be separated from his hands; when Adam is pictured correcting essays, the camera does not focus on his concentrating face, but on his hands: his right handles a pen, his left lays patiently on the paper as if to show that he is not wearing a ring. When Adam and Anthony eventually meet, Anthony first asks to compare Adam's hands to his. This interesting close-up proves the two pairs of hands to be perfectly identical.

Several harmless occurrences separate the *doppelgängers*'s faces from their hands[17] until the story takes an unexpected turn: while Anthony sleeps with Adam's girlfriend, a pale mark shows on his hand – once more, it is filmed in close-up – which the girl notices. In this scene, their fate is fixed as they will both die in a car accident, the consequence of their fighting. Therefore, the presence or absence of the ring does not only indicate which side of the character is filmed (Adam or Anthony?), it also shatters both individuals and provokes the public's inference: if Adam does not have a mark on his finger, is Anthony really his *doppelgänger* as his hand is marked? Rather than a product of Adam's imagination, could Anthony be his actual double, negating the *doppelgänger* option?

iii. Sicario: *reflection and duplicity*

Presenting protagonists through a car window or reflected in a mirror indicates duplicity, actual or potential. Such a statement could be drawn from a cautious analysis of *Sicario*, Villeneuve's thriller establishing a conflict between two drastically different ethics: Macer's, an FBI agent who desires to conduct her work legally and ethically, and Matt's (Josh Brolin) and Alejandro's (Benicio del Toro), who consider all means permissible as long as they help solve a case. From *Sicario*'s opening sequence onwards, close-ups show the protagonists filmed either through a surface or reflected by a mirror, two types of frames that illustrate reticence to give direct access to the human face.

I extracted three examples from the large quantity of such close-ups[18] in order to underline the fact that they express the characters' actual or future duplicity. Firstly, one of the first shots presenting Alejandro is through the rear window of a car, which raises a doubt about his faithfulness although the public has of yet no proof that he is a double agent.[19] Other close-ups show what is happening off-screen, as a reminder that there is a whole world, potentially dangerous, outside the shot. In the sequence I already quoted, Macer is placed in a situation where she is about to be killed – a furtive close-up of the car side-mirror shows a man aiming at her. By killing him, she consequently betrays her oath and places herself halfway to becoming another dual character, which she will confirm to be at the end of the movie. One last example involves Matt, the CIA officer heading up the cartel operation. In order for Matt to get crucial information about the cartel's *cheffe*, Alejandro tortures a mole working both for the mafia and the police. The scene is presented through a close-up on the rear-view mirror of the car where Matt repeatedly peeks, therefore protected from direct eye-contact with the torture scene. In this last occurrence, Matt's dual identity too is foreshadowed: he is a coward who wants to put a hand on the head of the mafia without personally crossing the line.

Spreading through the recurrence of close-ups indirectly picturing characters, duplicity spreads from Alejandro to Matt to Macer, who will end up signing a paper where she swears nothing unethical was perpetrated during the mission, sealing her defeat.

iv. Arrival *and the 'weapon/tool'*

Possession is to be taken literally in *Arrival*, a science-fiction movie representing the encounter between the linguist Louise Banks and the Heptapods, alien visitors landing on Earth in order to give a 'weapon,' also called 'tool,' to the human race. The human obsession with possession strikes immediately upon their first intrusion into the spaceship: both Banks and her colleague Donnelly (Jeremy Renner) touch the vessel with their gloved hands. While focusing on the hands, these close-ups dispossess humans from their faces and depict the team's greed through these inquisitive gloves patting the unidentified material of the ship. Such frames punctuate the whole movie as a parallel to Banks's progressive learning of the Heptapods' language.[20] In fact, as soon as she gets into the ship, she puts her whole apparatus down and caresses the glass-window separating her from the aliens with her bare hand. This second close-up echoes the previous, while possession is getting more concrete. In this shot, Banks's hand spreads on the glass as the inverted other of the blurred figure appearing in the background: the Heptapod's body. As soon as she understands how the logograms function, in a following sequence, she puts both of her hands on the screen and expresses herself by shifting the inky material forming the aliens' language. Finally, she enters their spaceship alone and, surrounded by an aerial foam, grasps the ink with her fingers, and learns clairvoyance. Through close-ups on Banks's hands, possession becomes explicit, a human desire she shares with everyone interested in knowing what the Heptapod's presence is about – *Arrival*'s real question that she is the only one to fully understand.

v. Blade Runner 2049: *Replicants and the individual's fragmentation*

Villeneuve's second science-fiction movie, *BR 2049*, pictures a final type of fragmentation due to the close-ups' insistence on (pairs of) eyes.[21] Diegetically, the eye is the most important part of a Replicant's body as their code is inscribed under this orb – explaining why K needs to collect one of each 'retired' victim's eyes. Moreover, K and his peers are inspected after their missions, and the inspector – a very efficient camera – detects anomalies by looking at their pupils. Such scenes, sometimes filmed in close-ups, punctuate the movie and are indubitably important when one considers that the Replicants' creator, Wallace (Jared Leto), is blind: his vacant stare skims through the frame in many key sequences. Another anecdotical detail is the (wrong) colour of Rachel's copy's eyes: when Deckard is tempted by Wallace to give away information about the resistance, he argues that his beloved Rachel used to have green eyes while the copy's are brown.[22] Such emphasis on this important part of the characters' body diegetically impregnates the movie and such close-ups are more interesting – and confusing – when noticing that *Blade Runner 2049*'s very first image is an extreme close-up of more than 10 seconds picturing the slow opening of an eyelid to a blue iris. Whose blue eye is that? How does it link with the next scene where K retires the farmer who witnessed the 'miracle'? Without a doubt, this frame represents the most undecipherable of the 3,330 close-ups I found in Villeneuve's œuvre.

CONCLUSION

In this study, I strove to shed some light on several of the particularities of close-ups within Villeneuve's filmography in order to prove that this type of frame is not solely interested in the actors' beautiful faces but, more importantly, that it draws one's attention to a large variety of objects or no objects altogether. In order for one to efficiently grasp their function, the close-ups need to be put in context – and sometimes in conflict – with other types of images or other close-ups. Some of them, disregarded by the public as banal, eventually prove to be paramount. Accordingly, this all but anodyne technique becomes even more important when it foreshadows a cultural shift: as I have shown, Villeneuve handles *gros plans* quite differently than he does close-ups – transcendence and possession sweep his œuvre although there is a predominance of the former in his French-language production, and of the latter in more recent English-language movies. This study more globally addresses Villeneuve's interest in size, while scholars have underlined the clash between the micro and the macro. As Doane puts it, 'the apparent collapse of the oppositions between detail and totality, part and whole, microcosm and macrocosm, the miniature and the gigantic, is crucial to the ideological operation of the close-up, that which makes it one of our most potent memories of the cinema' (108). After all, quoting Jean-Luc Godard, Villeneuve considers that '[i]n cinema, the most important thing is to confront blurry ideas with clear images' (Amsdem 24). I believe that my investigation of close-ups and *gros plan* aligns and elicits, in many aspects, such a purpose, despite and against those who thought otherwise.

NOTES

1. 'Jamais je ne pourrais dire combien j'aime les gros plans américains. Nets. Brusquement l'écran étale un visage et le drame, en tête à tête, me tutoie et s'enfle à des intensités imprévues. Hypnose. Maintenant, la tragédie est anatomique. Le décor du cinquième acte est ce coin de joue que déchire sec le sourire' (Epstein 93; English translation mine), Epstein, Jean, *Bonjour Cinéma*, Siren Publishing, 1921.
2. *Un 32 août sur terre* (1998, sixty close-ups); *Maelström* (2000, 210 close-ups); *Polytechnique* (2009, 215 close-ups); *Incendies* (2010, 355 close-ups); *Prisoners* (2013, 400 close-ups); *Enemy* (2013, 340 close-ups); *Sicario* (2015, 440 close-ups); *Arrival* (2016, 460 close-ups); *Blade Runner 2049* (2017, 850 close-ups). At the time of writing, *Dune* had not yet been released on streaming platforms; it therefore does not figure in this study.

3. Comte, Joanne, 'Denis Villeneuve – Portrait surréaliste d'un cerveaunaute en vol', *Séquences*, no. 175, 1994, p. 11.
4. Deleuze, Gilles, *L'Image-Mouvement*, Éditions de Minuit, 1983.
5. Thérien, Gilles, 'La critique et la disparition de son objet', *Cinémas*, vol. 6, no. 2–3, Spring 1996, pp. 142–63; Doane, Mary-Ann, 'The Close-up: Scale and Detail in the Cinema', *Differences: A Journal of Feminist Cultural Studies*, vol. 14, no. 3, 2003, pp. 89–111.
6. At least two scholars formulated their frustration regarding the discrepancy between 'photogenia' and vacant content in *Maelström*: 'the characters are deprived of compasses and appear as only taking roots in the void [. . .] but one never feels, in his movies, the need for discourse nor the true singularity of one's point of view' (Lavoie 61); 'Everything happens in this movie [. . .] as if the beauty of some images or the strength of some procedures really only serve a function that is essentially cosmetic, have been used to camouflage a discourse that is often shallow or superficial' (Barrette 51). 'Personnages dépourvus de boussoles et n'apparaissent qu'enracinés dans le vide [. . .] mais l'on ne sent jamais chez lui l'urgence d'un discours et la véritable singularité d'un point de vue' (Lavoie 61); 'Tout se passe dans ce film [. . .] comme si la beauté de certaines images ou la force de certains procédés remplissaient en réalité une fonction essentiellement cosmétique, visaient à camoufler un propos souvent creux ou superficiel' (Barrette 51). Lavoie, André, '*Maelström* de Denis Villeneuve', *Ciné-Bulles, Le cinéma d'auteur avant tout*, vol. 19, no. 1, Fall 2000, pp. 61–2; Barrette, Pierre, 'Le désert de l'âme – *Un 32 août sur terre* de Denis Villeneuve', *24 images*, no. 95, Winter 1998–1999, p. 51.
7. My translation; 'L'image affection, c'est le gros plan, et le gros plan, c'est le visage'.
8. My translation; 'Tantôt le visage pense à quelque chose, se fixe sur un objet, et c'est bien le sens de l'admiration ou de l'étonnement, que *wonder* anglais a conservé. [. . .] Tantôt, au contraire, il éprouve ou ressent quelque chose, et vaut alors par la série intensive que ses parties traversent successivement jusqu'à un paroxysme, chaque partie prenant une sorte d'indépendance momentanée'.
9. Ransom, Amy, 'Deterritorialization and the Crisis of Recognition in Turn of the Millenium Québec Film', *American Review of Canadian Studies*, vol. 43, no. 2, 2013, pp. 176–89.
10. See Lavoie; 'De la banalité, on le constate très rapidement, Villeneuve ne réussit pas complètement à s'échapper. Et tous les subterfuges utilisés pour la masquer, du poisson philosophe aux lumières chatoyantes qui enrobent Marie-Josée Croze, une créature de rêve dépourvue de mystère, ne font que confirmer le caractère dérisoire de tout ce cirque [. . .] dont il reste si peu de choses après son passage', 2000, p. 62.
11. Marchessault, Janine, 'Versioning History: *Polytechnique* as vector', *Canadian Journal of Film Studies*, vol. 22, no. 1, 2013, pp. 44–65.
12. Such questions are raised in Brenda Longfellow's and Kinglsey Marshall's chapters in the present volume.
13. Longfellow, Brenda, 'The Practice of Memory and the Politics of Memorialization: Denis Villeneuve's *Polytechnique*', *Canadian Journal of Film Studies*, Spring 2013, vol. 22, no. 1, pp. 86–106.
14. Mélon, Marc-Emmanuel, 'Quand les fantômes viennent à notre rencontre . . .', *Revue Belge du Cinéma*, vol. 10, Winter 1984, pp. 75–84, 'La lecture du gros plan est de type archéologique: elle procède à l'exhumation (progressive et infinie) des différentes images que le gros plan superpose' (p. 76).
15. Amsdem, Cynthia, '*Maelström* – Much Ado about a Fish', *Take One*, no. 29, Winter 2001, pp. 22–4.
16. 'Il est vain de se demander dans *Persona*, si ce sont deux personnes qui se ressemblaient avant, ou qui se mettent à se ressembler, ou au contraire une seule personne qui se

dédouble. C'est autre chose. Le gros plan a seulement poussé le visage jusqu'à ces régions où le principe d'individuation cesse de régner', 1983, p. 142.
17. According to my transcription, more than twenty shots are indeed focusing on either Adam or Anthony's hands, in *Enemy*, a technique that can also be found, although to a lesser extent, in *Incendies*, *Arrival*, and *BR 2049*.
18. I indeed counted some twenty-six of them.
19. Another occurrence of this technique indirectly filming Alejandro takes place during the second half of the movie, when he is following Macer outside her working time. While she comes out of the club together with a man she does not know to be a mole, the camera insists, in a close-up, on the screen of car, waiting outside. Although the audience cannot see who the driver actually is, because the light is reflected by the screen, one soon understands it was double agent Alejandro.
20. According to my transcription, there are at least twenty close-ups dealing with human possessivity in *Arrival*.
21. According to my transcription, some ten shots are drawing attention to this body part in *BR 2049*.
22. Which is, actually, a lie. On this element, see Christophe Gelly and David Roche's article in the present volume.

CHAPTER 4

Reproductive Futurism and the Woman Problem in the Films of Denis Villeneuve

Brenda Longfellow

The release of Denis Villeneuve's *Blade Runner 2049* (*BR 2049*) in 2017, the long-anticipated sequel to one of the late twentieth century's most iconic films, was met with a swooning chorus of four-star reviews, many hailing the film as 'one of greatest science fiction films of all time'.[1] Much of the swoon stemmed from the way in which the film functions as a canvas for philosophical speculation, raising core questions of traditional philosophical inquiry: 'What is reality?' and 'What constitutes the authentic human being?' (Shanahan 8).[2] Indeed, the seductive philosophising of BR 2049 animated a score of video essays[3] and no fewer than two scholarly anthologies.[4]

In one feisty corner of the internet however, feminist bloggers and critics have asked a different kind of question, namely: 'Does *Blade Runner 2049* have a woman problem?'[5] While the response to this question has frequently focused on Joi, the sexbot who, for Sara Stewart and many others represents 'a sci-fi fanboy's wet dream',[6] feminist critiques have taken issue with the presumed gender neutrality of *BR 2049*'s philosophical turn as Rosie Fletcher and Sam Ashurst wryly observe: 'The original film made us question what it means to be human. *Blade Runner 2049* explores what it means to be a man'.[7]

I want to suggest that this 'woman problem' is not unique to *BR 2049* but, in fact, might be traced through much of Villeneuve's œuvre, from his early films rooted in the independent art film habitus of Quebec to his blockbuster globalised Hollywood endeavours. Villeneuve's woman problem, however, is not so much about the objectification of the female body, the traditional animus of feminist critique. The multiple female protagonists in his films are provided with agential purpose and are often, in his latter Hollywood work, centred as a film's moral centre in militarised worlds of hyperbolic masculinity. The issue inheres in the ways in which these female protagonists are consistently figured in relation to variants of what Lee Edelman has named 'reproductive futurism',[8] a cultural dominant, heterosexist phantasm and disciplinary technology that represents the child, procreation and domestic biological lineage as a utopian and redemptive embodiment of the future. Indeed, one can follow a recurring narrative compulsion from Simone's (Pascale Bussières) determination to have a baby in response to a near fatal car crash in *Un 32 août sur terre* (1998) to Bibiane's (Marie-Josée Croze) existential crisis precipitated by her abortion in *Maelström* (2000), to Valérie's (Karine Vanasse) pregnancy which signals the resilience of survivors in *Polytechnique* (2009) to Nawal's (Lubna Azabal) pregnancy with twins in *Incendies* (2010) that posits the figure of the child as a life-affirming symbol against the prevalence of soulless consumerism, misogynist violence and militarism. As Edelman, Rebeka Sheldon[9] and writers of feminist technoscience have argued, however, reproductive futurism domesticates sexuality and pathologises non-procreative sex and queer modes of being and becoming, with eugenic implications given how only certain children (white, middle class and non-racialised) are capable of embodying beatific innocence and futurity.

This chapter will argue that while the figuration of reproductive futurism haunts much of Villleneuve's early work, it reaches a certain kind of apogee in both *Arrival* (2016) and *BR 2049* (2017). In *BR 2049*, themes of fertility and reproductive futures are central as the narrative is triggered by the story of the child born from the human/Replicant union of Deckard and Rachael. In *Arrival* Dr Louise Banks (Amy Adams), a university linguistics professor seconded by the American military to communicate with aliens, succeeds in apprehending and inhabiting the alternate episteme of Heptapod cosmic consciousness. Her ascension to this consciousness, however, is domesticated and exclusively limited to flash-forwards featuring her progeny, a beautiful, white, and precocious child. Here the child forecloses the possibilities of Louise's queer encounter with the tentacular otherness of the Heptapods, domesticating her ability to occupy simultaneous time by returning her to the familiar and familial time of procreation and maternal investment.

DOES *BLADE RUNNER 2049* HAVE A WOMAN PROBLEM?

Both the original *Blade Runner* (1982) and *BR 2049* harness film noir and science fiction tropes to conjure storyworlds whose central character, a Blade Runner, functions as the embodiment of taciturn grizzled masculinity. Neither film would obviously pass the Bechdel test[10] as female characters are distinctly secondary to the main narrative arc of the male anti-hero whose journey through the murky underworlds of dystopian horror is resolved through the surrender to heterosexual love or through the acknowledgement of the truth of his own birth. But while Ridley Scott's version enacted this gender hierarchy through a studied faithfulness to generic noir conventions, in *BR 2049*, gender apartheid is relayed with an equally studied reflexive irony. Among the pirouetting ballerinas and replicant sex workers, there is no more ironic an apparition than Joi, the hologram sex bot played by Ana De Armas, whose faint 'exotic' accent[11] and wide-eyed anime look convey a plasticised attractiveness. Joi has been designed to provide 'everything you want to see' and 'everything you want to hear'. Joi, in fact, seems like a parody of an adolescent fantasy where women exist only to serve and bolster the male ego, taking up little space, switched on and off at whim, endlessly servile and adoring. The ironic implications are immediately apparent in Joi's first onscreen incarnation as a 1950s housewife in button- down collar, pencil skirt and apron, who serves K (Ryan Gosling) a steak hologram as he returns home after a hard day at work. She exists only to please K, even arranging a threesome with a 'real' Replicant body so he can have a physiological orgasm (do Replicants have orgasms?). The irony of sexist caricature reaches its apogee in the hologram version of Joi, a 90-foot high advertisement with blue skin, a pink wig, naked body and a robotic come on, where she is ultimately recast as a manufactured and endlessly reproducible product of the Wallace corporation.[12] Other female caricatures include the Replicant Luv (Sylvia Hoeks), the ruthless muscle of the Wallace Corporation and Lieutenant Joshi (Robin Wright), K's superior at L.A.P.D., both of whom meet gruesome and violent ends, though hardly unexpected given the noir tradition of punishing or eliminating the phallic woman. Finally, there is Dr Ana Stelline (Carla Juri), the real miracle child who serves as the embodiment of sexless purity, intelligence and humanity. As Fletcher and Ashurst observe, 'women are present in the narrative, while simultaneously absent. *Blade Runner 2049* has the illusion of women, with nothing solid for them to do. It makes its female characters feel as hollow as holograms.'

While Ashurst and Fletcher provide an apt observation, I want to argue that the androcentricism of *BR 2049* runs at a deeper level than the recirculation of conventional female stereotypes and is related to the film's thematic and discursive reflections on reproduction and fertility. Narratively, these reflections are attached to the story of the child born from the human/Replicant union of Deckard, the original blade runner, and Rachael, his Replicant love interest. In *Blade Runner*, the category breakdown between human and Replicant centred around the question of whether Replicants could experience 'real' feelings, empathy and love. In *BR 2049*, this ambiguous ground is replaced by an assertion of biological facticity: the 'truth' of Rachael's fertility, womb, ovaries, eggs and hormonal cycles, whose functionality blurs the distinction between human and Replicant. How a Replicant could conceive, gestate and give birth is never explained but remains shrouded in mystery, 'a miracle' as Sapper Morton, the first Nexus 8 Replicant assassinated by K, puts it. For Lt Joshi, a bio-physiological birth through a Replicant womb represents an existential threat to the bio-political order, threatening chaos as the distinction between humans and Replicants dissolves. For Freysa (Hiam Abbass), the leader of the Replicant resistance, the birth substantiates the Replicant political claim to rights as sentient beings, rights withheld by casting Replicants as slave-objects, as less-than-human others.

Rachael/Deckard's 'miracle' child signifies the possiblity of the simulacra becoming organic, the Replicant transmogrifying, beyond appearance, into a hybrid sentience that incorporates the bio-reproductive facilities of the human but whether this child is an aberration or a result of the transforming power of heterosexual love, the film never makes clear. Rachael's putative fertility, however, is paralleled by the macabre obsessions of Niander Wallace (Jared Leto) the creepy head of the Wallace Corporation who dreams of manufacturing self-replicating Replicants as the final measure of biopolitical industrial efficiency, one that would entirely remove human women from the process of reproduction. Wallace's dream provides the film's alternative model of reproductive futures as the realisation of a neoliberal logic of somatic capitalism which sustains a corporate regime based on slavery and the absolute colonisation of life. While Wallace's reproductive meglomania represents the most glaring embodiment of a dystopian ruin of the social and the cunning ruthlessness of capital, the birth of the 'miracle' child provides an idealised vision of reproductive futures as it consolidates a chimeric hope enshrining the possibility of Replicant becoming human through the mediation of bio-reproductivity.

What is the significance of shifting narrative momentum to the bio-reproductive? Joi intimates to K that he is 'of woman born', initiating the film's intensely Œdipal journey as K seeks knowledge of his origins only to discover that he is, ultimately, not 'of woman born' but is, rather, manufactured as a Replicant. *Blade Runner* left the distinction between Replicant and human an open question; the sequel, by contrast, moves toward narrative closure to establish the irrefutable truth of biological reproduction through Sapper and Freysa's eye-witness accounts and evidentiary images such as the scan of Rachael's pelvic bones which show traces of an emergency C section, or the photograph of Freysa holding the child. Whether we agree with Helen Lewis or not that '[f]ertility is the perfect theme for the dystopia of *Blade Runner 2049* because of the western elite anxiety that over-educated, over-liberated women are having fewer children or choosing to opt out of childbearing altogether',[13] her provocation reminds us of just how contentious, fraught and overdetermined the notion of reproduction is, and how easy it is to amplify social anxieties around this volatile terrain.

Richard Dyer, in his ground-breaking study of the historical constitution of whiteness,[14] is one of the first in a range of film and cultural theorists who address how issues of reproduction in *Blade Runner* are complexly articulated within existing racialised problematics. For Dyer, *Blade Runner* exercises a primordial racial dynamic where the search for life, humanity and meaning on the part of its white characters is set against a background filled with anonymous 'Orientals' eking out bare life on the fringes of what remains of society. The spectre of Oriental hordes, of course, is an enduring and ancient racist trope, and Dyer sees it employed here to signal the putative waning of the white man whose status as an endangered species is what lends the film its poignancy and generates much of its continuing cult status. Edward Chan argues that this racial logic of othering continues in *BR 2049*, given how a 'hypermulticultural' underclass is constituted as the abject horizon against which white reproduction remains the privileged genealogical hope.[15] This hope, of course, is embedded in the narrative resolution of *BR2049* which involves the sentimental reunion of the white 'biological' father and daughter who are seen to constitute the rightful familial reproductive unit. Their union is only made possible through the tragic excision of the artificial Replicant's claim to human status and, thus, K dies on the steps of the institute, his body artfully shrouded in white snow, as he reconciles himself to the properness of his sacrifice on the altar of biological reproductive truth.

The gendered and racialised implications of reproduction are rarely addressed in the scholarship exploring the philosophical resonance of *BR2049* which tends to focus on an exploration of the distinction between the authentically human and the non-human. But as we have learned from anti-colonial, post-humanist, queer and black feminist scholars, the category of the human itself represents a particular historical phenomena which emerges during the European Renaissance as a core component of an episteme that is intimately and inextricably bound to the history of European expansionism and colonialism.[16] Within this episteme, as Sylvia Wynter insists, the 'human' only attains semantic substance through the co-constitution of its abject Others: 'peoples of the militarily expropriated New World territories . . . as well as the enslaved peoples of Black Africa [who] were made to reoccupy the matrix slot of Otherness – to be made into the physical referent of the idea of the irrational/subrational Human Other' (266).

The 'human', as such, is always and already marked by the colonial matrix of white supremacy built around the categorisation and exclusion of its others. As a conceptual category and philosophical subject, the 'human' is also foundationally androcentric and occludes the process whereby hierarchies of gender also assign certain populations to the side of abjection and otherness. The critique of the persistent binary logic of othering will be crucial to my reading of *Arrival* whose narrative of alien encounter is already scaffolded by the opposition between the human and its others.

THE MATERNAL ENCOUNTER WITH ALIENS

While *Prisoners* (2013) marked Villeneuve's transition into globalised Hollywood studio filmmaking, *Arrival* signalled his arrival as a superlatively bankable A-list director charged with helming high profile genre adaptations.[17] Working within the legible boundaries of genre but transcending these, *Arrival* is, as one witty critic put it, 'sophisticated, grownup sci-fi: a *movie about aliens for people who don't like* movies about *aliens*' (Lansky).[18] In contrast to the schlocky or campy excesses of the genre, *Arrival*'s narrative is elegantly restrained, focused less on action than on a quest for enlightenment and understanding. Spectacular action happens off-screen or is relayed through faux news reports of looting, demonstrations, and the growing spectre of military retaliation on the part of 'rogue' powers like China, Sudan, Pakistan and Russia as the narrative focuses on Louise's inventive efforts to decipher Heptapod intent and the meaning of the logograms they squirt into the atmosphere which embody a form of cosmic consciousness.

True to the genre of speculative fiction, *Arrival* embodies a dense meditation on language and temporality. Villeneuve's films have always functioned as a palimpsest of layered meaning in their allusiveness, metaphoric play, intertextual referencing and semiotic density and *Arrival* is no exception, inspiring a range of radically diverse textual encounters. Francesco Sticchi, for example, reads the film through the frame of competing linguistic theories, advocating for the superior hermeneutic power of a 'Spinozistic-experiential account' over that of the 'Sapir-Whorf' theory which the film references in expositional dialogue.[19] David H. Fleming and William Brown turn from the nuances of linguistic theory to explore how *Arrival* reconciles two 'counter-intuitive' philosophical theories of time: Gilles Deleuze's 'third synthesis' of time and J. M. E. McTaggart's a-temporal 'C series' of 'unreal' time, concluding that *Arrival* provides a validation of both models as it embodies a temporality beyond the linear conceptual frames of the Anthropocene, joining a 'burgeoning chthulucinema' (341).[20]

Very few of these textual encounters take up the issue of difference, and even fewer comment on the signifying content of the proleptic hallucinations themselves which haunt Louise and whose temporal ambiguity mediates the film's play with time. One exception is Anne Carruthers who argues that the alternate temporality evoked in *Arrival* suggests an approximation of reproductive time, the 'not-yet' reproductive body, and the 'not-yet' child.[21] Carruthers turns to Iris Marion Young's much referenced essay, 'Pregnant Embodiment: Subjectivity and Alienation',[22] to recover a feminist phenomenological theory of alternate time grounded in the experience of actual pregnant women.[23] Young's innovation was to argue that pregnancy inaugurates 'a unique temporality of process and growth in which the woman can experience herself as split between past and future' (Young, 2). However, as Carruthers argues, this is not the temporality figured in *Arrival* where Louise's pregnant body and the maternal labour of giving birth occur are never represented. The child miraculously appears as an infant swaddled in a hospital blanket and the proleptic flashes exclusively chart her development from precocious young girl to dying teenager. As Carruthers notes, '[p]lacing pregnancy and the growth of the child in a temporal ellipsis unravels the representation of the maternal body and pregnant embodiment' (Carruthers, 325). Carruthers' analysis suggests that *Arrival* represents a missed opportunity to complicate reproductive timelines by imagining an alternative to the dominant cultural fantasy of an unfolding future 'held in place by heteronormative familial trajectories' (Carruthers, 327).

I'd like to amplify Carruthers' insights here by exploring how *Arrival*'s staging of an encounter with otherness represents an endeavour to move outside the logics of colonialism, speciesism and anthropocentrism but is, nonetheless, narratively eclipsed, tamed, and domesticated through this familiar/familial narrative resolution of the heterosexual imperative and the figuring of the white precocious child as the embodiment of human futurity. Like Carruthers, I'm intrigued by the fact that the original Chiang story and Villeneuve's adaptation, mediate cosmic consciousness exclusively through the personal, the domestic and maternal reproduction. While both story and film are narratively focalised through the character of Louise Banks and, in fact, the narrative conceit of 'The Story of Your Life' is a letter written by Louise to her daughter, Louise's future as represented in the proleptic visions never seems to intersect with worlds, ecologies or others outside her narrowly circumscribed life. The only future sequences that do not focus on the familial involve Louise lecturing at a university and opening up a box filled with copies of her newly published treatise on translating Heptapod B. These glimmers of the future are never dystopian; they don't gesture toward visions of climate apocalypse, advanced technology, the imperial reign of AI or freakish humanoids and genetically modified animals,[24] the kinds of tropes that have richly populated speculative fiction, they are far more prosaic and limited to the near future: nine months after the Heptapods leave and fifteen or so years into the future.

At some level, *Arrival* defies the optimism of reproductive futurity as the child dies, the promissory note to the future is cut short and the genealogical line is terminated. However, the child does live on in memory as an ethereal figure, an idealised vision. Her untimely death and the way in which unbearable loss is inscribed as an inevitable future event leverages the affective charge of the film. Here it is useful to point out that in Chiang's original story the daughter dies in a freak avalanche at twenty-five having graduated from university as a financial analyst (much to the chagrin of her mother), while *Arrival* layers additional melodramatic resonance by staging the child's death much earlier, so that the child expires as young teenager, an embodiment of pure white innocence, untrammelled by any coarse interactions with the wider world. The most sustained and frequent representations of the child in the proleptic hallucinations feature a six-year-old Hannah (Abigail Pniowsky) running through pastoral settings in nature, hunting frogs, losing a rubber boot by the lake, dressed in a cowboy hat and vest, sporting a toy gun and hobby horse that feel like artefacts of the 1950s. But, perhaps, that is exactly the point, as this vision represents a throwback to a deeply conversative and romantic ideal of childhood. Unlike contemporary children of privilege, Hannah is not glued to her iPad or transfixed by screens; she writes poetry, tells stories, demonstrates artistry, expresses wonder at the natural world (Figure 4.1). Within the narrative diegesis of the film, her death does not signal the end of life on Earth, either for the planet or for Louise, who presumably fashions a wistful life that is ongoing, without Hannah, without Heptapods, without a partner but with a newly minted wisdom and reconciliation to loss.

In its representation of the precocious child as the affective harbinger of the future, *Arrival*'s investment in mainstream representations of reproductive futurity seems remarkably consistent with the way in which the trope figures in Villeneuve's early films. Yet there is something I find deeply seductive about *Arrival* that is particularly related to its mesmerising scenes of alien encounter, their visceral haptics and the non-anthromorphised representation of the Heptapods that haunts. I don't want to let go of the film or entirely dismiss it as yet another iteration of hetero-patriarchal storytelling. *Arrival* unsettles, it is deliberately ambiguous and, as such, has the makings of a cult movie, defined so memorably by Umberto Eco: 'To become a cult, a movie should not display a central idea, but many. It should not exhibit a coherent philosophy of composition. It must live on in and because of its glorious incoherence' (4).[25] The open-ended incoherence of *Arrival* is precisely what invites compulsive and arcane readings, so let me venture my own, an attempt to read against the grain, inspired by the possibility of locating buried or alternate figurations of futurity.

Figure 4.1 Hannah (Abigail Pniowsky), the precocious child in *Arrival*.

Arrival features a strong female protagonist who is not a blank cipher like Bibiane in *Maelström* or Simone in *Un 32 août*, but is narratively established as a renowned linguist, a university professor, a woman of deep intelligence and capability who can navigate her way through complex conceptual matters and narrowly avert an intergalactic war single-handedly. The narrative is focalised through her, established through aural and visual cues and consolidated in Louise's subjective proleptic hallucinations, and in her voice-over narration heard near the end of the film. Her face and the exaggerated sounds of her rapid breathing inside the hazmat suit and breathing apparatus are foregrounded the first time she and her co-worker, theoretical physicist, Dr Ian Donnelly (Jeremy Renner) are inducted into the communication chamber of the alien spacecraft, and throughout it is Louise's embodied physical presence that provides a key haptic interface and point of identification for spectators. Louise has agency and, unlike Bibiane or Simone, who have quit meaningless jobs, she has an intellectual and rigorous commitment to her calling as a linguist. She has no other human contacts than her mother (indicated in a cursory phone call) and her university students: professional life is, presumably, what drives her. Dressed in frumpy clothing or army fatigues, void of makeup or any conventional feminine artifice, hair held in a prim bun or ponytail, she is largely rendered as an asexual, although not ungendered character. Among the crew of scientists and intelligence specialists, Louise's methodology is bound up with her ability to intuit, and to create an affective and empathetic connection to the aliens, a modus operandi set against the rigid rationality, inflexible mechanistic thinking of the CIA, and the American military complex.

Opposed to the hard science approach of her academic co-worker Ian Donnelly, Louise's humanistic linguistic interpretative frame represents a strongly female coded mode of relating and knowing. When Ian suggests the cornerstone of civilisation is not language but science and starts to read the kinds of questions that would interest a theoretical physicist, she retorts 'How about we just talk to them before we start throwing math problems at them'. Although the army has established strict protocols around protective gear, decontamination sprays and inoculations against the potential biohazard of alien atmosphere, in her very first encounter with the aliens, Louise throws scientific principle and caution to the wind, removing her protective gear and breathing apparatus in order that the aliens can see her face and connect with her emotionally.

In the outer communication chamber of the alien spacecraft, Louise, Ian and the crew are separated from the Heptapods by a giant transparent screen which enables them to see into the white foggy atmosphere where the Heptapods live and approach the screen to squirt black ink from their tentacles, an emission which resolves into exquisite forms of ephemeral calligraphy. In their symmetry, delicacy and evanescence, these striking black and white Heptapod emanations could be easily read as high concept installation art, at home in any A-list global art biennial. We might even read these scenes in the communications chamber in relation to Laura Marks's elaboration of haptic cinema, a multisensory visuality that engages spectators in an embodied sensorium.[26] Indeed, the guttural texture of alien vocalisations, the intimacy of Louise's breathing, and the tactile intensity of the scene where Louise holds her hand against the screen and a Heptapod throws up a tentacular high-five on the other side of the screen barrier, add layers of intense visceral affect to the scenes of alien encounter.[27]

In a later scene, Ian helpfully provides exposition that this 'writing' of the aliens is semasiographic: 'Like their ship, or their bodies, their written language has no forward or backward direction. Linguists call this non-linear orthography. Which raises the question, is this how they think?' Ian's question, of course, orders the narrative quest to arrive at a deeper understanding of alien being and much screen time is subsequently devoted to the research process of Louise and Ian as they mass data and categorise screen grabs of the logograms, all the while balancing time pressures and the trigger-happy crudeness of their military overseers. Ultimately though, it is only when Louise transgresses the boundary of the screen separating humans and aliens, and is enveloped in alien atmosphere, that the real leap in understanding takes place, one that is mediated by her bodily surrender, her vulnerability, permeability, and willingness to intimately engage with otherness.

This transgression, and really, the climax of the film, takes place at the 90-minute mark, when Louise rushes to the docking site after rogue soldiers have triggered a bomb in the main space ship. The aliens send down a mini space pod that transports Louise, unencumbered with PPE or a breathing mask, into the depths of the mothercraft, gently floating her into the other side of the screen, into the foggy whiteness of the Heptapod atmosphere. The scene is marked from the very beginning as a kind of oneiric hallucination occurring in a unique warp of time and space. Louise's hair floats loose from its restraints, undulating in slow motion as she floats through the atmosphere and lands in the cavernous hull. Shrouded in the foggy atmosphere, her body and face radiate an incandescent glow (Figure 4.2). With her head tilted up toward the light, Louise appears years younger, as if a child herself, her face moulded in an expression of erotic surrender.

The visual staging of this encounter is coded around a complex binary of whiteness and darkness where the blinding whiteness of Louise's skin, the dense white fog of the alien atmosphere and the white quartz-like ground of the spaceship are contrasted with the dark, elephantine, wrinkled otherness of a Heptapod appendage, seen for the first time in close-up and in detail. In *White*, Richard Dyer insists that 'true whiteness', as a culturally invented racial category, 'resides in the non-corporeal (also associated with) the soul, the mind, and also emptiness, non-existence and death, beauty, virtue' (33). Dyer sees mainstream Western cinema as a potent contemporary purveyor of these racial associations which

Figure 4.2 Louise (Amy Adams) floats in the Heptapod atmosphere.

are baked into the technologies of photography, film stock and lighting conventions. Cinema, he argues 'permits a construction of the human person that discriminates between those who have a large amount of lighting shining through them and those who have next to none – the radiant white face and the opaque black one' (69). Moreover, the 'radiant white face' is a recurrent attribute of the white female actor, he points out, who is frequently lit so as to appear as the apogee of immateriality, spirituality and transcendence.

I'd like to think that this scene of intimate alien encounter (Figure 4.3) is deliberately designed to represent Louise's ascension into cosmic Heptapod consciousness through association with the long history of Western Renaissance depictions of female religious ecstasy, particularly those devoted to the ecstasy of Mary Magdalene or Saint Teresa of Avila. Head thrown back, eyes closed, lips parted, Louise receives this gift like the saints before her, as a form of spiritual impregnation, a transmission that occurs without the messy mixing of material bodies. Lost in alien space, Louise enters another dimension, her hair released from the restraints of gravity and propriety to ripple in slow motion, like a halo around her head. We hear her rapid breathing as the scene plays out like a deep erotic phantasm.

Fleming and Brown hint that *Arrival* might be read as an allegory of first contact (341). Fleming amplifies this insight in an essay where he returns, obsessively, to a single scene he describes as a worrying 'cine-splinter' of intense and complex reference (252).[28] The scene in question involves the confrontation between Colonel Weber (Forest Whitaker) and Louise who points out the danger of mistranslation by relaying a story around the encounter between Captain Cook and the aboriginal peoples of Australia. As Louise narrates it, 'One of the sailors pointed at the animals that hop around and put their babies in their pouch, and he asked what they were. And the aborigines said "Kangaroo."'

Figure 4.3 The Heptapod Costello and Louise meet.

Weber asks what the point is and Louis responds that 'It wasn't until later that they learned that kangaroo means "I don't understand."' Apart from this literal reference to a colonial encounter (which Louise later admits she invented as a salvo to buy more time), Fleming reads the scene's signifying elements, its lighting design, costuming, and blocking as a 'a series of dialectical Manichean binaries,' in which 'the scene's bold black/white aesthetics virtually prime viewers to perceive Weber as being – to paraphrase Fanon – simultaneously African-American, Aboriginal and Zulu' (258). I'm not convinced that all viewers would make that kind of association[29] and I'd like to move beyond the epidermal schema that Fleming evokes as key to the racial manicheanisms in the film to think about a more obvious reading of *Arrival* as a reversed form of colonial contact where the explorers are not white Europeans but 'blackened'[30] Heptapods who seek not world domination, dispossession and territorial land grab but relation, the guarantee of friendship with humans who they hope will come to their assistance 3,000 years into the future. In contrast to the magnanimity of the Heptapods who come bearing the gift of their language as a portal to advanced consciousness, humankind, as embodied by paranoid military complexes or the looting mobs and suicidal cults we see featured in the news reporting, seems dangerously crude, primitive and unenlightened. This reversal does a number of things: it undermines species aggrandisement which considers the human as the pinnacle of evolution, and relativises humanity as but one form of life that exists in a much larger cosmic frame of multiplicity and difference. In highlighting the advanced form of Heptapod intelligence and consciousness, the reversal privileges another other mode of being and ordering relations with others, based in generosity, reciprocity and the primacy of the gift over ruthless competition and militaristic aggressiveness. Louise, of course, takes on the role of conduit for communicating this model to the world. She intercepts Chinese military aggression by stealing a satellite phone, contacting General Shang and repeating the words his wife had uttered on her death bed, pointing out the real cost of war. She publishes a book which documents the linguistic process of translating Heptapod B and at the glittering gala where she is to receive a peace prize, we learn that her accession to cosmic understanding has been translated into a *Realpolitik* of banal liberal internationalism. Chinese aggression has been tamed by appealing to the heart and the twelve countries where the aliens had docked have now agreed to share information and work for the betterment of all.

This vision of world peace lends a certain tepid idealism to the film's narrative resolution where the brutality of colonialism is reduced to misunderstandings and mistranslations, the military industrial complex is softened by a female touch and a humanistic conceptual fame ushers in new forms of co-operative internationalism. We might be tempted to end our reading there, and yet the scene of Louise's intimate encounter with the Heptapods on the other side of the barrier is my 'cine-splinter' and one that provokes a search for textual possibilities that might also reflect a deeper or more radical inversion of colonial and racial tropes of otherness.

QUEERING THE HEPTAPOD

As argued above, the acoustic and visual design of the scene bears a haptic and visceral intensity, drawn from the tactile swirl of the dense white fog of alien atmosphere, the guttural drone of Heptapod vocalisations, the acoustic focalisation on Louise's nervous breathing and the muted base drone of the musical score. The scene is built around a dialectic of shot/reverse shots, alternating images of 'Costello', the remaining Heptapod, with close-ups of Louise's incandescent face or high angle long shots, presumably mapped onto the point of view of Costello which emphasise Louise's vulnerability as a tiny human female body. While previous glimpses of the Heptapods in the communication room had only featured murky body parts, here we are treated to a full long shot of the towering alien, replete with close ups of the elephantine texture of its tentacles, towering spherical trunk and faceless top with some kind of orifice on top of it. Costello and Louise never touch, although she attempts to grasp the ethereal logogram as it dissipates into the atmosphere, but it is precisely her surrender and physical proximity to the otherness of the alien that accelerates her understanding of Heptapod language and consciousness.

As spectators, we are also aligned with the evolution of Louise's fluency by means of the subtitles which are used for the first time to render the meaning of Heptapod logograms. From these we learn that Abbott is 'death process' and that the purpose of the alien visit is finally enunciated as a message of friendship and solidarity: 'We help humanity in 3,000 years. We need humanity's help.' Throughout the exchange, Louise remains bewildered by the cryptic nature of the Heptapod's utterance and by the sudden flurry of proleptic hallucinations which the utterances seem to provoke. Emerging back on Earth, transformed by her encounter, she walks back through the military tents as the soldiers and intelligence personnel are preparing to evacuate, logs into her computer, calls up a graphic screen shot of the logograms and has a monumental epiphany: she can read Hetapod B.

How anti-climactic, then, is the exchange between Ian and Louise when she returns from her transcendent encounter and Ian, in a rare moment of personal revelation, tells Louise the most amazing part of the alien adventure was meeting her. Notably, Louise doesn't respond with a passionate kiss but with a companionate hug and this embrace is montaged with a flash forward to a similar embrace in Louise's living room several months later where Donnelly delivers the rather unsexy come on: 'Do you want to make a baby?' How much more interesting if Louise had been impregnated by the remaining Heptapod, inspired by a queer and deviant bonding over their joint recognition of death and loss, the loss of Abbot and the future death of the child to come. Such a coupling would of course throw a wrench into the dominant cultural script of heteronormative futurities but it might begin to grapple with the fact that in our current moment, the future, as Franco 'Bifo' Berardi has caustically noted, is not what it used to be.[31]

The most exciting work being done today in the fields of feminist technoscience, black feminism, Indigenous philosophy, animal studies and queer theory is, precisely, imagining the future outside of the logics of reproduction, heteropatriarchy and colonialism, beyond what Donna Haraway calls the 'old saws of Western philosophy and political economics': 'human exceptionalism and bounded individualism' ('Tentacular Thinking').[32] Haraway's point is pertinent here because while this work emerges from a broad range of diverse and distinct agendas, it shares an insight that Man or the Human as the anthropocentric subject of history is a necessarily retrograde, if not dangerous presumption. The point then is not to simply expand the concept of the Human to include those who have been historically excluded (Africans, the Indigenous, Replicants, etc.) but to develop expansive ecological thinking, grounded in materialities and relationalitites with others, including non-human others.

Haraway muddles over an appropriate slogan for the Chthulucene, a speculative new ecological epoch marked by a profound recalibration of relations between humans and their non-human others. She finally lands on: 'Make Kin, Not Babies!' (*Staying* 102).[33] Making kin involves multispecies relationality and alternative 'tentacular' models of being and becoming, knowing and thriving. Kin is never restricted to the human but incorporates all forms of vitality and life which are bound in intimate physical and conceptual relations to each other. In this, Haraway is a partisan of many tentacled entities, 'cnidarians, spiders, fingery beings like humans and raccoons, squid, jellyfish, neural extravaganzas, fibrous entities, flagellated beings, myofibril braids, matted and felted microbial and fungal tangles, probing creepers, swelling roots, reaching and climbing tendrilled ones' ('Tentacular Thinking'), precisely because of their inherent multiplicity, their embeddedness in networks and nets of difference which defy the monological thinking of humanist Man.

Making kin with tentacular others, seems to me to perfectly encapsulate Louise's encounter with the Heptapods, whose tentacular physical being, investment in nurturing relations and cosmic intelligence seem like a perfect instantiation of Haraway's weird and wonderful cnidarians. This alternative mode of knowing and relating, however, is never given full primacy in the film whose narrative resolution yields to a proscriptive reproductive futurity and instrumentalised liberal internationalism. Of course, *Arrival* is a blockbuster genre film, indebted to a global corporate entertainment complex: to imagine that the film might fully commit to a revolutionary weirdness, is, obviously, wishful thinking. But, as I've argued elsewhere,[34] Villeneuve's films are frequently riven by two opposing impulses: one which drives the breathtaking immersive hapticity of images and sounds, apparent from the elegaic landscapes in *Un 32 août*, *Maelström* and *Polytechnique* to the inventive dystopian worlding in *BR 2049* and the other embodied in the centripetal forces of narrative. Even as he transitions into studio filmmaking and is charged with working with scripts or adaptations written by studio-appointed authors, Villeneuve retains an art cinema sensibility which tempers narrative action with a kind of meditative solemnity and conceptual layering embedded in performance, and in the ingenuity of art and sound direction. That his films from the early art house offerings to the franchise blockbusters consistently embrace reproductive futurity as a normative resolution and humanist aspiration seem to me to reveal as much about Villeneuve's auteurist preoccupations as they do about the narrative constraints and demands of a mainstream film industry. *Arrival* bears the marks of all of those constraints and yet the complex, compelling and layered nature of the film has provided a rich invitation to speculation and a provocation, grounded in its haptic representation of an encounter with aliens, to imagine otherwise.

NOTES

1. Debruge, Peter, 'Film Review: *Blade Runner 2049*', *Variety*, 29 September 2017, available at: https://variety.com/2017/film/reviews/blade-runner-2049-review-1202576220 (last accessed 28 June 2021).
2. Shanahan, Timothy, 'We're All Just Looking for Something Real', *Blade Runner 2049: A Philosophical Exploration,* edited by Timothy Shanahan and Paul Smart, Routledge, 2020, pp. 8–26.

3. See in particular: Like Stories of Old, 'In Search of the Distinctly Human/the Philosophy of *Blade Runner 2049*', YouTube, 29 January 2018, available at: https://www.youtube.com/watch?v=O4etinsAy34&ab_channel=LikeStoriesofOld (last accessed 28 June 2021). See also Jack's Movie Reviews: '*Blade Runner 2049 – The Evolution of Humanity*', YouTube, 6 January 2018, https://www.youtube.com/watch?v=LxIBv_XS3ls&ab_channel=Jack%27sMovieReviews (last accessed 28 June 2021).
4. In addition to the Shanahan and Smart anthology referenced above, see Bunce, Robin and Trip McCrossin (eds), *Blade Runner 2049 and Philosophy: This Breaks the World,* Open Court, 2019.
5. Response to the feminist critiques of *BR 2049* on the internet was highly vociferous and predictable. Multiple blog entries and video essays by (male) fans took offence at the challenge to a beloved cult object. One of the more interesting of these is: 'Novum', '*Blade Runner 2049* *Does Not* Have "A Woman Problem"', YouTube, 11 March 2019, available at: https://www.youtube.com/watch?v=6GsXBh5PGZU&ab_channel=Novum (last accessed 28 June 2021).
6. Stewart, Sara, 'You'll Love the new *Blade Runner* – Unless You're a Woman', New York Post, 4 October 2017, available at: https://nypost.com/2017/10/04/youll-love-the-new-blade-runner-unless-youre-a-woman (last accessed 28 June 2021).
7. Fletcher, Rosie and Sam Ashurst, 'Can we talk about *Blade Runner 2049*'s problem with women?', *DigitalSpy*, 9 October 2017, available at: https://www.digitalspy.com/movies/a839916/blade-runner-2049-gender-issues (last accessed 28 June 2021).
8. Edelman, Lee, *No Future: Queer Theory and the Death Drive*, Duke University Press, 2004.
9. Sheldon, Rebekah, 'Somatic Capitalism: Reproduction, Futurity, and Feminist Science Fiction', *Ada, A Journal of Gender, New Media & Technology*, no. 3, 2013, available at: https://adanewmedia.org/2013/11/issue3-sheldon (last accessed 28 June 2021).
10. The Bechdel test was posed by queer graphic artist Alison Bechdel who suggested a low bar for assessing the status of women in fiction film: 'two women who talk to each other about something other than a man.'
11. De Armas is of Cuban descent.
12. For a detailed analysis of the hologram scene in *BR 2049*, see Christophe Gelly and David Roche in this volume.
13. Lewis, Helen, '*Blade Runner 2049* is an Uneasy Feminist Parable About Controlling the Means of Reproduction', *The New Statesman*, 9 October 2017, available at: https://www.newstatesman.com/culture/film/2017/10/blade-runner-2049-uneasy-feminist-parable-about-controlling-means-reproduction (last accessed 28 June 2021).
14. Dyer, Richard, *White: Essays on Race and Culture*, Routledge, 1997.
15. Chan, Edward, 'Race in the *Blade Runner* cycle and demographic dystopia', *Science Fiction Film and Television*, vol. 13, no. 1, Spring 2020, pp. 59–76.
16. See: Wynter, Sylvia, 'Unsettling the Coloniality of Being/Power/Truth/Freedom: Towards the Human, After Man, Its Overrepresentation – An Argument', *The New Centennial Review*, vol. 3, no. 3, Fall 2003, pp. 257–337; Mignolo, Walter, 'Decoloniality and Phenomenology: The Geopolitics of Knowing and Epistemic/Ontological Colonial Differences', *Journal of Speculative Philosophy*, vol. 32, no. 3, 2018, pp. 360–87; and Jackson, Zakiyyah Iman, *Becoming Human: Matter and Meaning in an Antiblack World*, New York University Press, 2020.
17. *Arrival* is based on the 1998 celebrated science fiction story by Ted Chiang, 'Story of Your Life,' adapted by Eric Heisserer. The film was shot for a budget of $47 million, released by Paramount and Sony Releasing, and went on to gross $203 million worldwide. Chiang, Ted, 'Story of Your Life.' (1998), in *Stories of Your Life and Others*, Vintage, 2016, pp. 91–146.

18. Lansky, Sam, 'In *Arrival*, Amy Adams Takes a Listening Tour of the Universe', *Time*, 10 November 2016, available at: https://time.com/4565975/amy-adams-arrival (last accessed 28 June 2021).
19. Sticchi, Francesco, 'From Spinoza To Contemporary Linguistics: Pragmatic Ethics In Denis Villeneuve's *Arrival*', *Canadian Journal of Film Studies/ Revue canadienne d'études cinematographiques*, vol. 27, no. 2, Fall 2018, pp. 48–65.
20. Fleming, David H. and William Brown, 'Through a (First) Contact Lens Darkly: *Arrival*, Unreal Time and Chthulucinema', *Film Philosophy*, vol. 22, no. 3, October 2018, pp. 340–63.
21. Carruthers, Anne. 'Temporality, Reproduction and the Not-Yet in Denis Villeneuve's *Arrival*', *Film-Philosophy*, vol. 22, no. 3, October 2018, pp. 321–39.
22. Young, Iris Marion, 'Pregnant Embodiment: Subjectivity and Alienation', *The Journal of Medicine and Philosophy: A Forum for Bioethics and Philosophy of Medicine*, vol. 9, no. 1, February 1984, pp. 45–62.
23. Young points out that her analysis is restricted to the specific experience of women in technologically sophisticated Western societies and presupposes that the pregnant woman subject she writes about is one who has chosen pregnancy, a generative anomaly, given as she writes that '[m]ost women in human history have not chosen their pregnancies'.
24. Who can forget Margaret Atwood's headless, multi-appendaged Chickienobs in *Oryx and Crake*? Atwood, Margaret, *Oryx and Crake*, McClelland and Stewart, 2003.
25. Eco, Umberto, '*Casablanca*: Cult Movies and Intertextual Collage', *Substance*, vol. 14, no. 2, issue 47, 1985, pp. 3–12.
26. Marks, Laura U., *The Skin of the Film: Intercultural Cinema, Embodiment and the Senses*, Duke University Press, 2000.
27. John Richardson et al. also draw attention to *Arrival*'s immersive and sensory-rich qualities, noting how the sound designers 'deliberately sought to *envoice* the aliens as living, agentic creatures by creating their sound effects from natural materials' including slowed down birdsong and camel snorts. Richardson, John, Anna-Elena Pääkkölä, and Sanna Qvick, 'Sensing Time and Space through the Soundtracks of *Interstellar* and *Arrival*', *The Oxford Handbook of Cinematic Listening*, edited by Carlo Cenciarelli, Oxford University Press, 2018, pp. 1–25.
28. Fleming, David H., 'Race and World Memory in *Arrival*', *Science Fiction Film and Television*, vol. 13, no. 2 Summer, 2020, pp. 247–67.
29. I'm actually always impressed with Whitaker who, no matter how macho a character he plays, always manages to depict a kind of wounded masculinity, but perhaps that is because I've been imprinted with his portrayal of Jody, the black queer soldier in *The Crying Game* (Neil Jordan 1992).
30. Jackson develops the concept of the 'blackened' humans in her rich *Becoming Human: Matter and Meaning in an Antiblack World* in order to highlight the fact that colour assignation results from an ongoing process, not from an immutable essential identity.
31. Berardi, Franco, Gary Genosko, and Nicholas Thoburn, *After the Future*, AK Press, 2011.
32. Haraway, Donna, 'Tentacular Thinking: Anthropocene, Capitalocene, Chthulucene', *E-flux*, no. 75, September 2016, available at: https://www.e-flux.com/journal/75/67125/tentacular-thinking-anthropocene-capitalocene-chthulucene (last accessed 28 June 2021).
33. Haraway, Donna, *Staying With the Trouble: Making Kin in the Chthulucene*, Duke University Press, 2016.
34. Longfellow, Brenda, 'The practice of memory and the politics of memorialization: Denis Villeneuve's *Polytechnique*', *Canadian Journal of Film Studies/Revue canadienne d'études cinématographiques*, vol. XXII, no. 1, Spring, 2013, pp. 86–106.

CHAPTER 5

Filming Missing Bodies: 'Bodiless-Character Films' and the Presence of Absence in Denis Villeneuve's Cinema

Emily Sanders

In the following pages I will explore the function of absence aesthetics in four of Villeneuve's films: *Maelström* (2000), *Polytechnique* (2009), *Incendies* (2010), and *Arrival* (2016). In order to conduct this investigation, I will frame my focus through Christian Metz's discussion of absence in narrative fiction films, and the 'bodiless-character films' theory of Odeya Kohen Raz and Sandra Meiri. For Kohen Raz and Meiri, bodiless-character films are defined by three characteristics: '(1) the absence of actors and objects from the spectator's space; (2) the role of seeing in spectatorship vis-à-vis this absence; and (3) cinema's ability to embellish its imaginary objects, the latter playing the role of fantasy objects' (63).[1] They employ this theory in films whose characters are always already missing, and it is their status as a 'missing person' that propels the film's narrative forward. By denying the sight of the object missing (here, the character), the films 'frustra[te] the spectator's desire to see', without a grand reveal of the person who has been missing at the films' end (Kohen Raz and Meiri 63). The loss of the missing person is permanent. For Kohen Raz and Meiri, this is the case in films such as Alfred Hitchcock's *Rebecca* (1940), *North by Northwest* (1959) and *Psycho* (1960), and Spike Jonze's *Her* (2013), but also true in films such as Michelangelo Antonioni's *L'Avventura* (1960), where the missing person that starts the film gets discarded, never to be found.

Some of Villeneuve's narratives – such as *Prisoners* (2013), *Incendies*, and in a different manner, *Sicario* (2015) – are about recovering bodies, but mostly they are an exploration of the feelings of loss. Structured through absence, the films focus on the characters' changing relationship to their surroundings, to their environments, and, most importantly, to their bodies. To begin this analysis, I will explore Metz's idea of good cinematic objects that inspire, upon viewing them, a viewer's fantasy. These good cinematic objects will heretofore be called fantasy objects, and they play a significant role in the function of absence aesthetics. Then, I will describe three main features of absence aesthetics: cyclical metonymies, the disruption of linear narrative structure, and the emotional and social isolation of the films' main (female) characters. Following this description, I will then look at how these three main features are embodied or exhibited through three different tropes – motherhood, surrogacy, and artefactualisation – which recur throughout Villeneuve's cinema. I will then engage in close readings in these four films to describe how these configurations of absence aesthetics work within and across each film.

ABSENCE AESTHETICS

Absence aesthetics are fuelled by fantasy objects. In this context, fantasy objects are the fictional characters on screen through which the spectator seeks identification but, because of their fictional status as signifiers, are themselves perpetually absent. For Metz, the cinema creates tension between loss and desire for its audience members. Viewers of cinema feed their desire through watching cinema and identifying fantasy objects in the main characters:

> Similarly, in order to understand the film (at all), I must perceive the photographed object as absent, its photograph as present, and the presence of this absence as signifying. The imaginary of the cinema presupposes the symbolic, for the spectator must first of all have known the primordial mirror. But as the latter instituted the ego very largely in the imaginary, the second mirror of the screen, a symbolic apparatus, itself in turn depends on the reflection and lack. However, it is not phantasy, a 'purely' symbolic-imaginary site, for the absence of the object and the codes of that absence are really produced in it by the *physis* of an equipment: the cinema is a body (a *corpus* for the semiologist), a fetish that can be loved. (57)[2]

In this explanation of the workings of the ego and the imaginary of the spectator when watching a film, Metz considers the cinema a fabricated space that mimics the symbolic and the Lacanian mirror, in which the viewer identifies with the cinema's fantasy objects – the photographed object – in order to dream their ideal self. Cinema, especially narrative cinema, is a waking dream-space for spectators. Cinema is more than a fantasy, more than a 'purely symbolic imaginary site' since the cinema offers a dreamscape we can replay and revisit, embodied by the artefact of film. The underlying contract of this relationship is the acknowledgement of the audience that this cinematic space is fictional. This awareness of fiction becomes, for Metz, what structures desire for the viewer: the cinema's inherent lack, the attractive fiction that keeps audiences returning.

I take this idea of fantasy objects further in applying it to Villeneuve's cinema. Villeneuve's fantasy objects are the characters who are constantly referenced in dialogue and action, but are (almost always) absent from the screen. In *Maelström*, the fantasy object is Bibiane's (Marie-Josée Croze) mother. Many are fantasy objects in *Incendies*: Simon (Maxim Gaudette) and Jeanne's (Mélissa Désormeaux-Poulin) unknown father and their missing older brother are the most prominent fantasy objects, but their emotionally absent and recently deceased mother, Nawal (Lubna Azabal), becomes a fantasy object as well, since the narrative also contains her within the irretrievable past. The fantasy objects in *Polytechnique* and *Arrival* are different in their representation but not in their function as perpetually missing. *Polytechnique*'s fantasy objects are direct references to the real-life bodies of those missing, or lost, during the 1989 École Polytechnique Massacre, which resulted in the murder of fourteen women. *Polytechnique* uses surrogates to represent those deceased (the film states at the beginning that it will not refer to its characters by the victims' real names). From the outset of the film, there is already a gulf of absence between the real-life victims of the massacre and their referents. Somewhat similarly, *Arrival*'s missing fantasy object is Louise's (Amy Adams) daughter Hannah (at various ages played by Jadyn Malone; Abigail Pniowsky; Julia Scarlett Dan), whom we only witness through brief, slightly distorted memories that interrupt the linearity of the narrative.

Villeneuve's absence aesthetics are located in the formal elements of his films. There are three components to absence aesthetics: cyclical metonymies, narrative sequences that disrupt the films' linearity in order to oscillate between memory/the past and the 'present' day, and the depiction of emotional and social isolation in Villeneuve's main female characters. A series of tropes demonstrate these three components, and it is these tropes that I will later discuss in detail in order to theorise Villeneuve's function of absence aesthetics.

The main characters' fantasy objects, like the viewers of the film in Metz's paradigm, are also missing. Their absence comes from trauma: parental neglect, death brought on by war, or another traumatic encounter which creates a void within the characters, one that the narrative seeks to fill. These missing fantasy objects for the main characters emphasise how 'unattainability' becomes necessary in Metz's film taxonomy. For Metz, 'narrative film's paradoxical nature lies precisely in the unattainability of the object on the screen making it possible for spectators to let the camera inscribe them into an imaginary space, compatible with an unconscious inscription in the primal scene fantasy' (Kohen Raz and Meiri 63). In *Maelström, Polytechnique, Incendies* and *Arrival*, the unattainable fantasy object can never be retrieved, or brought back in a satisfactory way to those who desire its return; it therefore haunts the protagonists. Haunting occurs through cyclical metonymies: reminders of who once was but is no longer. Furthermore, the way in which those missing haunt the screen in each film produces a similar kind of desire as described between the audience and screen in Metz. Desire impels the characters towards their emotional and social isolation. This interplay of desire and isolation is shaped by the formal characteristics of the film, and the way Villeneuve defies or undermines linear convention in narrative film. Additionally to the three formal components I have detailed above that structure absence aesthetics (cyclical metonymies, disruptive linear narrative structure, and social/emotional isolation), Villeneuve constructs three different recurring tropes in order to emphasise these formal features in his film. The three aspects of absence aesthetics I will examine below are: motherhood, surrogacy, and artefactualisation. These tropes triangulate the structure of absence throughout Villeneuve's œuvre and they present themselves similarly, although with notable varying inflections, in each film.

MOTHERHOOD

Motherhood is a recurrent theme throughout Villeneuve's œuvre that represents all three of the components in absence aesthetics. In terms of cyclical metonymies, the pregnant body signals ancestry that has been lost and impossible or inaccessible futures. As I will look at more closely in what follows, the temporality of the pregnant body and its various cultural significances disrupts the narrative's progression forward, since pregnancy destabilises the ideas of past, present, and future. The pregnant body inscribes women as more than themselves – they contain futures and carry within their womb the trauma of the past. Most of Villeneuve's leading female characters have been or become pregnant within the diegesis. It is clear that Villeneuve imbues within them the same weight of cultural expectation during their pregnancies. However, this does not help the women create community or collaboration. Instead, motherhood and pregnancy are a lonely affair, and thus they also design the absence aesthetic of emotional and social isolation.

Villeneuve almost exclusively characterises women as people who can, or will, get pregnant. This treatment of an essentialised, reproductive woman's body as 'woman-as-hopeful-womb' follows the trajectory of previous theorists in feminist biopolitics.[3] Villeneuve's treatment of women perpetuates this idea of the womb 'as a national space that contains the future/foetus citizen' (Sparling 166). Hope generates through the treatment of the woman's womb as a vessel of futurity. As Heather Latimer states, 'women and other pregnant people are usually assumed to "enfold futures, both individual and the future of peoples"' (430).[4] Certainly, Villeneuve's œuvre constructs the product of the womb as a potential and hopeful departure from past institutionalised routines of violence and suffering which at points have been sites of violent impregnation and failed abortion, with the idea that the offspring might create a better future. But, as is evident in *Maelström, Polytechnique, Incendies,* and *Arrival,* women's generative capacities also signal a past. In this sense, 'woman-as-hopeful-womb' relates to Pierre Nora's theory of *lieux de mémoire* (sites of memory). Conceptualised in relation to the way in which the erasure of history – through colonial forces, rapid technologisation, changing political structures, and more – Nora uses this term to indicate tactile or imaginary sites, rather than actual environments, 'where memory crystallises and secretes itself' during 'a particular historical moment, a turning point where consciousness of a break with the past is bound up with the sense that memory has been torn – but torn in such a way as to pose the problem of the embodiment of memory in certain sites where a sense of historical continuity persists' (7).[5] The hopeful womb becomes this site of a 'historical moment' where memory and history are embedded within the very process of reproduction. In its ability to reproduce futures, the hopeful womb also becomes a liminal space that intertwines various temporalities, but its inherent status as hopeful is engraved in how the narrative writes the foetus as producing a better future (although, we must ask, better for whom?). And yet, Villeneuve's figuration of motherhood is that the mother births loss. Pregnancy, in his films, is always immediately indicative of an irretrievable pastness and hopeful future. In all four films, this idea of futurity is intimately tied to the main character's reproductive capacity. Therefore, the womb becomes a cultural site that produces hope – a child – a *lieu de mémoire* that fills in the absences of the past and future.

Maelström, Villeneuve's second full-length feature, follows Bibiane, a young wayward daughter of a fashion icon in Montreal. Bibiane is future-less: the film opens with Bibiane getting an abortion, and we quickly learn she's mismanaged one of her family's fashion storefronts. Bibiane drives inebriated and consequently kills a fishmonger crossing the road, after which she also tries to kill herself. Her self-destructive tendencies seem to stem from the pressure of living in her mother's shadow. As such, Bibiane's mother is her fantasy object. Never materialised on screen, the mother haunts Bibiane, although whether it's a literal haunting remains unclear. One reviewer asserts the death of Bibiane's mother,[6] and yet at one point in the film Bibiane's brother (Bobby Beshro) comments how she has yet again avoided seeing their mother at a family gathering over the weekend. If Bibiane's mother is not actually dead, she at least seems figuratively dead to Bibiane. Either way, her mother's status as missing is clear. Additionally, Bibiane's choice to terminate her pregnancy at the very beginning of the film denotes her as a different kind of 'absent' mother.

Bibiane's inability to access the future is visualised especially poignantly during one scene in the film. A magazine – appropriately called *L'Avenir* – asks to photograph Bibiane for the cover of the magazine. When Bibiane is at the shoot, a photographer asks her to *become* her mother. In French, the photographer tells Bibiane 'I'd like you to do it as slowly as possible. I want you to transform, but slowly. Very slowly, gently. Let her come out. Let your mother out. I want you to become transparent. Now I don't want to see you anymore.'[7] Several fantasy objects emerge and fold into each other: Bibiane's mother, whom she must 'let out', but also Bibiane, who must vanish herself, leaving another absence in trying to fill the original. These absences are linked to motherhood; it is motherhood that is commanded, that must 'come out', and that Bibiane refuses to perform. These aesthetic constructions – the haunting absent mother and Bibiane's abortion as a metric of her purposelessness – characterises Bibiane as 'a void waiting to be filled with meaning' (Longfellow 'Counter-Narratives' 74).[8] If this void can be filled at all, the film tells us it is with Evian (Jean-Nicolas Verreault), the son of the fishmonger she killed, who provides Bibiane a new life through sealing her within the bounds of heterosexual monogamy at the end of the film.

One of the most unique features of *Maelström* is its talking fish (Figure 5.1). Voiced by Pierre Lebeau, the fish is the omniscient narrator who lives in the story only to die again and again at the hands of a nearly-naked butcher in a blood-soaked darkly lit dungeon-like location. The ceiling of the dungeon is concave, with prominent beams that give the sense as if the fish is in the belly of a whale. The fish gasps to the camera in the opening shot, 'I have little time left. I would like to take advantage of my final breaths to tell you a story. A very pretty story.'[9] The camera then cuts to a medical lighting apparatus, and we find Bibiane in the

Figure 5.1 The dying fish/the narrator (voiced by Pierre Lebeau), giving voice and form to Bibiane's abortion in *Maelström*.

process of having an abortion. I contend that the highly stylised dungeon, full of grime, with low lighting that emphasises the imminent death of the fish, is actually the 'belly', or womb, of Bibiane. The slightly destabilising cuts from the dungeon to the abortionist's office link the two sites so that the film provides a reading of the fish as Bibiane's abortion. While Villeneuve apparently inserted the figure of the fish to represent 'storytellers from the beginning of time' (Melnyk 96),[10] I posit the fish serves as one of the absence signifiers, and is Bibiane's abortion made flesh (and viscera). Indeed, Melnyk states that Villeneuve's 'desire' for making the film is 'to explore the emotional trauma of having an abortion' (Melnyk 94). Although the film does open with the abortion, the abortion doesn't seem to be the main concern for Villeneuve. If anything, it seems as though it's Bibiane's own life that she is trying to abort. Her high-rise apartment in downtown Montreal matches the sterility of the abortion clinic. Bibiane's carelessness of her own life and future, evident in her frequent use of drugs, loss of company funds, drunk driving, accidental killing of Evian's father, and eventual suicide attempt all give the sense that Villeneuve is more concerned with the meaninglessness Bibiane feels in her own life, because she can't live up to the expectations of her family. Perhaps the gulf between Villeneuve's impetus for creating the film and the messages he actually transmits comes from the fact that, as Melnyk states, '[Villeneuve's] reading of the trauma comes from someone who can never experience it other than as an observer' (94). The film becomes an exploration of the feeling of loss positioned through this aesthetic and narrative lens of the hopeful womb. The fish/abortion, as a *lieu de mémoire*, can't quite live within the *mise-en-scène* that depicts Bibiane's struggles. Pulled from its primordial body of water, the fish tells us, in a rhetorical structure of 'pastness', the story of Bibiane and Evian. The fish, like the aborted fœtus, like Bibiane before she meets Evian, has no future. Motherhood, or the potential for motherhood, as signified by the abortion, is the key fantasy object of the film.

Woman as 'hopeful womb' returns again as a theme in Villeneuve's 2009 film, *Polytechnique*. The film follows Valérie (Karine Vanasse), a fictionalised version of one of the female survivors targeted during the 1989 Polytechnique Massacre.[11] Valérie's 'hopeful womb' is, of course, a threat: to The Killer (again played by Maxim Gaudette), who seeks revenge on the women whom he perceives thwarted his success, but whose violent outburst is in reality related to his perceptions of his own mother as pathetic and controlling. It is also a different kind of threat to Valérie's potential employer, Mr Martineau (Pierre Leblanc), in mechanical engineering. Mr Martineau hints that Valérie is a liability because she might get pregnant and quit. Motherhood disrupts time: for Mr Martineau, Valérie's hypothetical motherhood diminishes his perceived value of her since she would not be a constant source of labour. The feminist statement of the film tries to recognise the persistent gaps that remain despite feminist achievements. Valérie may eventually be permitted access to the patriarchal spaces of mechanical engineering, but before she is an engineer – as she is reminded by Mr Martineau and The Killer – she is first a woman. The film, which reinforces a heteropatriarchal ideology even as it tries to reveal its inherent violence, nonetheless solidifies Valérie as a precarious subject in that it maintains she is always first a womb waiting to be filled.

Valérie does become pregnant at the end of the film. The ultimate scene of the film features Valérie in voice-over, reciting a letter she has written to The Killer's mother. She reads:

> [F]or the second time in my life, I am afraid. The first time was when I faced your son. Your son opened my eyes to how much hatred can be in this world [. . .] Love has brought me a gift: a child grows inside me. I want with all of my heart for this child to be happy, but I'm afraid. And I'm tired of being afraid. I have to learn to have faith again, and give life another chance, so I can stand on my own. And I will stand on my own. If I have a boy, I will teach him how to love. If I have a girl, I will teach her the world is hers.[12]

Valérie's pregnancy seemingly becomes the final event that will heal the trauma The Killer has inscribed within her. With her child, Valérie births a new hope for the future.

Incendies also visualises the expectant nature of pregnancy, particularly poignant in this story since pregnancy emerges out of the rubble of war. The story revolves around twins Jeanne and Simon Marwan, who learn in their deceased mother's will that they have a brother. Their mother, Nawal, tasks each twin to find, respectively, their father and brother. They must travel back to their mother's home country, unnamed in the film (although the film is adapted from the stage play by Wajdi Mouawad, which clearly sets the story in Lebanon), in order to fulfil their mother's (re)quest. The mother's promise – the reunion of the family – is a hope that emerges in flickering moments, but is just as quickly snuffed out through acts of violence. The man we initially believe might be the twins' father is shot mercilessly in the face when he and Nawal attempt to flee their village. We learn that Nawal is pregnant with his child, and that the child she births is the twins' missing older brother. Nawal gives him up for adoption, where his orphanage is bombed and the surviving children collected to be trained as soldiers. Despite these brutal moments, the reunification of the family remains a persistent thread of hope throughout the narrative.

Images of Nawal searching for her missing son concern a part of the film, but it is really Jeanne's retracing of her mother's steps that leads her to find the missing brother. This is the most prominent absence aesthetic of the film: Jeanne, through her search, both visually and metaphorically becomes her mother as she traverses the Lebanese landscapes.

Often, the camera jumps between the past – Nawal in various locations of Lebanon, searching for her missing son (Figure 5.2) – to the present, where Jeanne re-visits the same sites her mother once occupied (Figure 5.3). The camera purposefully deceives the viewer and flits from past and present through matches on form: the body of Nawal replaces the almost identical body of Jeanne, who dons the same necklace and often similar clothes as her mother throughout the journey. Jeanne becomes her mother, but always only partially: her inability to speak Arabic leaves her lost and ignorant to the potentially useful information that surrounds her.

Eventually we learn, in an overtly Œdipal twist, that Jeanne and Simon are the children of their older brother, Nihad (Abdelghafour Elaaziz). Nihad, now known as Abou Tarek, a renowned torturer, rapes his mother (not knowing he is her progeny), while she's imprisoned as an assassin. Once Nihad is located by the twins, they deliver him a letter from Nawal. In it, she tells Nihad 'you were born of love, so your brother and sister were born of love, too'.[13] This triadic structure establishes each as their corresponding fantasy objects: the traumatised Nawal is emotionally unavailable to the twins and physically absent in Nihad's life. Nihad also serves as a fantasy object for the twins, whose status as father/brother means that he can be neither, given the trauma that structures his relation to them. Moreover, the twins serve as Nihad's fantasy object, but a 'bad' one, since they are the product of his own abuse that he is trying to repress. In the end, Nihad visits his mother's gravesite. He returns to his mother through their children: it is motherhood that brings each of them 'home'. Jeanne and Simon return 'home' to their ancestral country but also to

Figure 5.2 Nawal (Lubna Azabal) leaves her village in *Incendies*.

Figure 5.3 Jeanne (Mélissa Désormeaux-Poulin), practically identical to her mother, retraces her mother's steps decades later.

the truth of their birth, and Nihad to his mother and his repressed traumatic past. Their reunification breaks a trauma cycle. There are no more flashbacks, and instead the film ends optimistically.

Arrival is perhaps the most overt in its depiction of the hopeful womb. The film revolves around Dr Louise Banks, a highly skilled linguist who is sought out by the US government to communicate with aliens who have arrived at twelve different locations on Earth. The alien spacecraft is an onyx oblong structure – a quite literal gaping void – that hovers over the expansive green fields of Montana. Louise is taken here to do her work. Similarly to almost all his other films – especially *Incendies, Sicario, Enemy* (2013), and *Prisoners* – Villeneuve performs a great deception: the film opens with shots of Louise remembering her young daughter, Hannah, who has died. These memories ceaselessly interrupt Louise as she tries to decode the language of the aliens, named Heptapods because of their seven squid-like tentacles. Louise's increasing fluency in the Heptapod's language rewires her brain to the degree that she experiences time differently.[14] Her flashbacks of her dead daughter grow in frequency. The images of her daughter are not flashbacks, but rather flashforwards. Louise is actually thinking in, or remembering, the future.

Anne Carruthers reads *Arrival* as negotiating pregnant embodiment as an ethics, a question with which the film grapples, which I align with the concept of the hopeful womb. Pregnant embodiment accounts for pregnancy as a social phenomenon that splits and decentres the pregnant subject, and also places the subject in a state of the 'not-yet'.[15] Louise's status as mother 'anchors temporal boundaries within the film' (Carruthers 324). Only when it is revealed to the viewer, and Louise, that her memories of her child actually exist in the future, and that the Heptapods' language has facilitated Louise's emergent ontology, do we understand the destabilising temporalities that the film wishes us to experience. Most importantly in terms of theorising an absence aesthetics represented in the hopeful womb, however, is the fact that, throughout the film, we read Louise as a mother, both through her recurring memories but also through her emotional status and the way she interacts with other characters. As Carruthers states, '[t]he viewer is encouraged to "see" Louise's character as a mother, as a grieving mother, and therefore "see" her character not as she is but as something she has only the potential to become at the end of the film' (333). It is precisely this 'potential' motherhood status that performs Louise as the (doomed) hopeful womb. When she eventually births Hannah at the end of the film, it is as much a reunion as it is a long goodbye: the film's temporal circuit closes, the end of the film is also its beginning.

The hopeful womb signifies desire for these lead characters, as the womb holds the liminal space of the fantasy object. The womb's potential as healing – both personally and politically – contains Villeneuve's leading women to the role of mother. Mayer writes that *Arrival* 'ends by securing Louise's normative gender as spectacle, as sexual partner, as mother' (36).[16] This is true in each film, to a degree: Bibiane's happy ending stems from her partnering with Evian, even though she has not (yet) become a mother; Valérie's pregnancy signals both the end of The Killer's traumatic hold on her life and, consequently, furthers hope for the future of Québécois feminism; Nawal fulfils her promise in that she reunites her family and finally allows herself to be buried as a mother; and Louise births the daughter of whom she has always (n)ever dreamed.

CASTING SHADOWS: SURROGACY

The surrogate works as a figure that disrupts linear structure and as a metonym within absence aesthetics in Villeneuve's œuvre. Closely related to the mother's function as a hopeful womb, surrogates reveal the absence aesthetics throughout the films in that they point to the films' representative lack. These surrogates – Bibiane and Jeanne for their mothers; all those that die in *Polytechnique* – disrupt the temporal specificities of the diegesis through their mis-recognition by other characters and the audience members. All surrogates operate as signifiers, and their statuses as such is paramount: they must stand in for those that are missing, and yet their presence only underscores the narrative's irresolvable absent figures.

If the mother is a hopeful womb, then the daughter is a surrogate. As mentioned earlier, Bibiane's self-destruction is largely informed by the shadow her mother casts over her. The photoshoot, in which the photographer asks her to 'become her mother', cages Bibiane as a signifier of her mother. In effect, Bibiane is lost because she cannot know who she is. Jeanne's relationship to her mother is similar. Unlike her twin brother, Jeanne dutifully departs to Lebanon to begin the search, and it is primarily through her that we revisit Nawal's history and traverse the landscape, including the jail cell where she is violently impregnated. Both Bibiane and Jeanne are asked, in different ways, to become their mother in order to realise a truth about themselves. For Bibiane, her truth is that she cannot follow her mother's path. For Jeanne, it is realising the true history of her birth, and ending the cycle of trauma her mother could not do herself.

In *Polytechnique*, surrogacy performs a two-fold process. Primarily, the film resurrects, through the process of acting, the victims of the Polytechnique Massacre. Canadian film theorist Janine Marchessault notes how the movie is aware of 'its epistemological status as a copy of a copy' (52).[17] Villeneuve consciously renames and thus partially fictionalises the victim; the actors are simulacra, not quite complete reproductions and not quite original characters. The film's monochromatic filter, like the black and white photocopier, is another way in which Villeneuve separates the signs from their referents. Blood that spills from the victims' bodies instead looks more like ink; we are reminded that this is a story being retold.

The relationship between fantasy and historical retellings through cinema becomes especially important in terms of understanding the role of the surrogate in Villeneuve's cinema. I invoke the surrogate as a trope that functions similarly to the process of reenactment. On *Polytechnique*, Marchessault writes:

> [T]he use of reenactment by such filmmakers gives the viewer the 'temporal knotting of past and present' that can be read as a kind of 'mise-en-scène of desire'. This is sustained through the creation of what [Nichols] calls 'the fantasmatic'. This notion of the fantasmatic helps us to situate the specificity of the cinematic image as an experience. In these instances, reenactment films are not about mourning what is fundamentally lost. Instead, the fantasmatic can create a specific form of gratification [. . .]. Thus documentary, like fiction films based on actual events, can help to create an affective experience of the past through these fantasmatic forms of *mise-en-scène*. (50)

Here, the fantasmatic is invoked in a similar way to how I describe the function of absence aesthetics in Villeneuve's œuvre. The surrogate, rather than reenactment's cinematic form, sutures temporalities that induce desire. The surrogates in *Polytechnique* are voids; we have already lost them before the film begins. It is thus the 'how' of loss that cleaves together a present affective experience with events from the past. *Polytechnique* moves within this place of loss through employing specific formal techniques that, in effect, design an aesthetics of absence.

The actors who play the murdered students represent a duality of absence, firstly through the indexical quality of the actor on film. Their surrogacy performs the 'temporal knotting of past and present' which produces the affect of desire for the spectator. Secondly, the actors perform superficial resurrections as they '[stand] in for a character [which] embodies a certain presence while at the same time, reminding us, in its difference, of irretrievable absence' (Longfellow 'Practice' 92).[18] In this way, it reflects the absent configuration of cinema in Metzian terms: the signifiers in the films reflect not only the desire for identification that is refused for spectators, since the actors only exist indexically, but also because the actors themselves play characters that have already died. *Polytechnique* crafts an 'illusion of presence', but, 'this illusion is not bolstered and intensified by an awareness, on a subliminal level, of the indexical veracity of the original recording process' (Singer 20).[19] The illusion of presence, in *Polytechnique*, incites mournful desire. The definitive loss of the film, the loss Villeneuve asks us to witness, is one that the audience, and certainly, a Québécois audience in 2009, would have already experienced prior to the film's screening. Because of this, the film takes the process of loss and contains it within the domain of narrative film. If there is a sense of gratification in the film, then it comes from the satisfactory ability for a narrative to control this defining, historic event and to contain it and explain within the realm of a highly aestheticised narrative film. Certainly, the aesthetics of the feature – the black and white format, the elliptical editing that returns to the subjectivities of Jean-François (Sébastien Huberdeau), the Killer, and Valérie and interrupts the linear structure, and the identification Villeneuve draws between this event and Picasso's *Guernica* – firmly establish *Polytechnique* as a film concerned with the art of filmmaking, rather than a documentary committed to facticity. Villeneuve's cross-filmic interest in representing – as Melnyk stated in regards to *Maelström* – what loss 'feels like' provides a container for the slippages between past and present, desire after death. These are absence aesthetics: they explore the irretrievability of those passed whose absence still structures the desires of those left behind.

ARTEFACTUALISATION

Multiple objects bear emotional weight throughout this selected corpus. They are smaller *lieux de mémoire*; like a fetish object, they signify more than their mere material because they stand for the person or a history that is trying to be recuperated. The transmogrification of these objects through the main characters' sense of desire and loss artefactualises objects and people. Some examples are the necklace Jeanne wears as she retraces her mother's journey, letters and documents in both *Incendies* and *Polytechnique*, Hannah's childhood artwork and toys, and hands in *Maelström* and *Arrival*. I will specifically look at the role of letters and hands.

The importance of artefacts throughout Villeneuve's œuvre is best represented through his character, Jean Lebel (Rémy Girard), the notary in *Incendies*. Lebel safeguards wills, testaments, personal letters, and other family documents in the film that bear specific emotional and legal weight. As a notary, Lebel is also a kind of *lieu de mémoire*: the columns of files in his office serve as indices to lives once lived. He tells Simon, 'Death is never the end of the story. It always leaves tracks.'[20] The written letters Nawal leaves behind for her twins in order to find their father and older brother signal part of the film's absence aesthetics. As part of Nawal's will, the documents stand in for the irretrievable loss of their mother, and are also the tracks she has imprinted on the world. Nawal's letters are also quite literally her final testament: they reveal the truth of her past and are also the final way she is able to reach her eldest child. And yet, the notary, too, is on the brink of vanishing. Lebel tells Simon that, following the footsteps of his father and his father before him, he is the last of the notaries in his family. The notary is future-less, a vanishing link to the past.

While letters represent a quite literal artefact, I also contend that there are more figurative artefacts Villeneuve produces that embody the same kind of impossibility of representation and retrievability as letters, necklaces, or toys. Hands perform this same function and are thus artefactualised by the camera. In *Maelström*, the camera tracks the hand of the photographer which points to – or rather, past – Bibiane as she asks her to become her mother. The camera severs the arm from the photographer in a medium close-up so that the pointing finger occupies the centre of the frame. Like the documents kept safe by Lebel, hands too point, signal, and identify that which is missing.

David Evan Richard notes how *Arrival* 'comments on the importance of gestural communication (perhaps further enhanced by the way that the Heptapods resemble hands), something that has perhaps been lost in our increasing contact with other people through the screen-sphere' (45).[21] The association between the Heptapods and hands is also notable, since the Heptapods and Louise communicate with each other through acts of writing. Louise communicates using a portable whiteboard through which she teaches the Heptapods English sentence structure. To respond, the Heptapods project from their tentacled 'hands' an inky substance that morphs into circular symbols which float in the air. These symbols are effectively the writing through which Louise and the Heptapods communicate. Richards' comment reflects how *Arrival* has been read by some scholars as striving towards world peace and the universalising aspect of cinema. As Tijana Mamula writes in her article on Villeneuve in *Screen*:

> Villeneuve equates Heptapod *with cinema* – through various references in the film's *mise-en-scène* and dialogue – and does so in a way that repurposes the 'universal language' thesis of the 1910s and 1920s. Like many early film theorists, Villeneuve embraces the notion that as a new, globally accessible, visual language, cinema may trigger profound changes in cultural and phenomenological perception as well as overcoming the obstacles to communicate erected by humanity's many languages. (543)[22]

Vision and hand signals become the initial, universal forms of communication between Louise and the Heptapods. On a more metaphorical level, the Heptapods point and thus signal to the perpetual absence that structures Louise's existence. The Heptapods' language reveals to Louise what she will both gain and lose. Louise's lover, a theoretical physicist (Jeremy Renner) who assists in communicating with the Heptapods, leaves her when he learns that she has always known Hannah will die young. He is always gone and at her side, her daughter is always dead and alive, the Heptapods have always already arrived and departed. Each presence coexists with their absence. Villeneuve lingers on hand imagery in these specific instances as a way to further denote the distance that separates the desiring subject from its object. As pointing hands tend to do, they remain always at a distance, always out of touch, always reaching for that which is beyond their grasp.

CONCLUSION

Throughout this chapter I have offered the term 'absence aesthetics' in an attempt to produce a theory surrounding the ubiquity of absence in Villeneuve's cinema. Absence aesthetics contains two tripartite layers. Firstly, absence aesthetics are formed through three narrative 'patterns': cyclical metonymies, disruption of linear structure, and the emotional and social isolation of the main characters. Secondly, these patterns manifest through the recurring characterisations of mothers, surrogates, and artefacts. Each of these three players act to disrupt these narrative patterns through their connection to the irretrievable past, the isolation of the present, and the hopeful future. Moreover, Villeneuve's absence aesthetics visualises Metz's theories on the feeling of loss and the configurations of absence inherent in cinema's imaginary signifiers. Villeneuve is thus uniquely attuned to the way cinema remains connected to traditional semiotic theory.

Motherhood, a recurring characterisation in practically all of the female characters in Villeneuve's cinema, encapsulates all three absence aesthetic properties. As a 'hopeful womb', the pregnant woman contains the traumatic past in her ability to produce a 'better' future. In doing so, she also disrupts time, since her body constantly references the inescapability of both temporal realms. Because of her ability to link together temporalities, the mother is one of many examples in Villeneuve's cinema of *lieux de mémoire*. Additionally, the mother is a mournful body: not only is the mother often the leading character in Villeneuve's cinema, but she is also emotionally 'abandoned' and isolated as an effect of her trauma. Subsequently, the mother produces surrogates. The surrogate, interestingly often (but not always) a daughter, attempts to represent and bring into the present temporally those who have died. The surrogate, although 'present' to the desiring subjects of the film (both the other characters and the audience members) thus always signals absence. They fill in the absent voids, but always only partially. Finally, numerous objects, although seemingly meaningless and disparate, become 'artefacts' through their association to their absent referents. The notary remains permanently in the past, amongst the fetishised documents that trace the lives of those dead. Hands are also artefacts: severed from their originating bodies, they point towards the fantasy object, always unable to grasp that which they desire. They endeavour to constantly signify or retrieve those who have been lost. All of these figures work together to design Villeneuve's cinema as a cinema of absence.

NOTES

1. Kohen Raz, Odeya and Meiri, Sandra, 'Revisiting Metz: bodiless-character films and the dynamic of desire/fantasy in narrative cinema', *New Review of Film and Television Studies*, vol. 16, no. 1, 2018, pp. 62–80.
2. Metz, Christian, *The Imaginary Signifier: Psychoanalysis and the Cinema*, translated by Celia Britton, Annwyl Williams, Ben Brewster, and Alfred Guzzetti, Indiana University Press, 1977. Original French: 'De même, pour comprendre le film (tout court), il faut que je perçoive l'objet photographié comme absent, sa photographie comme présente, et la présence de cette absence comme signifiante. L'imaginaire du cinéma présuppose le symbolique, car le spectateur doit avoir connu d'abord le miroir primordial. Mais comme celui-ci instituait le Moi très largement dans l'imaginaire, le miroir second de l'écran, appareil symbolique, repose à son tour sur le reflet et le manque. Il n'est pourtant pas le fantasme, lieu "purement" symbolique-imaginaire, car l'absence de l'objet, et les codes de cette absence, y sont réellement produits par la *physis* d'un outillage: le cinéma est un corps (un *corpus* pour le sémiologue), un fétiche que l'on peut aimer.' (41), italics in original text.
3. Creed, Barbara, *The monstrous-feminine: film, feminism, and psychoanalysis*, Routledge 1993; Haraway, Donna, 'Manifesto for Cyborgs: Science, Technology, and Socialist Feminism in the 1980s', *Australian Feminist Studies*, vol. 2, no. 4, 1987, pp 1–42; Płonowska Ziarek, Ewa, 'Bare Life on Strike: Notes on the Biopolitics of Race and Gender', *South Atlantic Quarterly*, vol. 107, no. 1, 2008, pp. 89–105; Silverman, Kaja, *The Acoustic Mirror: The Female Voice in Psychoanalysis and Cinema*, Indiana University Press, 1988; Weheliye, Alexander G, *Habeas Viscus: Racializing Assemblages, Biopolitics, and Black Feminist Theories of the Human*, Duke University Press, 2014.

4. Latimer, Heather, 'A queer pregnancy: affective kinship, time travel and reproductive choice in Denis Villeneuve's *Arrival*', *Feminist Theory*, vol. 22, no. 3, 2021, pp. 429–42.
5. Nora, Pierre, 'Between Memory and History: Les Lieux de Mémoire', *Représentations*, no. 26, Spring 1988, pp. 7–24. Original French: 'où se cristallise et se réfugie la mémoire est liée à ce moment particulier de notre histoire. Moment charnière, où la conscience de la rupture avec le passé se confond avec le sentiment d'une mémoire déchirée; mais où le déchirement réveille encore assez de mémoire pour que puisse se poser le problème de son incarnation.'
6. Holden, Stephen, 'Film Review: Fathoming Meaning From a Talking Fish', *The New York Times*, 25 January 2002.
7. 'Je voudrais que vous me fassiez ça le plus lentement possible. Ok? Je veux que tu transformes, mais lentement. Tranquillement, doucement. Laisse-la sortir, laisse sortir ta mère. Je veux que tu deviennes transparente. Eh? Je veux plus te voir, toi.'
8. Longfellow, Brenda, 'Counter-Narratives, Class Politics, and Metropolitan Dystopias: Representations of Globalization in *Maelström*, *waydowntown* and *La Moitié gauche du frigo*', *Canadian Journal of Film Studies*, vol. 13, no. 1, March 2004, pp. 69–83.
9. 'Il me reste peu de temps. J'aimerais profiter de mes derniers souffles pour vous raconter une histoire. Une très jolie histoire.'
10. Melnyk, George, *Film and the City: The Urban Imaginary in Canadian Cinema*, Athabasca University Press, 2014.
11. The École Polytechnique Massacre occurred on 6 December 1989. Fourteen women were killed by Marc Lépine, who also injured ten women and four men. The massacre was an overt act of misogyny and hatred towards feminism. It was the deadliest act of gun violence and terrorism in Canada up until the Nova Scotia shooting rampage in 2020.
12. '. . . pour la deuxième fois de ma vie, profondément peur. La première fois, c'est quand j'ai rencontré votre fils, votre fils qui m'a ouvert la porte sur ce que le monde peut contenir de haine. [. . .] L'amour vient de me faire un cadeau. J'ai un enfant dans mon ventre. Je voudrais de tout mon cœur que ce soit joyeux, mais j'ai peur. Je suis fatiguée d'avoir peur. Il faut que j'arrive à retrouver assez confiance dans la vie pour sauter dans le vide. Il faut que je me tienne debout toute seule. Et je vais me tenir debout. Si j'ai un fils, je veux lui apprendre l'amour. Si j'ai une fille, je veux lui apprendre que le monde lui appartient.'
13. 'Tu es né de l'amour. Ton frère et ta sœur sont, donc, aussi nés de l'amour.'
14. As is often mentioned in articles on *Arrival*, this phenomenon for Louise demonstrates the Sapir-Whorf hypothesis, in which different languages inform the way their speakers think.
15. Carruthers, Anne, 'Temporality, Reproduction and the Not-Yet in Denis Villeneuve's *Arrival*', *Film-Philosophy*, vol. 22, no. 3 October 2018, pp. 321–39.
16. Mayer, Sophie, 'Girl Power: Back to the Future of Feminist Science Fiction with *Into the Forest* and *Arrival*', *Film Quaterly*, vol. 70, no. 3, 2017, pp. 32–42.
17. Marchessault, Janine, 'Versioning History: *Polytechnique* as Vector', *Canadian Journal of Film Studies/Revue canadienne d'études cinématographiques*, vol. 22, no. 1, Spring 2013, pp. 44–65.
18. Longfellow, Brenda, 'The practice of memory and the politics of memorialization: Denis Villeneuve's *Polytechnique*', *Canadian Journal of Film Studies/Revue canadienne d'études cinématographiques*, vol. 22, no. 1, Spring, 2013, pp. 86–106.
19. Singer, Ben, 'Film, Photography, and Fetish: The Analyses of Christian Metz', *Cinema Journal*, vol. 27, no. 4, Summer 1988, pp. 4–22.
20. 'La mort c'est jamais la fin d'une histoire. Il y a toujours des traces.'
21. Richard, David Evan, 'Film Phenomenology and the "Eloquent Gestures" of Denis Villeneuve's *Arrival*', *Cinephile*, vol. 12, no. 1, 2018, pp. 41–7.
22. Mamula, Tijuana, 'Denis Villeneuve, film theorist; or, cinema's arrival in a multilingual world', *Screen*, vol. 59, no. 4, December 2018, pp. 542–51.

CHAPTER 6

Life, Risk and the Structuring Force of Exposure in *Maelström*

Terrance H. McDonald

Differences between insides and outsides unfold in a manner of degrees in Denis Villeneuve's *Maelström* (2000). In the film, a series of talking fish (voiced by Pierre Lebeau) narrate the story of Bibiane (Marie-Josée Croze) as she experiences a series of events, which include an abortion, a failure in business, a fatality caused while driving under the influence, an attempted suicide, and a plane crash. Eventually, with the support of her friend Claire (Stephanie Morgenstern) and a stranger (Marc Gélinas) in the subway, Bibiane develops a romantic relationship with Evian (Jean-Nicolas Verreault) even though she accidently killed his father (Kliment Denchev). A melancholic malaise caused by day-to-day experiences within globalisation, late capitalism, and citification may be a key theme within the film, but *Maelström* also challenges our assumptions about the roots of this condition by exposing that the potentiality for a world outside of these experiences always already exists within us. In relation to this key theme, Brenda Longfellow eloquently argues that *Maelström* represents the uneasiness of living within a milieu determined by globalisation, late capitalism, and citification.[1] However, building on Longfellow's insights, I contend that films do not simply represent postmodern conditions or theory, but can also unfold cinematic forms necessary to imagine the potentialities beyond such circumstances. Rather than connecting the film as evidence of what exists in the world, reading *Maelström* with a methodology inspired by radical formalism[2] – as opposed to a representational methodology – can open up a potential world or, at least, potentialities beyond the conditions of globalisation, late capitalism, and citification, even if fleeting. On the promise of radical formalism, Eugenie Brinkema maps a methodology that generates 'a reading without guarantee that secures nothing, whose rhythms unfold a contingent world instead of being for the sake of evidencing a necessary truth taken to be already fully lodged in the world' ('Form' 265).[3] Launching from this position, my chapter maps how the cinematic forms of *Maelström* generate the capacity to rethink life through exposures and the risks that accompany them.

One tenet of poststructuralist theory – and theory in general – takes shape by exposing alternatives to our assumptions about the world. Gilles Deleuze's philosophy of immanence mobilises this principal through a reconceptualisation of subjectivities and being by foregrounding an ontology that refuses to be structured by external, transcendent ideals. Therefore, Deleuze's immanence relies on a transcendental empiricism that posits our being in the world cannot be known or given in advance.[4] In *The Fold*, he works through a section of this reconceptualisation by rethinking the ways in which bodies relate to the world.[5] Through this theoretical exploration, he maps how the world does not exist prior to bodies, or before bodies. Nor does a body exist prior to, and simply receive, the world. Rather, a body takes shape through relations as the world: 'It is not the body that realizes, but it is in the body that something is realized, through which the body itself becomes real or substantial' (Deleuze 120). This position – which we may attribute to poststructuralism – challenges our understanding of the world as something that we encounter as bodies. Instead, for Deleuze, the body exists through the encounter and the world unfolds in relation to the body via realised and potential encounters. Deleuze challenges the notion of a pre-existing world by insisting on the power of bodies to express the world:

> On its own account each monad conveys the entire world independently of others and without influx, while every body receives the impression or influx of others, and that is the totality of bodies; that is the material universe that expresses the world. (120)

Therefore, a stable and knowable world can never be grasped by a body – a monad – because the conditions that a body will experience remain in process which depend not only on its relations with other bodies but also the many tiny bodies within that body. From bacteria-unfolding processes within us to trees generating oxygen for us to breath, many bodies – both inside and out – determine the potentiality of our world.

Any perspective contains the entire world for that body even though it finds itself amongst and within a flurry of other perspectives. 'Dividing endlessly, the parts of matter form little vortices in a maelstrom,' states Deleuze, 'and in these are found even more vortices, even smaller, and even more are spinning in the concave intervals of the whirls that touch one another.' (5) In *Maelström*, Bibiane has an experience of being inside of herself while in the shower after dinner at Claire's house: 'Paradoxically, she loses touch with time and the world around her.'⁶ Despite being 'inside' of herself in this moment, she remains within some perspective of a world which becomes informed by the perceptions within her body as opposed to the influx of the outside. This endless succession of vortices demonstrates a ceaseless expanse of insides as well as outsides. For every inside finds itself outside of the vortices within it, such as the body that contains a multiplicity of relations within itself. Rather than a rigid and knowable difference between inside and outside, we find a degree of difference that depends entirely on a perspective which possesses a fluidity with the capacity to recognise each outside as an inside and vice versa. In the scene prior, for example, Bibiane finds herself in touch with time and the world around her as she tastes a pasta sauce prepared by Claire which places Bibiane's perspective on the relations around her. There are insides and outsides in this moment, too, such as when the sauce becomes consumed by Bibiane. In other words, differences between inside and outside, following Deleuze, become a matter of folds.

This conceptualisation extends to a range of material relations experienced by Bibiane. 'Flanked by a wall of clear glass, through which the city is constantly visible,' states Longfellow, 'the distinction between inside and outside, the world of territorialized capital and her intimate domestic space is completely attenuated.' (75) While Longfellow notes this characteristic to argue that, for Bibiane, there is no attainable experience outside of globalisation, late capitalism, and citification, this lack of distinction between inside and outside illuminates the ways in which *Maelström* takes shape through exposing insides to outsides and outsides to insides in order to transform perceptions of the world. Current discussions of the film tend to connect Bibiane's experience to the conditions of globalisation, late capitalism, and the cityscape.⁷ Moreover, the limited interpretations of the film tend to analyse how the characters and setting represent socio-cultural issues in 'an emancipatory, secular, and economically dynamic post-Quiet Revolution Québec' (Melnyk 92). This existing scholarship tends towards representational interpretations that posit urban spaces as less appealing to humans than nature (Melnyk 96) or that claim the film reflects changing identities within contemporary Quebec (Ransom 179). However, in addition to representing these experiences, I argue that Villeneuve's *Maelström* takes shape through (over)exposures in order to unfold meanings and life yet to come beyond the conditions of globalisation, late capitalism, and citification. In this sense, Villeneuve's film reveals not what a future Quebec might look like but rather the inescapable risks that are crucial in order to increase capacities for transformation.

The form of *Maelström*, through my mobilisation of radical formalism, flattens expanses that may be considered as separate, divided, distinct, divergent, contradictory, or incongruous. In other words, reading *Maelström* through the collapsing of the marked boundaries between inside and outside allows for a mapping of relations that do not exist a priori and demonstrates the potentialities created by exposures. In part, this theoretical move may be viewed in relation to post-poststructuralism in the sense of a return to poststructuralism that, in some ways, repeats the poststructuralist return to structuralism. Both of these returns aim to push the tenets of structuralism (and, by extension, poststructuralism) to their extreme, or logical conclusion. 'In the history of film theory,' states Brinkema, 'one shorthand for this switch to poststructuralism would be the shift from codes-in-texts to texts-in-process.' (*Forms* 42) *The Forms of the Affects*, Brinkema's mapping of a radical formalism, advances the argument that a turn to affects within film and media theory requires a commitment to close reading to illuminate the capacity to unfold theoretical speculation which returns to poststructuralism with a reinvigorated attention to form. *Maelström* provides a vibrant text through which to explore such a commitment precisely because the film foregrounds this shift from codes-in-texts to texts-in-process via Villeneuve's creation of images. Responses to the film have generally relied on interpretations that identify codes-in-texts despite employing theory intimately tied to poststructuralism. Longfellow outlines such a position when she claims:

> In *Maelström*, however, the oral narrative is delivered by a fish in a space of campy art direction, an excessive symbolic rendering that hints at depth while its very hyperbole acknowledges that, in a disenchanted, post-sacral world, the archaic-allegorical can only be represented from a space of extreme irony or naïveté. (72–3)

While Longfellow's theoretical commitment and ideas launch my thinking in relation to the film, I want to tease out the implications of her interpretation in relation to a representational analysis that upholds some notion of inside and outside through distances, boundaries, impossibilities, and detachments.

There appear to be varying levels of distinction between insides and outsides in the film. While Longfellow notes the almost non-existent barriers between the global, commodified public of the city and the private, domestic space of Bibiane's apartment, she sees a much more of an expansive distance between the setting of the film – contemporary Montreal – and the unidentified locations in which a series of dying fish offer exposition while being butchered (Figure 6.1). Longfellow identifies these fish-narrated spaces as belonging to or calling to mind an archaic-allegoric realm: 'Yet the conjuring of an archaic-allegoric in *Maelström* feels much like Jameson's catalogue of postmodern angst with its longing for deep memory, long history, real tradition.' (73) This position stands in as a fairly standard interpretation of subjective experiences within globalisation and late capitalism (a longing for an authenticity that is, perhaps, forever lost), but there appears to be a shortcoming within this claim which becomes visible through the forms of the film. If we are to embrace a poststructuralist (or postmodern) position that pushes the tenets of structuralism to a logical conclusion, the existence of some more authentic moment of the past becomes fraught with instability, whether it is thought of as real or even if it remains an imaginary projection. Can there be a longing for what is not there or not possible or not reachable if that 'what' was never actually there? In other words, a poststructuralist position does not simply replace a previous experience of authenticity that has become eroded by globalisation and late capitalism in a continued theoretical move away from liberal humanism. Instead, poststructuralism, through structuralism, reveals that any notion of authenticity, or of stable and knowable meaning, was always already arbitrary and fragile. If anything, the longing Longfellow speaks to that composes the general malaise and discontent of a global, late capitalist, postmodern moment would be a longing for ignorance of such a fact: the ability to return, not to a moment of authenticity, or to the real, or to stable and knowable meaning, but to a moment where one could still imagine those concepts to exist. Poststructuralism does not erode those concepts; liberal humanism and other theoretical positions simply constructed the illusion of their existence.

If codes-in-texts can no longer be relied upon, we may ask: what if a signifier no longer connects to its assumed signified? After Bibiane spends the night at Claire's house early in the film, she vomits the next morning. Claire tells her that her body still thinks it is pregnant – she has just had an abortion the day prior – and she reassures her that the feeling will eventually pass in a few days once the body adjusts. Bibiane knows she is no longer pregnant, yet inside her

Figure 6.1 The dying fish narrator (voiced by Pierre Lebeau) in *Maelström*.

tiny vortices continue to spin believing that a fœtus remains growing inside her. From this early moment in the film, Villeneuve illuminates even biological messages fraught with fragility and instability. Then, at breakfast, Bibiane asks Claire about the song she sang to her the night before because it was so gentle. Bibiane does not speak Norwegian (the language of the lyrics) and asks Claire what the meaning of the song is. She says that she does not remember, but she learned it from her grandmother. Without access to a predetermined meaning, Bibiane and Claire can only speculate. Gentle. Pretty. In other words, they must rely on the form of the song by reading the ways in which the lyrics take shape rather than connect to an established known. The film then cuts from this scene to another fish sequence where a fish protests, while being chopped to bits, that the song 'is all but . . . gentle'.[8] The fish exposes that the assumption the women make about the song does not align with the Norwegian denotation. Nonetheless, Bibiane experiences the song through a connotation of its form in that moment. Pretty. Gentle. Later in the film, Bibiane will ask Evian, who speaks Norwegian, if he knows the what the lyrics mean. 'Rip their heads off, empty their skulls,' he recites, 'drink from the skulls of our enemies.'[9] Not quite gentle. Without delicacy or grace. Perhaps, if sung before a battle it would terrify enemies while, at the same time, it would be a rousing song for the warriors chanting these lyrics. However, when Claire's grandmother sang to her there was a different experience which one might assume was soothing. Can a song be terrifying, rousing, and soothing? Even if the intended meaning of the lyrics is known, the song may elicit differing responses in the same moment. Terrifying. Rousing. In another moment, soothing. Responses to the song and its lyrics differ based on perspective, but the form remains stable. Or, conceivably, it does not. One might anticipate that the folklore origins of the song as well as its rousing delivery before battles would employ a melody, a pitch, a tune quite divergent from Claire or her grandmother's delivery. In short, the meaning and, moreover, the experience of listening to the song depend on a set of relations in a given moment: it must be read for.

Turning to the same chapter in Frederic Jameson's *Postmodernism* as Longfellow references, there emerges the potential to think through this move from codes-in-texts to texts-in-process within *Maelström*. In a discussion of space and photography, Jameson outlines how the new allegory is horizontal as opposed to vertical and 'now profoundly relational' (168).[10] This position reveals a key tenet of poststructuralism: the signifying systems sketched out in structuralist theories are arbitrary, fragile, deconstructable, and very much so relational:

> When we add to this the inevitable mobility of such relations, we begin to glimpse the process of allegorical interpretation as a kind of scanning that, moving back and forth across the text, readjusts its terms in

constant modification of a type quite different from our stereotypes of some static medieval or biblical decoding. (Jameson 168)

In this passage, Jameson speaks to the same switch as referenced in Brinkema earlier: from codes-in-texts to texts-in-process. Of importance here, in relation to *Maelström*, Jameson parses out the inability to read a text according to what it represents because the static codes troubled by structuralism become forever fractured by poststructuralism. Clichéd illusions, such as the snake equals evil, now become a matter of degree. Consequently, a snake – or any other sign, symbol, character, or the like – can no longer be assumed in advance and, by extension, a new demand arises in the wake of constant modification: close reading. However, this mode of close reading differs from the type of observations made through the process where a snake can be decoded as representing evil. Jameson notes that 'the attention of the viewer is now engaged by a differential opposition within the image itself, so that he or she has little energy left over for intentness to that older "likeness" or "matching" operation which compares the image to some putative thing outside' (179). *Maelström* unfolds a particularly vibrant opportunity to explore 'a differential opposition within the image' as opposed to an interpretation based on likeness or matching precisely because of the seemingly disparate and distinct sections of the narrative.

If they are part of a text-in-process, what do the talking fish do? The first scene in the film, after the credit sequence, takes place inside a vessel (perhaps in the hull of a ship) where a fish lay exposed on a table. The scene moves from a medium-long shot of the infernal fishmonger sharpening a blade to a close-up on the blade griding on the wheel and then a rack focus exposes the fish. Out of water, the fish gasps for air before another cut centres the fish in a close-up and then an extreme close-up. The flesh of the fish, mutilated on one side, has been exposed. Absolutely, as noted by Longfellow, the image can be linked to a campy aesthetic (72–3), which remains far from a Canadian and Quebec cinematic legacy of documentary realism – outrageously artificial, we may say. This observation becomes more obvious when the fish states that it wishes to use its last moments to tell a story. 'A very pretty story',[11] states the fish. This first fish sequence, through a representational methodology, may be connected to the qualities of irony or naïveté, but the fish does not seem to find its situation funny, nor does it seem unaware of its present situation as it knows it will die. By pushing beyond what these images may represent or connect to in terms of a world that we know, the initial fish sequence – in all of its particularity – takes shape through exposure. The fish lays exposed to the elements – out of water – with a section of its flesh exposed and, in the scene, it first becomes visible through a rack focus which exposes it in the background of the close-up on the sharpening wheel. Moreover, the fish offers exposition. The fish introduces, or makes known, the story. Following Longfellow, if the fish is said to be connected to extreme naïveté, it might only be of its apparent separation from the world of which it speaks: Bibiane's world. A cut from the fish sequence moves into the world of Bibiane, perhaps not that distant from the archaic world as expected. One cut exposes a pathway between these two worlds, which may be, conceivably, not two but only one. In this fish sequence, the disjuncture that exists does not arise between the archaic and the contemporary, as they both occupy images in the film, but between signifiers and signifieds. 'A very pretty story', states the fish, but the next scene, with a washed out and too bright quality, can hardly be said to denote a delicate image or event. Cold. Sterile. Medical. The overexposed images in the following sequence reveal Bibiane, exposed on an examination table, in an abortion clinic. In these two initial scenes, the images and the events, the style and the narrative, of *Maelström* unfold through exposures.

The city of *Maelström*, as an extension of the conditions within globalisation and late capitalism, has been identified as a space that restricts authenticity and leaves Bibiane within a melancholic malaise. The abundant images of water and other elements connected to nature as well as the archaic fish sequences are linked to this restriction and discontent that she feels. These images and elements are decoded as representing an authentic space and experience that cannot be reached. 'In the post-sacral, secular zeitgeist of metropolitan Montréal', states Longfellow, 'what confronts the soullessness of everyday life in corporate capital is a patently faux archaic and a particular sense of affect grounded in unresolvable loss and melancholy.' (78) A core, a real, a truth remains forever out of reach because everything becomes determined by a series of relations within a signifying system which turns out to be in and of itself fragile and arbitrary. Yet, despite the embrace of these basic tenets of poststructuralism to inform interpretations of Villeneuve's film, the methodologies employed to conduct these readings remain wedded to decoding or, as Brinkema frames it, codes-in-texts. George Melnyk, in his substantial work on the cities in Canadian films, employs a similar methodology in his interpretation of *Maelström*. In the film, states Melnyk,

> Villeneuve seems to be contrasting water as a symbol of organic nature with the waterless or lifeless city, which is portrayed as being composed of concrete buildings, concrete underground parking garages, concrete streets and sidewalks, and a concrete dock in the city's port. (96)

This idea fits well with the general notion that experiences within the cityscapes of globalisation and late capitalism lack authenticity. In Melnyk's reading, the water is taken to signify the real or the truth sought by subjectivities, but which remain unavailable within the inorganic materiality of the city. However, within the conditions of poststructuralism (or postmodernism), the authentic, the truth, the real are exposed as something that is inaccessible, impossible, unreachable or, even, constructed, imagined, fabricated. Not only, in the case of Melnyk's reading, does the link between water and organic nature become forever fractured – arbitrary, fragile, undone – but, taking that tenet of post-structuralism to its logical conclusion, it was always already the case. We cannot manufacture such a position through the very logic that such a position undermines. In short, we need to take risks.

The life of Bibiane unfolds by taking risks within a capitalist system which becomes structured by exposures. In an early scene in the film, Bibiane's business risk becomes exposed by her brother, Philippe (Bobby Beshro), after she takes another risk by lying to him about her supplier, Mr Koumsawout (voiced by Zhenhu Han), in Jakarta. It turns out, Philippe has the supplier on hold, and he quickly exposes the lie Bibiane has told – she has not spoken to Koumsawout in two months. Later, fearing being alone, Bibiane takes ecstasy which exposes her to new experiences but can also be a risk. Furthermore, within the rave sequences and the sexual rendezvous that follows, many close-ups reveal a shoeless, sockless Bibiane with her bare feet exposed – a risk she does not seem to discern (Figure 6.2). In other situations, she also seeks to limit her risks. In the sexual encounter that follows the rave sequence, Bibiane and the man she engages in intercourse with choose to use a condom. Whether she makes the choice to avoid another unwanted pregnancy or due to the unfamiliarity she has of his sexual history, the condom minimises risks. Regardless, taking risks and exposing oneself to new experiences, new connections, new potentialities do not guarantee a positive outcome. The lie to her brother may have aimed to quell his concerns, but it accelerated her removal from their joint business

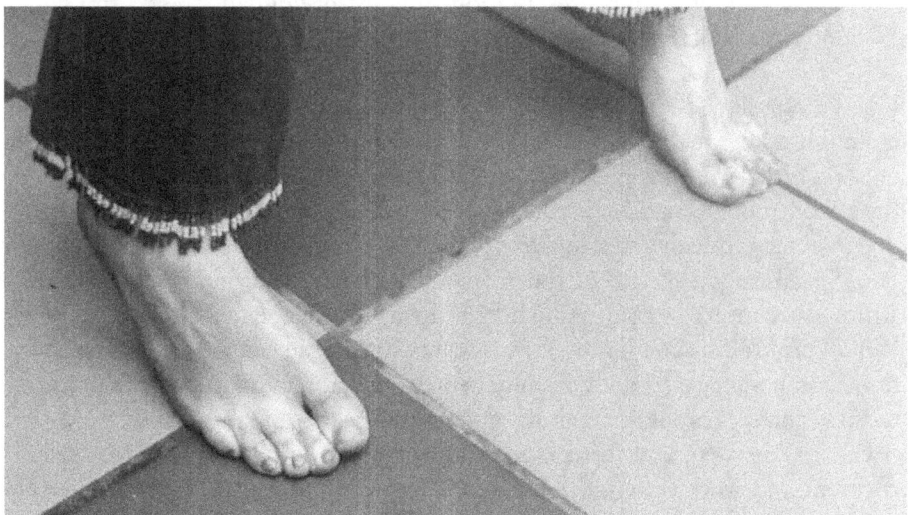

Figure 6.2 Bibiane (Marie-Josée Croze) with her bare feet exposed in *Maelström*.

venture. Consuming ecstasy and going to a rave may have sought to alter her experience, which seemed to be successful, eventually, for at least a period of time. A condom can limit the chance of pregnancy and the odds of contracting a sexually transmitted infection, but a condom is not 100% effective. Ultimately, no one can know the outcome of a risk in advance. All that can be said of taking, or not taking, a risk in advance will be the degree of exposure.

A general position on *Maelström* appears to be determined: it reflects a general experience of uneasiness within globalisation, late capitalism, and citification. David L. Pike highlights how this reflection is a core focus of contemporary Canadian films:

> Exactly how a local cinema can depict the radical changes brought by globalization and the postmodern cityscape is an open question, but it is also a question at the heart of much of the interesting film-making at the turn of the millennium. (167)[12]

Here, Pike comments on *Maelström* and other contemporary Quebec films, in order to outline how life transforms in the wake of these conditions. While Pike does not offer a sustained engagement with Villeneuve's film, he does make a key observation about the ways in which these contemporary Quebec films seek to express these conditions:

> One of the effects of the stylistic tricks of the multimedia generation is to provide a visual correlative for this change and when we see that style reckoning with the spatial iconography of the province we can get a glimpse of how such representations might work outside the traditional confines of documentary realism. (167)

Pike's discussion identifies key characteristics associated with Canadian cinemas, including a lineage of documentary realism that is considered a substantial influence on narrative films produced in the 1970s and 1980s. In the 1990s and into the 2000s, more Canadian directors began to challenge and rethink the legacy of documentary realism and *Maelström* provides a vibrant example of this endeavour. Specifically, Pike notes the role of 'the surrealistic talking fish-narrator within the context of the local fishing industry in Villeneuve's *Maelström*' (167). While this brief discussion by Pike remains within the confines of a representational methodology, he does illuminate the role that style plays to draw attention to these changes brought about by globalisation, late capitalism, and citification. Stylistics, visuality, and form illuminate processes within the film that seek to confront and work through these issues. However, much like a break from the documentary realist tradition that *Maelström* embodies, there also emerges a force that seeks to break from the current experiences within the contemporary, global city. More than simply representing what these current experiences are like, *Maelström* opens up potentialities to think beyond these constraints and restrictions.

There is clearly a break from the conventions of Canadian cinemas which unfolds through Villeneuve's images. The story itself might be recognisable within the general lineage of Canadian cinemas – the film does visibly take place within Montreal, after all – but the style of the film puts pressure on preconceived formal and stylistic conventions. As Geoff Pevere states, 'the talking fish heeds us not to expect a story that honors the rules of conventional romantic storytelling, a fact that the creature's brutal filleting certainly stresses' (100).[13] Do the fish do more than simply occupy a location of inaccessible authenticity? Villeneuve begins the film by setting up a departure that throws recognisable elements into new contexts. An undermining of static meaning unfolds through the move away from established conventions. 'Weirdness, understood here as the deliberate departure from realist convention for the sake of undermining convention itself', states Pevere, 'has long struggled to maintain a foothold on the stubbornly docudramatic surface of Canadian movies' (101). The style of the film, as outlined by Pevere, seeks a departure from the restrictive and limiting conventions of Canadian film by way of fracturing the notion of tradition or a lineage linked to documentary realism. Seeking a departure from what exists, what has been done, what is expected, Villeneuve's film explores the capacity to rethink the available, stylistic pathways that a Canadian film may take. Of course, other films before *Maelström* have pursued breaks from these conventions as well, but what specifically does Villeneuve's film do and how can a close reading unfold a contingent world beyond what the film is taken to represent in terms of an established world?

Images of Bibiane in *Maelström* unfold through risk that include her actions in the narrative as well as the stylistic risks chosen by Villeneuve. While it is proposed that her actions correspond to feelings of uneasiness and discontent within globalisation, late capitalism, citification, and a general malaise, Bibiane never explicitly voices such feelings: they must be read for. If Bibiane feels such feelings then we may posit that she takes a series of risks in an attempt to break from the constraints, the restrictions, the limitations that she encounters within such a milieu. However, more than simply reflecting her experience, discontent and uneasiness, the film maps the pursuit of, the creation of, the unfolding of a world beyond the one Bibiane knows. She does not remain within her world; Bibane seeks a world yet to come. Initially, these risks are, perhaps, more noticeably risky, as Amy J. Ransom states:

> Partying and promiscuous sexual activity offer Bibiane Champagne (Marie-Josée Croze) an outlet for her frustrations, but also repeatedly bring her into contact with death, from the graphic opening sequence

of an abortion, her hit-and-run accident while driving drunk, and an attempted suicide fueled by her sense of guilt. (177)

Death may be an outcome, or a possible outcome, that results from the situations Bibiane engages in, but these situations take shape through risks which involve exposures. Though Ransom does not identify such activities as risks or as risky, her article does point to a motivation that launches the actions of Bibiane as well as other protagonists within the contemporary Quebec films she discusses. Ransom sketches this motivation as a desire to seek out difference:

> These films force their characters out of familiar territory, or bring 'the foreign' onto the territory of Québec, not as a threat to unity and identity in the homogenous society that the province's Francophone populace used to view itself as being, but rather to facilitate positive change in these individuals' sense of self and being in the world and in the community. (179)

The doubling of struggle, of change, of transformation, of the new becomes evident within Ransom's interpretation. Not only does the film undertake a stylistic move – as discussed by Pike and Pevere – that seeks a difference outside of the documentary realist tradition, *Maelström* also launches a narrative move through which Bibiane pursues change beyond the restrictions levied by her global, capital, urban milieu.

A set of moves occurs, through form, from familiar to difference which seeks to open up the new. The stylistic move might be easiest. 'The stylistic excess of the fish dungeon sequences', reaffirms Longfellow, 'signals an immediate departure from any realist tradition of Québec cinema' (72). Villeneuve's style becomes a departure. Yet, Longfellow does not view Bibiane's narrative as a departure. She argues that the films do not 'forecast the possibility of a utopian radical disjuncture from contemporary conditions of globalization' (80). The style moves; the characters do not. Stylistically, *Maelström* breaks from the restrictions of the realist tradition. Narratively, Bibiane remains stuck, constrained, entombed by the conditions of globalisation and late capitalism. The standard approach to Bibiane's experiences is to link them to an established view which understands these conditions to be far reaching, all encompassing, unchangeable, and as saturating all aspects of life. In short, from this perspective, there appears to be no outside of these conditions. Longfellow frames this interpretation by arguing that 'the emotional texture of everyday life is one of a generalized melancholia explicitly tied to the colonizing and territorializing flows of corporate capital into all aspects of life – the intimate as much as the work environment' (71). While the documentary realist tradition of Canadian (and Quebec) cinema does not permeate all potentialities available to Canadian directors, which Villeneuve's film visibly demonstrates, the same cannot be said for potentialities outside of late capitalism.

Or can it? Longfellow notes that these conditions saturate all aspects of life. Nevertheless, Villeneuve's film seeks a pathway: 'I would like to explore the manner in which the resistance to the omnipresence of global corporate culture in *Maelström* is compromised by its recourse to this romantic fantasy of non-coded, non-territorialized spaces of nature.' (71) The film does resist globacapitalism. However, following Longfellow, there appears to be a flip. Where the local, the rural, the natural, the private, the archaic, and all other vibrant modalities before and outside of globalisation, late capitalism, and citification have become inaccessible which signifies the loss of authenticity, the contemporary conditions lived by Bibiane, which are saturated in the flows of capital, have blocked any route to this authenticity. A longing for authenticity lost becomes the only possibility for resistance, but such a longing exists as an infinite deferral. Moreover, any production of such archaic forms can only ever be in and of themselves inauthentic:

> In a post-sacral world where collective 'deep' traditions have been eclipsed by ubiquity of American consumer culture founded on the principles of immediate gratification, sappy optimism, anti-intellectualism, and infantilism, so humourously captured in the song that plays as Bibiane exist from the abortion clinic ('Gliddy glub gloopy nibby nabby noopy, La la la lo lo . . .'), what is left in the absence of depth, are beautiful seductive surfaces. (Longfellow 74)

From this perspective, what was authentic can now only ever be experienced as inauthentic – the absence of depth. Therefore, globacapitalism has either forever destroyed the possibility of authenticity or it has become a new authenticity through the permeation and saturation of all experiences. Yet, there remains another potentiality, which was discussed above: authenticity was always an illusion.

Projecting back through a linear conception of time, the standard conclusion becomes life was authentic before globacapitalism. Conversely, living within the conditions of globalisation, capitalism, and citification throws us into a moment where authenticity no longer exists. Longfellow frames this position through a discussion of Quebec cinema from the 1980s:

> While the films assert the impossibility of a simple return to a rural mode of life as a means of reconciling alienation, the landscape nonetheless functions as a melancholic reminder of all that is lost by the travails of modernity and technological rationality. (77)

Past modes of life, of experience, are impossible. Current modes of life no longer possess the authenticity of the past. Thus, in Villeneuve's film, Bibiane is characterised as embodying the effects of this loss and the uneasiness that is felt living in such discontents from the loss of authenticity. This view is a fairly standard notion in terms of Quebec cinema and, moreover, culture that, as discussed by Longfellow, has been established in Bill Marshall's work on Quebec cinema (77). Therefore, the fish sequences are linked to a world outside of our own and forever inaccessible outside of a fantasy or imagined space. Bibiane's narrative reflects our world where we are forever stuck in globacapitalism as either a perpetual inauthentic and frustrating experience or as a new mode of authenticity in and of itself. However, what if the archaic, the rural, the traditional and all else projected as outside the current milieu was always already inauthentic? What if that longing was there the whole time? To take this poststructuralist framing to the limit – and, perhaps, beyond – the real was eternally a myth, an illusion, a hallucination. The artifice has been stripped away. The depth was simply a willingness to believe in depth not actually depth itself. That said, the implications may be quite similar. Whether authenticity was possible or, conversely, only the belief in authenticity was possible seems to be a matter of degree. The vibrant potentiality unfolds when authenticity becomes always already a willingness to believe or the possibility of believing. Consequently, authenticity was never lost. And, more importantly, the present conditions of globacapitalism do not throw us into a depthless and eternal malaise from which authenticity remains forever lost. Nothing can be lost if it was never found. Therefore, through this recognition, the capacity to transform becomes visible and it becomes pure potential (or virtual). In this sense, the fish sequences do not represent the archaic or authenticity forever inaccessible; the fish sequences express the potentialities beyond, in spite of, always already outside the contemporary milieu produced by the conditions of globalisation, late capitalism, and citification.

My argument then becomes less about linking the fish or Bibiane to what they may tell us about our world. Rather, my reading seeks out what they do not. 'Readings cannot secure a gain on its investment through promises of prior and external affordances precisely', states Brinkema, 'because aesthetic objects do not immediately render the world.' ('Form' 267) This fact becomes obvious in relation to *Maelström* when we consider some of Bibiane's actions. It would be atrocious to suggest that the film promises that killing a person while driving drunk and stoned might change our lives for the better. Likewise, that driving your car into the river may, if you can escape, provide a new life. *Maelström* does not render our world, but a world. The film does foreground the necessity of risks for the potentialities of transformation. Whether the risks take shape stylistically through the overexposure of the film stock that may render the image completely washed out or narratively through the exposure of a truth that may cause a new lover to hate you, the changes that take place in the film require risks. Yet not all risks become necessary or even advisable. The stranger that Bibiane meets in the metro and that Evian meets in the bar attests to this fact. After a train passes by a platform in the metro, a shot exposes Bibiane sitting near a stranger. Bibiane tells the stranger in the metro that she has killed a man, and that nobody knows but her. Following this confession, which exposes her secret to the stranger, Bibiane asks if she should turn herself in to the police. 'If he's dead,' replies the stranger, 'what does it change? It changes nothing.'[14] He further suggests that she not tell anyone else. Later in the film, after Bibiane has confessed to Evian that she killed his father, Evian drinks heavily in a bar and tells the situation to a man next to him. While the man's identity has been concealed with his back to the camera, he becomes exposed via a cut to the opposite side of Evian as the man offers his advice. It is the same stranger that Bibiane met in the metro. 'Sounds compatible. Marry her and keep quiet . . .' says the stranger, 'especially in a bar.'[15] Through the stranger's straight forward reading of each situation, new perspectives emerge. What could exposing the truth transform in each of these situations? According to the stranger, only adverse outcomes are possible through these risks. Therefore, he advises both Bibiane and Evian to stop talking about it. Some secrets may be best kept inside.

Evian and Bibiane overcome the fact that she killed his father. At least the film suggests this outcome when he returns to her, and they travel together to scatter his father's ashes in the ocean. She killed his father, but she also saved his life by stopping him from getting on a plane that would later crash. Before Bibiane exposes the truth, Evian claims she is an angel for saving his life. Can Evian still consider her an angel after learning the truth? Bibiane takes a risk by exposing this truth to Evian despite the fact that no one else knows. The risk appears to unfold a new life with Evian and Bibiane embracing at the end of the film after exposing his father's ashes to the ocean, where they scatter them. Perhaps, following the advice of the stranger from the bar, Evian's perspective has changed. '*Every perception is hallucinatory*', states Deleuze, '*because perception has no object.*' (107, italics in original) In other words, only our view of the world, our vortex, determines our perspective. We may assume that the world exists as such because we see it that way, but a stranger in the metro or in a bar might view it quite differently. *Maelström* unfolds this condition of life through risks structured as exposures. Therefore, what we may assume to be outside or impossible or inaccessible may actually be a matter of degree, or of perspective.

In this sense, we are already outside of globalisation and late capitalism, we just do not know it. Or, in other words, we need a new perspective that seizes a virtual potentiality. While the conditions of globacapitalism may saturate all facets of life, *Maelström* seeks to expose the virtual potentialities beyond these conditions. The capacity to see an outside exists and we need to find a pathway to expose it. These exposures do not come without risk, nor do they offer readily available solutions. We cannot simply take the right risk and find ourselves in a transformed world. However, through the realisation that authenticity was always already an illusion, we can recognise the limitations of our perspectives and expose ourselves to new potentialities. The fish expose such a virtual potential. Evian and Bibiane embrace this virtual potential. 'Locked in a clinch in a space that is so utterly de-territorialized, de-racinated and de-nationalized as to be imaginary,' states Longfellow, 'the fairy tale ending remains just that, an empty allegory.' (78) Yet can an allegory be anything other than empty? When there are no longer codes-in-texts and, instead, texts-in-process then every allegory becomes empty in advance of close reading. All symbols remain empty until their relations generate meaning. Therefore, a cardboard box containing a foetus exposed to flames inside of a furnace or a cardboard box containing a person's ashes exposed to the ocean can be both endings and beginnings. These moments may take us outside of ourselves and outside of what we have come to know, but they also reveal more insides. Inside of a new relationship or a new path to somewhere we did not know we could go. Death may be linked to endings and endings may be linked to death. Nevertheless, death remains part of a process that may be seen from a different perspective to unfold new potentialities. To invoke the final fish sequence, no one can tell us the secret of life because life remains in-process. Never do we find ourselves outside until we are truly outside of ourselves. Yet, even then, we may well find ourselves in the vortices we never left behind.

NOTES

1. Longfellow, Brenda, 'Counter-Narratives, Class Politics, and Metropolitan Dystopias: Representations of Globalization in *Maelström*, *waydowntown* and *La Moitié gauche du frigo*', *Canadian Journal of Film Studies*, vol. 13, no. 1, 2004, pp. 69–83.
2. Brinkema, Eugenie, *The Forms of the Affects*, Duke University Press, 2014.
3. Brinkema, Eugenie, 'Form.' *A Concise Companion to Visual Culture*, edited by A. Joan Saab, Aubrey Anable and Catherine Zuromskis, Wiley Blackwell, 2021, pp. 259–76.
4. For scholarship that directly discusses Deleuze's transcendental empiricism, see Bryant, Levi R., *Difference and Givenness: Deleuze's Transcendental Empiricism and the Ontology of Immanence*, Northwestern University Press, 2008; Baugh, Bruce, 'Transcendental Empiricism: Deleuze's Response to Hegel', *Man and World*, vol. 25, no. 2, April 1992, pp. 133–48; McDonald, Terrance H., 'Posthuman Cinema: Terrence Malick and a Cinema of Life', *From Deleuze and Guattari to Posthumanism: Philosophies of Immanence*, edited by Christine Daigle and Terrance H. McDonald, Bloomsbury, 2022, pp. 129–46.
5. Deleuze, Gilles *The Fold*, translated by Tom Conley, London, Continuum, 2001.
6. 'Paradoxalement, la douche lui fait aussi perdre contact avec le temps et le monde qui l'entoure.'
7. See Longfellow; Ransom, Amy J., 'Deterritorialization and the Crisis of Recognition in Turn of the Millennium Québec Film', *American Review of Canadian Studies*, vol. 43,

no. 2, 2013, pp. 176–89; Melnyk, George, 'The Gendered City: Feminism in Rozema's *Deperanto* (1991), Pool's *Rispondetemi* (1991), and Villeneuve's *Maelström* (2000)', *Film and the City: The Urban Imaginary in Canadian Cinema*, Athabasca University Press, 2014, pp. 77–100.
8. 'Est tout sauf . . . douce.'
9. 'Hachons-leur la tête, vidons le crâne buvons dans le crâne de nos adversaires.'
10. Jameson, Fredric, *Postmodernism, or The Cultural Logic of Late Capitalism*, Duke University Press, 1991.
11. 'Une très jolie histoire.'
12. Pike, David L., *Canadian Cinema since the 1980s: At the Heart of the World*, University of Toronto Press, 2012.
13. Pevere, Geoff, 'Fishy', *North of Everything: English-Canadian Cinema Since 1980*, edited by William Beard and Jerry White, University of Alberta Press, 2002.
14. 'S'il est mort, qu'est-ce que ça change? Ça change rien.'
15. 'Ça me semble compatible. Marie-la et ferme ta gueule . . . surtout dans les bars.'

CHAPTER 7

The Self as Other and the Other as Self: Identity, Doubling and Misrecognition in *Incendies*, *Enemy* and *Blade Runner 2049*

Jeri English

Characters grapple with questions of identity throughout Denis Villeneuve's films, from Simone Prévost (Pascale Bussières) in *Un 32 août sur terre* (1998), who seeks to redefine herself after surviving a car crash, to Louise Banks (Amy Adams) in *Arrival* (2016), whose interactions with the alien Heptapods lead her not only to a new understanding of her future role as a mother, but to a whole new conception of being and time, to Paul Atreides (Timothée Chalamet) in *Dune* (2021), who grapples with his potentiality as the Kwisatz Haderach of the Bene Gesserit and the Lisan al Gaib of the Fremen. In three films specifically – *Incendies* (2010), *Enemy* (2013) and *Blade Runner 2049* (2017) – the question of identity is underpinned by explorations of intersubjectivity,[1] as it is the protagonists' quests for knowledge of the Other that inevitably lead to a profound shift in understanding of the Self.

These physical and symbolic quests all originate in a desire to know who someone is. In *Incendies*, twins Jeanne (Mélissa Désormeaux-Poulain) and Simon Marwan (Maxim Gaudette) are sent to the unnamed native country of their deceased mother to find their brother and father; to their horror, they discover that their father is indeed the very son their mother failed to find years previously. In *Enemy*, Adam (Jake Gyllenhaal) first spies his presumed *doppelgänger*, Anthony (again, Jake Gyllenhaal), in a minor role in a film and pursues this mysterious actor through an alienating Toronto until he himself becomes the object of Anthony's obsession; by the film's conclusion, the double has disappeared, leaving Adam in a state of disarray as both subject and object of the quest. In *BR 2049*, K (Ryan Gosling) is instructed by his boss, Lieutenant Joshi (Robin Wright), to hunt down the lost (half) Replicant child[2] of Rachael (Sean Young) and Rick Deckard (Harrison Ford) through a deeply dystopic Los Angeles, San Diego and Las Vegas; K's false belief that he himself is the miracle child whose existence may change the future for the Replicants and humans stems from his confusion of Ana Stelline's (Carla Juri) implanted memories for his own and demonstrates a breakdown in his narrative identity or, in other words, in the stories he tells and is told about his life.

These characters demonstrate a clear misunderstanding of the object of their quests: the dialectic between the *idem* and the *ipse* – between permanence in time and variable selfhood[3] – becomes a major plot point in all three films and a reason for the protagonists' misrecognition of both Self and Other. Perhaps unsurprisingly, given that these films deal with questions of selfhood, identity and misrecognition, they also all play with questions of seeing and not-seeing: characters in each film are either literally sightless (Niander Wallace [Jared Leto] in *BR 2049*), temporarily blinded (Simon in *Incendies*) or simply unable to see the truth they seek (Nawal, Jeanne and Simon in *Incendies*, Adam in *Enemy* and K in *BR 2049*). To amplify the mystery of the unknown son/brother/father, of the elusive *doppelgänger* and of the Replicant-born child, traces of certain female characters in all three films reverberate uncannily in others. Jeanne retraces her mother's steps through a fictionalised Lebanon in *Incendies* and, as we see in flashbacks that show young Nawal (Lubna Azabal) on screen in the same location as her daughter thirty years later, looks just like her. In *Enemy*, Adam's girlfriend, Mary (Mélanie Laurent), calls to mind Anthony's wife, Helen (Sarah Gadon); the blond sex worker who tantalisingly crushes a tarantula under her heel under Anthony/Adam's spellbound gaze in the first scene of the film suggests both women and foreshadows Helen's final uncanny transformation. In *BR 2049*, Rachael 2.0 (images of Sean Young projected onto body double Loren Peta)[4] briefly and imperfectly echoes the original Rachael, and K's hologram AI girlfriend Joi (Ana de Armas) literally maps herself onto and imperfectly merges with Replicant sex worker Mariette (Mackenzie Davis).

In the following pages, I examine key moments of misrecognition and doubling across *Incendies*, *Enemy* and *BR 2049* in order to shed light on Villeneuve's cinematic exploration of intersubjective identity. I will show how, despite their obvious differences in budget, language, location and plot, these films engage similarly with questions of identity, and of the recognition and misrecognition of Self and Other.

ONE PLUS ONE MAKES ONE: DOUBLING AND MISRECOGNITION IN *INCENDIES*

After their mother's death, Jeanne and Simon are initially tasked with finding their father and brother; their quest, however, necessarily begins with uncovering the truth about their mother's identity. The enigma of Nawal is made clear to Jeanne by a woman from her mother's village ('You're looking for your father. But you don't know who your mother is') and to Simon by Nawal's ex-employer, notary Jean Lebel (Rémy Girard): 'If you want to find your brother, you will need to follow the traces of your mother'.[5] The twins' initial distance from their mother is materialised in an early sequence where Nawal, having suffered a stroke brought on by her sudden understanding of the *idem* of her son and the father of her twins, lies dying in hospital. A full shot shows Simon and Jeanne seated in chairs angled towards each other underneath a window in a hospital room, Nawal lying motionless on a bed in front of them. After a cut, the camera shows Nawal in a medium full shot and the camera tracks slowly towards her as the intertitle 'NAWAL' appears in red over her body; with the intertitle still on the screen, there is a cut to a shot of a young woman running through a rocky landscape. The slow tracking shot towards Nawal shows the twins' desire to get closer to her, while the abrupt cut to a shot of her as a young woman in her home village highlights their ignorance of her life story. What Jeanne and Simon do not understand is that their physical proximity to their mother as her children does not give them privileged knowledge about her previous lived reality; it is Nawal's prior relations with others that have created the Self she is currently. Matthew Escobar's conception of the 'meta-body' as 'a dynamic which results from the interplay of our lived body, the images and spaces we encounter in the phenomenal world [. . .] and the temporally, spatially and affectively marked trajectories of the self' as well as 'a product of our relations with others' (82–3)[6] is useful here to conceptualise the ways in which Nawal's prior lived experiences are inaccessible to her children. Nawal's transformations and new identities are multiple: she is the illicit lover of Wahab (Hamed Najem), a Muslim refugee executed by her Christian brothers; the mother of a baby boy abandoned at an orphanage, fleeing her village and the shame she has brought to her family; the near-victim of a massacre of Muslim refugees on a bus by Christian nationalists; the assassin of this group's leader; 'The woman who sings' in the Kfar Ryat prison; and a trauma-marked mother of twins in Montreal. If we accept Paul Ricoeur's notion of narrative identity as a key element of personal identity[7] and if, as Escobar suggests, trauma plays a key role in displacing narrative emplotment,[8] then we can see that Nawal's own tragically failed identity quest ended by alienating her from her own meta-body and her own life story.

Nawal's unknowability by her children is reflected in the mystery of her lost son. Despite her repeated desperate and dangerous attempts to find him, he remains throughout the film unattainable and unrecognisable by his mother. This enigma of Nihad (Hussein Sami/Yousef Soufan) is foreshadowed in the final shot of the first scene of the film, where he figures among the dozens of filthy and blank-eyed orphans being transformed into child soldiers by the warlord Chamseddine (Mohamed Majd) and his men. In this shot, the camera tracks slowly towards Nihad's bowed shaved head as his gaze, both terrified and resigned, locks onto ours. The movement that hinted at Jeanne and Simon's belated desire to understand a dying Nawal in the hospital room here underscores Nihad's fundamental unknowability throughout the film. Nihad is himself ignorant of his own identity; Nawal's grandmother's counsel to 'Take a good look at your mother's face so you'll recognise her', spoken to the new-born infant moments before he is to be removed from Nawal's care is, of course, fruitless. Nawal searches for years for her lost child and cannot recognise him as her eventual torturer; nor does the spectator immediately recognise the child, Nihad, in the fearsome figure of Abou Tarek (Abdelghafour Elaaziz). In one scene, Villeneuve purposely misdirects our drive to solve the mystery of Nawal's missing boy: as the intertitle 'NIHAD' appears on the screen in red, we see a young boy sprinting through rubble in a war-torn street. He is soon joined by three others, all carrying plastic bags and sheltering behind burned out cars as they try to move to safety. As an older boy helps the younger ones move through the wreckage, the close-up shots on their faces cause us to assume one of them is an older Nihad, a desperate victim of war. Our worry for Nihad intensifies when, after a loud gunshot sound, in a POV shot through the sight on a rifle from a building above, we see that the smallest of the boys has been shot down and that the sniper is searching for more targets. It is only a subsequent shot that shows the three dots tattooed on the back of the shooter's heel that allows us to properly identify the sniper, and not his victim, as Nawal's lost child.[9]

The first time we see Nihad as an adult Abou Tarek, it is in a medium close up low angle shot where he is looking down and to the left as he circles around a figure that the next shot will reveal to be Nawal; the tilt of his head recalls Nihad's bowed head in the film's first scene. After a cut, we see a long shot of Abou Tarek standing in the prison torture room, gazing down at Nawal; although he watches her intently for several seconds, he does not recognise as his mother the woman he will beat, rape and impregnate. Nawal will only recognise him years later, where a glimpse of the three dots tattooed on a stranger's heel at a swimming pool leads to her sudden understanding of the identity of her prison rapist, precipitates her stroke and triggers the twins' journey. Once Nawal has solved the mystery of her missing son and acknowledged the identity of the father of her twins, she forges a separation between son and rapist by writing two letters to be delivered by her twins: one to her son and one to her twins' father. She thereby literally refuses the *idem* identity of Nihad and Abou Tarek, and solidifies her son and her rapist as two separate identities.

Nawal's creation of a double and unresolvable Nihad/Abou Tarek is foreshadowed in the film by the very existence of Simon and Jeanne; the first intertitle of the film, 'LES JUMEAUX', appears in red across the screen as they walk together into Lebel's office, conflating the identities of brother and sister.

Before Jeanne leaves to fulfil her mother's request, the twins are often shown in a two shot, side-by-side, centred in the frame. The dyad of Simon and Jeanne is broken, however, once Jeanne arrives in her mother's native country. As Jeanne retraces her mother's steps, flashback shots conflate the two women who, separated by thirty years, are dressed nearly identically in dark blueish-grey tops and who wear the same hairstyle and necklace. As Yana Meerzon remarks, the strong resemblance between actors Azabal and Désormeaux-Poulin creates not just an uncertainty with regards to the characters' identity, but also allows Villeneuve 'to create a type of cinematic magic, to reach the past/present simultaneity [. . .] normally impossible to achieve in film' (28).[10] The superposition of Nawal's meta-body onto Jeanne is emphasised by the intertitle 'DARESH' that appears in red writing on Nawal's back as she is leaving her grandmother's house after the birth and loss of Nihad; the same intertitle remains as the image of Nawal is replaced by a nearly identical image of Jeanne. In the shot following the revelation by the janitor that Nawal was indeed 'The woman who sings' in Kfar Ryat prison, Villeneuve films Jeanne in an extreme long shot, speaking outside on her mobile phone to Simon; although we know it is Jeanne we are seeing, it is the figure of Nawal who haunts the scene, an echo reinforced by the imprinting of the intertitle 'LA FEMME QUI CHANTE' on Jeanne who stands in the backdrop of her mother's youth. Villeneuve's use of Désormeaux-Poulin to uncannily bring Nawal to life on screen signals the return of a knowledge 'that was long familiar to the psyche and was estranged from it only through being repressed' (Freud 147):[11] the Œdipal reality of Nihad as both Nawal's son and Jeanne's father.

Throughout the first half of *Incendies*, Simon refuses to participate in seeking out the truth of his mother's story; once he joins Jeanne, there is a transition in which the twins reform their initial dyad. In the sequence titled 'SARWAN JANAAN', the twins are framed together in a tight medium close-up shot in the hospital as they learn from the elderly nurse that they are the babies who were born to Nawal in prison. The solution to this first mystery – they had originally misrecognised the child born in prison as their brother, Nihad – is marked by a symbolic return to their gestation: in the following shot, Jeanne and then Simon plunge, in fœtal positions, into a swimming pool as we hear underwater sounds. The final shot in this swimming pool scene, of the twins holding each other in the pool, suggests their embrace in the womb.

This union gives way once Simon takes over the active role in the quest for their brother; traces of Nawal appear in Simon as they did earlier in Jeanne. When Simon goes to the refugee camp in Deressa, we see a medium close-up shot of him squinting into the sun, wearing a greyish-blue shirt and looking very similar to both Nawal and Jeanne in earlier shots. In the following sequence, Chamseddine's men come to the hotel to fetch Simon. We see him get into a silver car and then, in an extreme long shot, we see a silver car pull up behind

Figure 7.1 Simon (Maxim Gaudette) blindfolded in *Incendies*.

an SUV on a desert road, and a figure gets out of the car and walks towards the SUV. Although we first understand this figure to be Simon it is, in fact, Nawal. Once Nawal gets into the SUV, the intertitle 'CHAMSEDDINE' appears in red over her face. The intertitle remains while the shot changes to Simon, blindfolded, sitting on a couch and backlit from hazy light coming in through curtains in the window behind him. The blindfold – used by Chamseddine's men so Simon will not know where he has been taken or be able to identify the men after – underscores Simon's unwillingness to learn the truth that is too awful to bear. As Simon unseeingly listens to Chamseddine, Villeneuve places the camera beside and slightly behind him on the couch; the shallow focus on Simon completely obscures the identity of the men in the background (Figure 7.1). In this scene, the spectator, like Simon, cannot immediately get a proper glimpse of the warlord or a grasp on what is going on: we are as much 'in the dark' as Simon. Once Chamseddine decides to tell Simon the story of how Nihad became Abou Tarek, he removes his blindfold. It is thus only near the end of the film that Simon recognises the *idem* of Nihad, the child lost by his mother during the country's civil war, and Abou Tarek, the prison rapist who impregnates Nawal. Simon captures the dialectic between sameness and selfhood with his horrified question, 'Can one plus one make one?'[12]

Once Jeanne and Simon have fulfilled their identity quest and returned to Montreal, the reflections of Nawal are no longer present in their dyad. The final shots of the twins as they read their mother's letter together in Lebel's office are two close-up profile shots, each of which has one twin in the foreground and the other in the background, using a rack focus. The changing depth of field, through which the twin in the foreground and the twin in the background become alternately in focus and blurry, highlights how their new tragic knowledge of the *idem* of their brother and their father has led them not only to a new empathic relation with the memory of their dead mother but also, finally, a new self-knowledge by bringing Nawal's lost narrative identity to life through their own bodies.

THIS IS A PATTERN THAT REPEATS ITSELF: SELF AND/OR OTHER IN *ENEMY*

While Jeanne and Simon attain an understanding of the Self by finding the object of their search, Adam spends much of *Enemy* in pursuit of or in flight from his *doppelgänger* who, as the film's conclusion seems to indicate, embodies his own repressed desires.[13] In other words, Adam's misrecognition of Anthony as Other shows his inability or unwillingness to grasp the dialectic of his own *ipse*-identity.[14] Adam is a history professor who is, in his own way, as unknowable as Nihad. His dominant character traits seem to be lethargy and repetition: day after day, he gives his lectures on totalitarianism and dictatorships in a brutalist concrete classroom in which he repeats the same ideas and even the same phrasings from class to class; he grades students' papers with a weary apathy; and he welcomes his girlfriend, Mary, to his dark, sparsely furnished apartment in the evenings for takeout and sex. Villeneuve uses an L cut to foreground the repetitive nature of Adam's life, replaying lines from his lectures during other moments of his day: we hear Adam say 'they kept the populace busy with entertainment' while we see him commuting home on a streetcar; we hear 'in other dictatorships, they have other strategies', while we see Adam reading student papers with Mary sitting, smoking, in a rocking chair by Adam's patio doors; and we hear 'To limit information, to limit ideas and knowledge. How do they do that? They lower education and limit culture', as we watch Adam and Mary have sex. The dreariness of Adam's professional life is accentuated through his rumpled beige suits, his economy-class car and his nondescript apartment in an anonymous tower surrounded by other hostile seeming towers ('What the fuck is this place, man,' asks Anthony, upon seeing the apartment for the first time, 'you live here?'). When asked by a cheerful colleague if he likes movies, an uneasy Adam seems only able to define himself in the negative: 'I don't know, I don't, I don't, I don't, I don't go out that much, I don't, I don't really like movies'.

Anthony is presented as diametrically opposed to Adam, although physically identical. A working actor with a stylish condo and a self-consciously slick style, Anthony exudes a virile, macho energy: he rides a motorcycle, travels, exercises, enjoys the organic blueberries that Adam hates, visits sex clubs and has extramarital affairs. The two men have distinct dwellings, romantic partners, jobs, wardrobes and personalities, and are shown on screen at the same time, corroborating the interpretation that Anthony is indeed Adam's *doppelgänger*.[15] However, key clues in the film – the torn photo Adam finds of himself in his apartment that, in its unaltered form in Anthony's condo, shows a smiling Anthony and Helen; the insistence by the mother, when speaking to Adam, that he does indeed like blueberries and that he should abandon his attempt to become a third-rate movie actor – serve to muddy this interpretation.[16] The film seems to suggest that Adam and Anthony – and their female counterparts, Mary and Helen – are at once defined by their sameness and by their difference.

The blurriness surrounding the identity of the two men – indistinguishable down to the scars on their chests – is established in the very first sequence of the film, where a man we will eventually understand to be Anthony (since he is wearing a wedding ring, which Adam does not do, as close-up shots of his hands later in the film, as well as Mary's panic when she sees a wedding ring tan line on Anthony's finger, confirm) visits a sex club, where he watches a naked woman masturbate on stage and then watches another prepare to crush a tarantula with her spike heel on stage. Before this scene, we hear a voice mail message while watching a slow pan across an endless series of apartment buildings against a hazy yellow sky: 'Hello darling, it's your mother. Well, thank you for showing me your new apartment. Um. I'm worried about you. I, I mean, how can you live like that?' Since it's Adam, we will learn, who lives in a sparse and unhospitable apartment, this ought to be his mother's voice; the man we see in the car after a cut, shot in a slow zoom from behind, his eyes visible in the rear-view mirror, would thus appear to be Adam, listening to his mother's voice mail. However, a later shot of Adam driving his car away in terror from his first meeting with Anthony shows that the headrests in Adam's car are different from the ones in the first scene of the film; the man we see in the car while we hear the mother's voice mail message would therefore seem to be Anthony. This interpretation is reinforced narratively by the following shot, which shows Anthony's pregnant wife, Helen, sitting naked on their bed; after this shot, we see the man we later identify as Anthony by his wedding ring enter the sex club.

If this first sequence serves to create confusion with regards to the identity of the son for whom the mother is leaving her voice mail, it also serves to create a link between Helen and the sex club workers. The reflection of Helen in these women is established when a blonde woman in a white silky robe – a robe that calls to mind the white silk sheets on the bed where Helen first appears nude – arrives on stage; the shallow focus on the backs of the men's heads makes it impossible to make out her facial features. A second woman follows, carrying a silver platter that, we will see, contains the tarantula one of the two women will crush with her heel. One woman removes her robe; again the shallow focus on Anthony's rapt face shot in a close-up profile shot, obscures the woman's facial features and even the form of her nude body. As the lid to the silver platter is lifted, we see shots of the swollen tarantula intercut with shots of mesmerised men staring at the stage, including Anthony with his fingers splayed over his eyes. The next shot shows the woman's body reflected imperfectly in the shiny surface of the stage; this is followed by a high angle shot of her body shadowed and backlit. The impossibility of assigning an identity to the blond sex club worker – who calls to mind both Helen and Adam's girlfriend, Mary – adds to the deep uncanniness of the film[17] and, in conjunction with the spider, gives a clue as to the hidden aspects of Self that push Adam to conjure Anthony. If Freud observes that 'neurotic men declare that they feel that there is something uncanny about the female genital organs' (151), this primal fear is often dramatised in cinema as both a fascination with the monstrous feminine, that is, 'what it is about woman that is shocking, terrifying, horrific, abject' (Creed 44),[18] and a terror of the figure of the archaic mother, sometimes represented as a spider figure that incarnates 'the blackness of extinction-death' (Creed 63). The brief scene where Adam rapes Mary while she is asleep reinforces the links between Adam's 'discovery' of Anthony and his own repressed Self. Seemingly out of character for a man we have seen represented thus far simply as an overworked, listless history professor, this scene hints at the existence of Anthony's aggression hidden under Adam's docile surface and prefigures the later scene where Mary will struggle to get away from Anthony after seeing his wedding ring tan line.

The initial sequence of the film, then, proves vital for creating a confusion around the identity of Adam and Anthony, and of Helen, Mary and the women in the sex club; at the same time, Anthony's intense gaze, combined with several lingering close-up shots of various men staring impassively at the women on stage, underscores the importance of looking and seeing as tools to confirm identity. While Adam is never literally blindfolded like Simon in *Incendies*, there are several scenes in which we see him covering his eyes with one hand, showing his unwillingness to truly grasp the truth of his *doppelgänger*'s existence. Adam 'sees' Anthony for the first time in a film; this recognition of himself does not occur the first time he watches the movie, however, but rather afterwards, in a dream. After Mary leaves angrily following Adam's non-consensual act, Adam falls asleep and, in his dream, replays the scene from the film in which the uncanny double appears for the first time: upon dreaming a clean-shaven Anthony dressed as a bellhop, Adam wakes with a start. It is significant that this moment of (mis)recognition happens in a dream sequence flashback; the first time the spectator sees the scene is not the first time Adam sees it, but rather when his unconscious replays it for him. Following this dream sequence, Adam looks to confirm his identity with Anthony through an accumulation of media: he frantically scrolls through the film until he finds his double's face on screen; he rents two more movies in which Anthony plays a small role and tracks down Anthony's actor profile online; and he compares a torn photograph of himself – clean-shaven – to the image of Anthony on his computer screen.[19]

The many shots of Adam and Anthony's eyes further reinforce the importance of seeing in confirming identity. As mentioned above, the first shot we see of either of the men is of Anthony's eyes reflected in the rear-view mirror of his car. Anthony is immediately portrayed as more willing to see than Adam, as he watches the sex club scene with his hands splayed open over his eyes; Adam, on the other hand, is often shown with one hand entirely covering his eyes. After he first speaks with Helen on the phone, looking for Anthony, he covers his eyes with his hands in the car; after meeting with Anthony for the first time, he repeats the same gesture (Figure 7.2). When he visits his mother after first meeting Anthony, we see him sitting at her table, his hand entirely covering his eyes, as she insists, 'There must be some difference'; he removes his hand from his eyes and answers, 'There isn't.' After this scene, in which the mother seems to confirm for us the *idem* of Adam and Anthony while insisting to her son they must be different, we see an extreme long shot of Toronto with a Louise Bourgeois-inspired spider towering over the skyscrapers,[20] followed immediately by a shot of Adam, leaning against his bathroom sink, again with one hand covering his eyes. Adam's covered eyes signal, then, his unwillingness to see that Anthony – with his aggression, violence and illicit sexual desires – is, indeed, part of himself.

The link between Helen/Mary and the sex club workers, initially suggested in the first sequence of the film, is what finally confirms the *idem* of Adam and Anthony. After Anthony and Mary's deaths in a catastrophic car crash, Adam reintegrates Anthony's life: he wears Anthony's clothes, sleeps in Anthony's

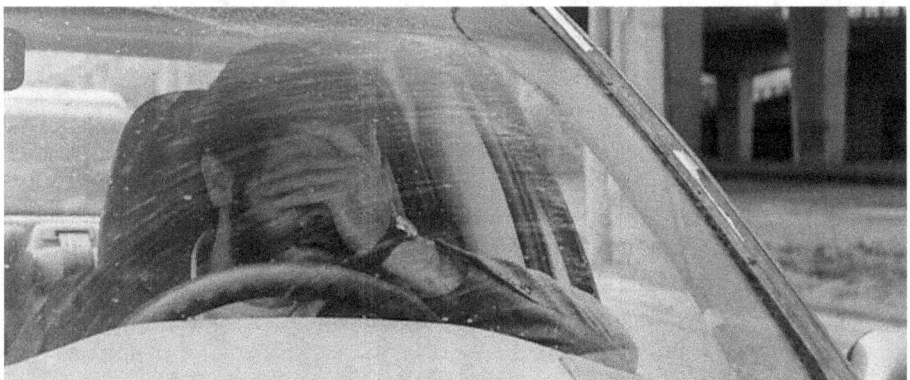

Figure 7.2 Adam (Jake Gyllenhaal) covering his eyes in *Enemy*.

bed, makes love to Anthony's wife and receives Anthony's most recent invitation to the sex club. Upon entering the bedroom where Helen has gone to dress after showering, Adam is confronted by a giant tarantula cowering in the corner of the room instead of the naked body of his wife. The resignation – not horror – on Adam's face upon seeing the spider in the bedroom recalls the men's impassive gazes in the sex club scene; his sigh shows that Helen's transformation is not a surprise to him. Helen is at once the woman in the sex club crushing the spider and the spider. The fact that Helen is six months pregnant surely plays a role in Adam's externalisation of his desires as Anthony, as 'the concept of motherhood automatically throws into question ideas concerning the self, boundaries between self and other, and hence identity' (Doane 27).[21] The 'object of terror' (Freud 143) that is the figure of the *doppelgänger* is thus less anchored in the supernatural or the fantastic in *Enemy* and more in a deep, existential dread. If, as Pilar Andrade suggests, 'the double and the appearance of the double should be perceived as the irruption of an unexpected threat in real life',[22] this threat for Adam is the incremental diminution of Self due to the banal repetition of everyday life and the repression of his primal urges.

DO YOU DREAM ABOUT BEING INTERLINKED? MEMORY AND MISRECOGNITION IN *BLADE RUNNER 2049*

Whereas Adam's projection of Anthony results from his refusal to integrate his *ipse* identity, K's misrecognition of himself as the object of his quest in *BR 2049* is linked to a desire to see himself as a distinct and unique subject. At the outset of the film, it is clear that K understands the limitations of his existence, conferred by his status as a Nexus 9 Replicant. In the film's initial sequence, before the fight that ends with his retirement of Sapper Morton (Dave Bautista), K apologises to him: 'I'm sure you knew it would be someone in time. I'm sorry it had to be me', to which Morton replies, 'Good as any.' The interchangeability of K with any other Nexus 9 Blade Runner is later affirmed by Joshi, who tells him 'You know, I've known a lot of your kind.' He is, as Replicant assassin and Wallace assistant, Luv (Sylvia Hoeks), reminds him, simply 'a gift, [. . .] from Mr. Wallace to the world'. In this world of manufactured humans, '[m]emory is a commodity' (Heersmink and McCaroll 87),[23] implanted in Replicants to provoke, as memory creator Dr Ana Stelline explains, 'real human responses'. Not only does K not have access to real memories, he is not allowed to hold dreams for his future; the Post-Traumatic Baseline Test, designed to detect whether K has become infected with feelings that would impede him fulfilling his duties, also looks to confirm his inability to dream and to imagine. The disembodied robotic voice spits a series of questions at K – 'What's it like to hold the hand of someone you love? [. . .] Do you long for having your heart interlinked? [. . .] Do you dream about being interlinked? [. . .] Do you feel there's a part of you that's missing?' and requires K to repeat back certain words – including 'cells' and 'interlinked' – throughout the test; if he is deemed to be 'off baseline', he is to be retired.[24] In answer to his hologram AI girlfriend, Joi's, question, 'It's okay to dream a little, isn't it?' K replies, 'Not if you're us.' Since subjectivity and consciousness are characterised by a '"temporal horizon", including in addition to the present, both expectations for the future and awareness of the immediate past' (Escobar 29), K, disallowed both real memories and future dreams, is condemned to live in an eternal present. Like all Nexus 9 Replicants, K is a being bereft of story and therefore of identity.

At the outset of the film, K knows that his mind holds the memories that have been created for him by the Wallace Corporation: 'I have memories but they're not real, they're just implants', he confirms to Joshi. His false new awareness of himself as the world-breaking Replicant child is based in a growing misapprehension of the nature of his memories and his subsequent creation for himself of a narrative identity. As Ricoeur explains: 'The narrative identity constructs the identity of the character, what can be called his or her narrative identity, in constructing that of the story told. It is the identity of the story that makes the identity of the character' (147–8). K's misrecognition of himself as a being with a story is initially grounded in objects: a wooden horse engraved with the date 6.10.21, a photo of Replicant rebel leader Freysa (Hiam Abbas) holding a baby in front of a living tree, and that same date engraved on the side of the tree at Morton's farm.

Although K initially understands that his memories of hiding the wooden horse in a furnace to keep it safe from other children in the orphanage are not actually his memories, this understanding is thrown into question once he visits Dr Stelline in her memory creation lab. Villeneuve reinforces the role that the transference of memories from Dr Stelline to K plays in K's creation of a narrative identity through the use of reflected images in this scene. Stricken with the fictional Galatian's syndrome – or, more likely, hidden away for safekeeping – Dr Stelline is confined to a sterile bubble where she makes memories for the Wallace Corporation. When K first enters the visiting area, we see Dr Stelline in an over-the-shoulder shot from behind K; his face is reflected on the glass that separates them. As she walks towards him, she moves into his reflection so that we see his reflected face imprinted on hers. After a cut, we see Dr Stelline in a close-up profile shot with the reflection of K's face and torso on the glass in front of her. Later in the scene, as she describes to K how real memories work, we see K in an over-the-shoulder shot from behind Dr Stelline and we see her face reflected onto his. Once she sits at her memory scanner with K facing her, on the other side of the glass, we briefly see the reflection of her face and torso mapped perfectly onto K's. As she views K's memory on her scanner, we see her in a medium close-up shot with K's intense stare reflected in the glass; moved by seeing her own memory playing on a screen, she wipes away her tears and

Figure 7.3 K (Ryan Gosling) with Dr Stelline's (Carla Juri) face reflected onto his in *Blade Runner 2049*.

confirms 'Someone lived this, yes.' The reverse medium close-up shot of K shows that he misunderstands her tears as validating his belief that the memory is indeed his: 'I know it's real', he declares. As he leans forward and puts his head in his hands, we again see the reflection of Dr Stelline's face and torso on his (Figure 7.3). This scene, where K watches Stelline watch her own memory and misinterprets the sense of her tears is the key moment where he becomes blinded to the truth of his existence: Ana Stelline implanted her own memory into his mind at his inception and it is she, not K, who is the miracle child. It is at this ultimate moment of misrecognition, where K imagines the orphan child with the wooden horse to be himself, that K begins to assume Stelline's narrative identity as his own; the reflections of each character onto the other in this scene highlights the changing nature of K's identity.[25]

As in *Incendies* and *Enemy*, confusion about the object of the main identity quest is amplified in *BR 2049* by the doubling of female characters. But whereas Jeanne and Simon's mapping onto Nawal brings their mother's metabody into their contemporary identity quest, and Helen's identity blurring with Mary and the unnamed sex workers serves to confirm the *idem* of Adam and Anthony, the imperfect doubling of female characters in *BR 2049* underscores K's misunderstanding of his narrative identity and his misidentification of himself as the object of his quest. The most striking example of the imperfect reproduction of female characters in other female characters occurs in the scene that Stephen Mulhall describes as 'the most uncannily powerful in the film – indeed, in the history of cinematic incarnations of sexual longing' (36),[26] where Joi literally maps herself onto and merges with Replicant sex worker Mariette in order to engage in intimate relations with K.[27] Although the two Replicants and the AI do spend the night together, the glitches in Joi's merging with Mariette – moments where, for example, Joi appears to have four arms – show both Joi's permeability and the unreliability of both Joi and Mariette's identities.[28] A crosscut during this scene shows a giant hologram of a Joi advertisement, towering in the night sky, as a woman's voice intones, 'Joi: Anything you want her to be.'[29] Once K's Joi is destroyed by Luv, the improbably tall hologram advertisement reappears to K to convince him to purchase a new model. But if Joi can be anything we want her to be – in endless iterations – this same statement does not apply to K, who can only be what he was created by the Wallace Corporation to be: a replaceable Nexus 9 Replicant. After fulfilling his real quest and reuniting Deckard with his lost daughter, K, bereft of past story and future dreams, has no further quest to fulfil.[30]

CONCLUSION

The knowability of Nawal and Nihad in *Incendies*, of Adam and Anthony in *Enemy*, and of K and the missing Replicant child in *BR 2049* is problematised by the inability of certain characters to properly see each other or themselves. The reflection of certain female characters in others is both destabilising and uncanny; these blurry identity boundaries signal a profound unease with regards to male subjectivity and selfhood, linked to a 'crisis and uncertainty in the relation of the self with itself and with the world' (Elsaesser 31).[31] In all three films, characters ultimately gain self-knowledge through the very inter-subjective relations that triggered the misrecognition of Self through a false understanding of the Other.

NOTES

1. I use the term 'intersubjectivity' in the Sartrian sense of conceiving one's subjectivity and one's self-knowledge in relation to the Other. Sartre, Jean-Paul, 'Existentialism is a Humanism' (1946), *Existentialism from Dostoyevsky to Sartre*, edited by Walter Kaufman, Meridian Publishing Company, 1989, available at: http://www.marxists.org/reference/archive/sartre/works/exist/sartre.htm (last accessed 18 July 2021).
2. Whether Dr Ana Stelline is understood as full Replicant offspring or as a half-Replicant, half-human hybrid depends on one's reading of Deckard from the original *Blade Runner* (Ridley Scott 1982) as Replicant or human. For a rigorous unpacking of this debate, see Shanahan, Timothy. 'What am I to you? The Deck-a-Rep debate and the question of fictional truth', *Blade Runner 2049: A Philosophical Exploration*, edited by Shanahan and Paul Smart, Routledge, 2020, pp. 228–47.
3. Ricoeur, Paul, *Oneself as Another*, The University of Chicago Press, 1995 (especially 'Introduction: The Question of Selfhood,' pp. 1–26).
4. See Graham J. Murphy for a description of how this scene was composed. Murphy, Graham J., 'Cyberpunk's Masculinist Legacy: Puppetry, Labour and *ménage à trois* in *Blade Runner 2049*', *Science Fiction Film and Television*, vol. 13, no. 1, 2020, pp. 97–106.
5. 'Si vous voulez retrouver votre frère, il va falloir remonter dans le passé de votre mère.'

6. Escobar, Matthew, *The Persistence of the Human: Consciousness, Meta-book-body and Survival in Contemporary Film and Literature*, Leiden/Boston, Brill Rodopi, 2016.
7. See Ricoeur, 'Personal Identity and Narrative Identity', p. 113–39, and 'The Self and Narrative Identity', p. 140–68.
8. 'It is precisely because of trauma's resistance to the emplotment of a logical narrative arc that it disrupts and undermines personal identity' (Escobar 28).
9. Mary-Jean Green notes how the three dots on Nihad's foot affirm 'the continuity of [his] identity', while also signaling 'a relationship to the ancient story of Œdipus' (106). Green, Mary-Jean, 'Denis Villeneuve's *Incendies*: From Word to Image', *Québec Studies*, vol. 54, Fall 2012/Winter 2013, pp. 109–10.
10. Meerzon, Yana, 'Staging Memory in Wajdi Mouawad's *Incendies*: Archaeolgoical Site or Poetic Venue?', *Theatre Research in Canada*, vol. 34, no. 1, Spring 2013, pp. 12–36. Claudia Kotte also notes how both Villeneuve's choice of actors for Nawal and Jeanne and the film's editing add to 'the puzzle of chronology, names and identities' in *Incendies* (290). Kotte, Claudia, 'Zero Degrees of Separation: Post-Exilic Return in Denis Villeneuve's *Incendies*', *Cinematic Homecomings: Exile and Return in Transnational Cinema*, edited by Rebecca Prime, Bloomsbury Academic, 2014, pp. 287–302.
11. Freud, Sigmund, *The Uncanny* (1919), Penguin, 2003. Freud describes the uncanny, or *das unheimlich*, as 'that species of the frightening that goes back to what was once well known and had long been familiar' (p. 124).
12. 'Un plus un, ça peut-tu faire un?'
13. This interpretation will be based on my reading of Anthony as the externalisation of Adam's repressed desire for chaos and violence. Bernd Leindecker, on the other hand, provides an analysis of *Enemy* according to which Anthony invents the personality of Adam in order to 'lead the careless life he thinks he desires' (202). See Leindecker, Bernd, 'Taking Split Personalities to the Next Level: Perturbatory Narration in *Enemy*', *Perturbatory Narration in Film: Narratological Studies on Deception, Paradox and Empuzzlement*, edited by Sabine Schlickers and Vera Toro, De Gruyter, 2017, pp. 199–208. Please also see Melanie Kreitler's chapter in this volume for a detailed analysis of narration and identity in *Enemy*.
14. Ricoeur explains that *ipse*-identity 'involves a dialectic complementary to that of selfhood and sameness, namely the dialectic of *self* and the *other than self*' (3).
15. Freud specifies that the motif of the double occurs with 'the appearance of persons who have to be regarded as identical because they *look* alike' (141, emphasis mine).
16. Leindecker adds to this list the sunglasses that Adam buys to disguise himself before going to Anthony's agency and that are also in Helen and Anthony's condo (204).
17. The figure of the double in literature and film has long been associated with an 'extraordinary degree of uncanniness' (Freud 143).
18. Creed, Barbara, 'Horror and the Monstrous-Feminine: An Imaginary Abjection', *Screen*, vol. 27, no. 1, January/February 1986, pp. 44–71.
19. We see also photos used to confirm Nawal's identity in *Incendies*; see Esther Pelletier and Irène Roy (114). Pelletier, Esther and Irène Roy, 'Évoquer pour susciter l'imaginaire et montrer plutôt que dire', *Nouvelles études francophones*, vol. 20, no. 2, Fall 2015, pp. 111–28. In *BR 2049*, K's horse statue and Sapper Morton's photo of Freysa holding baby Ana Stelline play similar roles. See Christophe Gelly and David Roche's chapter in this volume for a discussion of the significance of the horse in *BR 2049*.
20. The countless anonymous apartment towers combined with the surreal spider imagery layer the notion of 'the urban uncanny' into Adam's *doppelgänger* experience. Huskinson, Lucy, 'Introduction: The Urban Uncanny', *The Urban Uncanny: A Collection of Interdisciplinary Studies*, edited by Huskinson, Routledge, 2016, pp. 1–17.

21. Doane, Mary Ann, 'Technophilia: Technology, Representation and the Feminine', *Cybersexualities: A Reader on Feminist Theory, Cyborgs and Cyberspace*, edited by Jenny Wolmark, Edinburgh University Press, 1999, pp. 20–33.
22. Andrade, Pilar, 'Cinema's Doubles, their Meaning and Literary Intertexts', *Comparative Literature and Culture*, vol. 10, no. 4, 2008, article 8.
23. Heersmink, Richard and Christopher Jude McCarroll, 'The Best Memories: Identity, Narrative and Objects', *Blade Runner 2049: A Philosophical Exploration*, edited by Shanahan and Smart, Routledge, 2020, pp. 87–107.
24. Brian Treanor posits that K's decision to go against his Nexus 9 programming stems precisely from his 'desire to be interlinked' (77). Treanor, Brian, 'Being-From-Birth: Natality and Narrative', *Blade Runner 2049: A Philosophical Exploration*, edited by Shanahan and Smart, Routledge, 2020, pp. 68–86.
25. Heersmink and McCarroll relate K's misunderstanding of 'his' memory to the idea of 'vicarious memory' (101), shared memories with Ana Stelline that 'play the same functional roles as personal memories, for example, guiding decision-making, developing or maintaining social relationships, or being incorporated into one's identity' (102). For Heersmink and McCarroll, 'K's journey from replicant to human [. . .] is based on a memory, a memory that is socially shared and physically distributed' (103).
26. Mulhall, Stephen, 'The alphabet of us: Miracles, messianism and the baseline test in *Blade Runner 2049*', *Blade Runner 2049: A Philosophical Exploration*, edited by Shanahan and Smart, Routledge, 2020, pp. 27–47.
27. For an analysis of the 'threesome' between K, Joi and Mariette, and a discussion of the problematic aspects of Joi, see Murphy, p. 101–102.
28. Mariette is later shown to be a member of the Replicant resistance, led by the one-eyed Freysa.
29. It may be useful here to remember Doane's observation that our 'anxiety concerning the technological is often allayed by a displacement of this anxiety onto the figure of the woman or the idea of the feminine' (20).
30. Sean Guynes provides an interesting reading of the rejection of K's chosen-one status as 'a powerful and fundamental rejection of neoliberal rhetoric that designates individual action as the font of social change' (146). Guynes, Sean, 'Dystopia Fatigue Doesn't Cut It, or *Blade Runner 2049*'s Utopian Longings', *Science Fiction Film and Television*, vol. 13, no. 1, Spring 2020, pp. 143–8.
31. Elsaesser, Thomas, 'The Mind-Game Film', *Puzzle Films: Complex Storytelling in Contemporary Cinema*, edited by Warren Buckland, Wiley-Blackwell, 2009, pp. 13–41.

CHAPTER 8

Villeneuve's Hidden Monsters: Representations of Evil in *Prisoners* and *Sicario*

Alex Frohlick

As a director keen on deviating from the conventional parameters of particular genres, Denis Villeneuve presents an uncanny amalgamation of genre conventions and eclectic thematic perspectives throughout the worlds he creates. In discussing his approach to directing *Sicario* (2015), Villeneuve stressed his emphasis on avoiding the assumed 'paths' of specific genres and the refinement of their conventional processes (Lambie).[1] This appeal to the negation of genre conventions can be observed in both *Sicario* and *Prisoners* (2013) as, despite their common recognition under the genres of crime, action or drama, their idiosyncratic nature stems from the inclusion of horror and art-horror genre conventions. In this chapter, I will identify and analyse the role and representation of evil through the films *Prisoners* and *Sicario*. In conducting these observations, I argue that it is possible to extract a consistent representation of the central characters of these films through the introduction of the concept of 'hidden' monsters. Within this context I establish an action-, affect-, and motivation-based criterion of moral accountability as the foundation of the identification of evil agents within the context of *Sicario* and *Prisoners*. Through the development of this criterion, this chapter goes onto propose an alternate definition of the term 'monster' through an analysis of Noel Carroll's writing on art-horror, mainly addressing the text *The Philosophy of Horror, or Paradoxes of the Heart* (126).[2] This chapter argues in opposition to the strict 'entity-based' nature of Carroll's art-horror theory by departing from the 'fantastic biologies' required from this approach and turning to alternate theories of monsters through the work of Cynthia Freeland and Matt Hills (144).[3] The purpose of this approach is to detail a mode of analysis in which we are able to identify antagonistic characters or entities as 'monsters' based upon a moral criterion informed by the behaviours and attitudes of a character or entity as opposed to their biological or physiological representation. As this analysis will demonstrate, these characters exist within *Sicario* and *Prisoners* as monsters not in the biological sense Carroll demands, but as 'realistic' human monsters who nonetheless align with Carroll's notion of interstitiality through the corruption of their assumed sociocultural identities. This analysis therefore takes place in accordance with Freeland's equivocation of evil and monstrosity through the moral evaluation of a character's capacity for evil through an analysis of their actions, engagements, and desires. By establishing this concept, I present an alternative approach to the analysis and discussion of these texts by identifying the formal and philosophical intricacies of *Sicario* and *Prisoners*.

APPROACHING EVIL ON SCREEN

The term 'evil' can be an elusive subject given its rich philosophical history and diverse implications.[4] If we are to adopt Brian Horne's perspective of a Western society no longer concerned with the intervention of theology in explication of human action in favour of the 'language of ethics', we are left unable to simply refer to the term evil as an opposite to 'good' (30).[5] Instead the term evil can be approached as a rhetorical device drawn upon to express forms of moral outrage or disgust towards an entity or action. In his formation of evil as a concept removed from religion, Paul Oppenheimer makes reference to forms of human behaviour which escape definition through language such as 'criminal' or 'bad' and argues towards the existence of physical and mental forms of evil that reach 'beyond the mundane and ordinarily comprehensible' (1–9).[6] In developing this framework, Oppenheimer offers a platform in which events such as genocide, serial killings, and acts of torture can be defined as evil without an appeal to supernatural or transcendent causes, and instead proposes that such acts are a result of a specific combination of mental and physical attributes. Building upon the mysteries arising from Oppenheimer's physiological and psychological basis of evil, Horne argues that our greatest tool for exploring such ideas lies in the capabilities of 'the language of art' and the power of imagination in developing these ideas through the representation of evil in contemporary art (33). By following these notions as to the nature of evil and speculating as to its manifestation through artistic forms, it is possible to encounter endless possibilities as to the representation and depiction of this secular conception of evil. Amongst the boundless potential candidates lies Carroll's concept of art-horror, which aims to identify a specific notion of evil through the genre of horror fiction ('The Nature' 51).[7] As a genre dedicated to the idiosyncratic nature of horror texts that inherently engage with concepts of evil, 'art-horror' presents an ideal environment to explore Horne's desire to extrapolate and develop our understanding of evil both in fundamental philosophical terms, as well as through the language of its artistic representation.

Prisoners and *Sicario* are examples of film texts that adopt specific formal characteristics from the art-horror genre without holistically subscribing to its conventional forms of representation. The concept of 'hidden monsters' encapsulates the process of the adoption and adaptation of the monster principal from Carroll's art-horror definition and its transposition into texts outside of its original context. This conception of the term 'monster' therefore aligns with the work of Cynthia Freeland, who instead argues towards an understanding of the term 'monster' qualified by the evil qualities possessed by a figure or entity (10–11).[8] Following this approach, it is possible to argue for a concept of evil as a particular form of moral categorisation in which the actions, affectual responses, and given motivational accounts of actors stand as its philosophical foundations. In defining this foundation further we observe the first account, an action-based account of evil, as one by which 'a person with an evil character is one who is often prone to do evil acts' (Thomas 82).[9] The second account, affect-based accounts, proposes that 'an evil character is one that derives pleasure from pain and pain from pleasure' (McGinn 62).[10] Finally, the third of these key accounts of evil personhood is one based upon motivation-based accounts, which demonstrates the need for an individual to be motivated in specific ways to commit evil acts (Calder).[11]

A similar methodological approach can also be observed regarding the representation of a character's moral status through conventional narrative cinema, as David Bordwell demonstrates, 'we are encouraged to understand the actions of a character through their desires, personal traits, and perspectives as opposed to situational factors' (32).[12] As Bordwell observes, it is not only the actions of an individual that informs our perception of their moral character as affectual and motivational data also informs the relationships and reactions of characters to events and people around them. *Sicario* and *Prisoners* disrupt this process through the presence of what I define as 'hidden monsters', a concept that seeks to define specific morally ambiguous characters as threatening and impure figures, in accordance with Carroll's entity-based art-horror (*Philosophy* 42). By demonstrating this moral account of evil and the nature of its representation in conventional narrative cinema, it is possible to observe the ways in which assumptions pertaining to moral judgements and interpretations of cinematic form can be destabilised and subverted. The hidden monster and its nuanced representation therefore plays an essential role within both the narrative structure and the formal construction of *Sicario* and *Prisoners*.

IDENTIFYING THE HIDDEN MONSTER

In revisiting Carroll's theory of art-horror it is essential to highlight the dichotomy between his 'entity-based' account of art-horror and what Carroll would otherwise label 'art-dread' (Hills 138). The 'entity-based' art-horror is one that elicits 'characteristic audience emotions' such as disgust and horror in reaction to the impure monsters presented (Hills 140). Carroll posits that stories that lack such elements instead evoke general senses of unease or awe as to the implied presence of 'unavowed, unknown, and perhaps concealed and inexplicable forces' are texts of art-dread (*Philosophy* 42). In simple terms, the distance between these two theories relies upon the presence of a monstrous entity manifested in a conventional physical form and directly addressed as a source of affective audience responses such as repulsion or disgust. Despite making such a distinction, Carroll also concedes that it is possible for these two concepts to coexist throughout particular fictions in a range of forms (*Philosophy* 42).

As texts that possess the core tenets of both theories, *Sicario* and *Prisoners* are fictions that exist within this potential middle ground. Both films feature the presence of the 'hidden monster' characters to implicate the presence of 'unknown, and perhaps concealed and inexplicable forces', although they lack the central feature of 'disgust' Carroll associates with art-horror texts (*Philosphy* 42). In discussing the role of Norman Bates in Hitchcock's *Psycho* (1960), Carroll uses this approach to distance *Psycho* from the concept of art-horror due to Bates's incompatible aesthetic representation. Yet, further in this analysis, Carroll also reiterates the inherent proximity between Bates and the 'impure beings' required of art-horror (Hills 140). Carroll initially rejects the perception of Bates as a monster from a 'technical' perspective before detailing psychological characteristics which partially bridge this rift (Hills 140). If we are to extrapolate the characteristics afforded to Bates's character it can be argued that this technical distinction from the conventional aesthetic formation of 'monsters' lies in the lack of certain physiological or biological qualities and the presence of sociopathic or 'impure' psychological traits (Carroll *Philosophy* 38–9).

Observing this framework therefore allows for a definition of 'monsters' which exist outside of graphic fantastical biological representations and instead moves towards establishing the evil nature of a character as grounds to qualify one as a monster. A distinction of this nature directly implicates and informs the hidden monsters of *Sicario* and *Prisoners* as these are characters, like Bates, which can be understood as monstrous figures who are hidden from immediate recognition. Their identities are instead revealed through their own actions, motivations, and affectual responses and communicated through the cinematic representation of subsequent events through a process Hill defines as 'the aesthetic representation of horror cinema's narrative events' (Hills 140). By situating the term 'hidden monster' within an inclusive approach to the broader conceptualisation of the term monster, we can identify similarities to other like-minded concepts, such as Freeland's notion of 'realist horror' (Knight and McKnight).[13] By privileging the role of 'fantastic psychologies', Freeland allows for an account of monstrous entities or characters which exist outside of the strict representational parameters of art-horror (Carroll 'The Nature').

THE HIDDEN MONSTERS OF *SICARIO* AND *PRISONERS*

In *Sicario*, we are presented with forms of hidden monsters from the very first scene. Having been called to an innocuous suburban area as part of her FBI raid team, Kate (Emily Blunt) discovers an empty house with its walls and crawlspace full of rotting corpses and an explosive trap set in its garage. It is later revealed that the house belongs to Manuel Diaz, a leader of the Sonora Cartel. During the following scenes the film's first major hidden monster figure is introduced in the form of Matt (Josh Brolin), an unassuming government contractor running a covert specialist unit. Offering the chance to unmask and seek revenge on Diaz and the cartel, Matt recruits Kate despite her inexperience. In the following sequences, Kate meets the mysterious Alejandro (Benicio del Toro) and takes part in the extraction of a cartel leader from the City of Juarez, Mexico. The mission in Juarez is presented by Matt and the team as the first real engagement with the forces of the cartel, which pervades the dense cityscape.

As the mission infiltrates the city, Kate learns that she is amongst the aggressors in this hostile situation as Matt's covert squad enacts violence throughout the city. Having torn through the city, killing several cartel members in public, Kate confronts Matt and questions the purpose of both the mission and his team. In detailing the objective of the extraction to 'shake the tree and create chaos' Kate is exposed to the morally questionable intentions of the team and their violent methods. If we are to approach Matt as representative of his team, there can be a natural argument to perceive this character as an evil figure despite his proximity to the assumed protagonist. It is evident that the actions of this individual are indeed violent, malicious acts with the calculated intent to inflict harm on others including innocent bystanders caught in the crossfire. This perspective is reflected in the methods and objectives of Matt and his team as they aim to destabilise the precarious balance of order within the local communities exposed to the fallout and violence of the cartel war they are creating. As demonstrated by the story of local policeman Silvio (Maximiliano Hernandez) and his murder at the hands of Matt's team, the destructive nature of these actions is not once considered or valued in opposition to their objective. In *Sicario*'s closing scene, Silivio's son's soccer match is interrupted by gunfire serving as a harrowing reminder of Silvio's fate as well as the omission of these environments and communities in the consideration of the team's objectives.

The calculated maliciousness of Matt's actions and character can also be observed in his behaviour towards those supposedly closer to his own objectives and motivations as seen in his use of Kate as bait to lure an unsuspecting cartel operative into custody. In this instance, Kate's emotional vulnerability is manipulated as she becomes the victim of sexual and physical violence orchestrated by Matt to apprehend his target. In the following scenes, Matt gives little credence or acknowledgement of Kate's traumatic experience as she learns of the premeditated nature of the encounter, shifting blame for the events on her for not following his orders stating, 'you used yourself as bait, I told you not to go in the bank'. Indifferent to Kate's visibly shaking hands and bruises to her eyes and arms, Matt declares the situation 'good news', as his mission has succeeded with the order that Kate's involvement is omitted from her official report. From these examples it can be observed that Matt is presented as someone indifferent to the application and result of violent acts compared to their efficacy in achieving his objectives, which can be seen further during a later scene in which Kate's assailant, Ted (Jon Bernthal), is tortured by Alejandro to Matt's amusement. Throughout this scene, Matt sits in the driver's seat of a squad car, his face illuminated by streetlights whilst Ted and Alejandro sit in the darker rear section of the vehicle made visible only by the flashing police lights. In this scene, Matt is presented from two perspectives, initially head-on with his entire face visible in clear detail (Figure 8.1), and then from Ted's perspective of Matt's eyes in the rear-view mirror (Figure 8.2). The interrogation is gruesome in content and discussion as Ted is mutilated and his family threatened with rape and murder. Yet Matt's expression either remains unknown through the rear-view mirror, or vacant when returning to the wider head-on shot. Upon breaking Ted's resolve and obtaining a confession, Matt breaks into a coy smile and laughter; in this moment it is shown that his prior neutrality has been performative in place of his visible enjoyment in Ted's suffering. In returning to the wider shot of Matt's face in this moment we can observe that these emotions go beyond the simple satisfaction of achieving his objective, revealing a more emotive response in the methods deployed and harm inflicted throughout this process.

In each of the examples given so far and throughout Matt's general behaviour there exists an unsettling juxtaposition between his upbeat satisfaction and the violent repercussions and consequences of his actions, with this dissonance ultimately presenting Matt as a dangerous monstrous figure void of any apparent morality with the power and influence to operate unchecked. It is not incidental that Matt's true identity within the American military or justice system is only partially revealed as a CIA operative, with Kate's accusations of him being a 'spook' deployed by powerful political figures further muddying his

Figure 8.1 Matt (Josh Brolin) seen head-on in the car in *Sicario*.

Figure 8.2 Matt's eyes reflected in the rear-view mirror.

motivations and objectives. Through the art-horror terms defined by Carroll it is justifiable to assign our hidden monster terminology to Matt's character in this context, as a monster can be defined as an individual or entity which meets the criteria of impurity and dangerousness, indicating a means of identifying and describing individuals as unnatural in relation to one's cultural conceptual schema. In violating this ontological knowledge, monsters are 'cognitively threatening' beings as they directly challenge general ideas of 'common knowledge' as well as specific socio-cultural assumptions (Carroll 'The Nature' 34). Carroll qualifies the notion of impurity as an object or being defined as categorically interstitial or contradictory, incomplete, or formless. The impure being is therefore one which cannot be accounted for by common knowledge either in its physical form or in its cognitive behaviours but can yet possesses 'normally distinct' qualities ('The Nature' 34). Matt therefore exists as an embodiment of obscure, morally questionable forces without the form or characteristics of a normative personhood. He exists as a transient morally incongruent figure hidden amongst the complex workings of the US military industrial complex, as a monster to be secretly deployed in order to carry out monstrous acts of violence. As an individual prone to intentionally violent, malicious acts indifferent to their interpersonal or individual consequences who takes evident enjoyment from these actions, Matt meets this criterion given his ambiguous interstitial existence within the formal channels of military operations. He exists as a contradiction to the common knowledge of procedure and accountability known to Kate and to public expectations of ethical military practice. When searching for explanations as to the existence of Matt and the scale of his operation, Kate is told that, 'these decisions are made far from here, by officials elected to office, not appointed to them. So, if your fear is operating out of bounds, I am telling you, you are not. The boundary's been moved.'

As an individual with near operational omnipotence and ability to conduct indiscriminate acts of extreme violence, Matt represents a cognitive threat as a form of monster given his predisposition to behaviours and motivations we can identify as evil. Matt argues that his presence is a direct response to escalating cartel violence and that the methods of his team are apparently justified in their cause; however, this argument is yet another means of obfuscating the moral status of his character, as it is later revealed that Matt's team have been fighting the various branches of the Sinaloa cartel, only to help reinstate the Columbian Medellin Cartel in order to aid US control of cartel activity. Such a revelation only contributes to the contradictory interstitial nature of the character and his moral inconsistency as the ideological disguise afforded by the appropriated role of national security dissipates. As a result, Matt relinquishes the façade of righteousness and instead repositions his efforts as the less of two evils compared to the prospect of endless cartel violence. For Kate, this information only deepens the trauma inflicted throughout the mission as she learns not only of her role of working via proxy for the assumed 'enemy', but also of the moral vacuum at the heart of the military institutions she represents. She learns that, despite possessing the white heteronormative qualities of military cultures, Matt exists as a hidden monster created and concealed by the bureaucratic powers of the military-industrial complex as an unfortunate yet necessary evil.

An essential component of this mission to dethrone the Sinaloa Cartel involves yet another hidden monster figure, this time in the form of Alejandro, an unknown figure who accompanies Matt throughout his mission. As a prosecutor turned assassin working to avenge the murder of his family, Alejandro's murderous nature is initially represented as justified response to aggression, as seen during the escort mission through Juarez and the following scenes of torture and interrogation. Yet, we later learn during these scenes that Alejandro's predisposition to violence is that of one indifferent and numb to the context or purpose of such acts and that he will inflict harm upon anyone in pursuit of vengeance. As Matt details, 'Alejandro works for anyone who will point him toward the people who made him.' In reference to the criteria outlined so far, this insight alone can implicate Alejandro as an evil figure who shares the same operational or bureaucratic protections as Matt and his team of mercenaries upon the revelation of his affiliation with the Medellin Cartel. For a large part of *Sicario*'s narrative, Alejandro remains an incomplete figure; like Matt, he exists within a moral and legal vacuum inclined yet indifferent to extreme acts of violence.

Through Kate's journey with the team, she is first exposed to these figures as allies working towards the elimination of a shared target, the evil forces of the cartel. Yet, as she ventures deeper into the political and operational dimensions of the objective, these figures' evil monstrous qualities emerge as 'necessary evils'. *Sicario* therefore presents a story in which monsters exist not as otherworldly external threats to human existence, but as reflections of humanity's capacity for corruption and revenge hidden amongst the bureaucratic obfuscation of converging military institutions. *Sicario* can even be seen to present the process of monstrous transformation through the story of Kate and her experiences working for and alongside the monsters within her team. Upon joining the squad with honest intentions in finding those responsible for the attack on her unit, Kate is forced to confront her own moral integrity as the objectives of the team progress. Throughout this journey, Kate experiences stages akin to those of grief: initially outraged by Matt's methods, she then threatens to abandon the project and deny the possibility of its existence before confronting her senior officers and bargaining to bring an end or at least scrutiny upon its operation. Towards the end of the film and her subsequent realisation as to the true objectives of Matt and Alejandro's operation, Kate understands the futility of her objections and is forced to realise her acceptance of her involvement at gunpoint. Confronted by Alejandro in her apartment, Kate is faced with the reality of her situation and the consequences of her actions as she is given the choice between complicity and acceptance, or death. The terror in Kate's eyes as the gun is pressed to her chin comes not from the prospect of her own death, but rather through the confrontation of her new existence in which she must come to terms with her own monstrous actions. Alejandro presents this ultimatum shrouded in the shadows of the apartment in opposition to Kate who remains illuminated by daylight. This visual contrast represents the remaining distinction between these two figures, Kate who still clings to her own moral identity, and Alejandro, the monstrous predator who has sacrificed his own identity for survival and revenge. In signing the document, Kate makes a similar sacrifice as she is forced to abandon her remaining principles in subscribing to an alternate reality in which her own monstrosity and that of the team exists only in her traumatic memories. In attempting one final act of redemption, Kate points her pistol at Alejandro who is walking back to his car, only to flounder and lower the weapon as she begins to accept the futility of her position and newfound identity. Kate therefore represents a complex hidden monster figure who seems resilient in her opposition to the acts she is committing and facilitating until faced with a binary choice between confronting her own emergent monstrous identity and her own demise. Alejandro attempts to be gentle in this scenario under the guise of seeing qualities of his daughter in Kate, although it is also possible that he sees himself in her grief, anger and confusion. She may not be a 'wolf' like Alejandro in these moments, but Alejandro realises she is on the path to become such and pleads with her to leave 'the land of wolves' before she makes this monstrous transition for good.

From this character analysis, the role of hidden monsters proves to be an essential property of *Sicario*'s narrative formula which is built around the development of these complex moral identities. Yet it is important to acknowledge that these insights are not exclusive to *Sicario*, as it is possible to observe similar characteristics in Villeneuve's preceding 2013 film, *Prisoners*. *Prisoners* follows the story of Keller Dover (Hugh Jackman) and the abduction of his daughter Anna (Erin Gerasimovich), during which Keller and the case detective Loki (Jake Gyllenhaal) pursue various leads across Pennsylvania. The case initially points towards the owner of the suspected getaway vehicle, Alex Jones (Paul Dano). Despite Loki's questioning, Keller kidnaps and tortures Alex for days, convinced of his guilt and therefore keeping him trapped within a makeshift torture chamber and periodically dousing him with scorching hot water. During this time, Loki discovers the existence of a murderous religious cult, leading to the pursuit of multiple suspects. After Keller tortures Alex, he comes to learn that Alex's stepmother, Holly Jones (Melissa Leo), has abducted children, including Anna, in order to 'create demons' from the traumatised parents of kidnapped children.

Throughout the course of *Prisoners*, we observe Keller's transformation into a demonic figure blinded by his grief; in a similar vein to *Sicario*'s Alejandro, he is driven to seek forms of vengeance, first in the torture of Alex and later in his attempt to confront Holly and avenge the harm inflicted upon his daughter. We observe a hidden monster character developed through the form of a corrupted father figure, psychologically compromised by a thirst for vengeance. For Keller, his status as a hidden monster comes as a result of the transition that occurs during the search for his daughter as he begins to take matters into his own hands. Keller starts the film as a conventional father figure who appears to be cautious and meticulous in caring for his family, as seen in the collection of resources and supplies in the family basement. Keller is represented as a father who looks to protect his family against all possible threats, even those seemingly apocalyptic in nature. Upon Anna's kidnapping, Keller quickly descends into a state of hyper-focus and obsession on his own vigilante search. This process culminates in the kidnapping and torture of Alex in which he sacrifices his civilised moral principles and becomes a monster in his own right in order to rescue Anna. During the torture sequences, it is possible to observe Keller's sympathy and compassion for Alex begin to fade as he begins to resent and abuse his victim further. Initially, Keller is appalled by his actions and retreats from Alex's screams cowering into his own hands and arms, but as he continues, Keller moves closer to the chamber, taking a cathartic pleasure in inflicting pain upon the man he holds responsible for his daughter's disappearance.

This change is reflected in the later sequences through the repeated close-up yet obscured shots of Alex inside of the chamber illuminated by the single beam of light from the peep hole (Figure 8.3). Seeing these repeated shots reflects the greater comfort Keller shows in looking at Alex in this condition, something he was unable to bring himself to see in earlier scenes. Keller also grows in confidence of his resentment as he begins to drink heavily whilst berating Alex with questions and abuse. As a result, Keller undergoes a transformation into the very evil he has sworn to eliminate, kidnaping and detaining Alex just as Holly has abducted Anna. As Keller confronts Holly in a later scene, it is also discovered that both figures share similar motivations behind these actions. For Holly, the loss of her biological child has stoked her desire for vengeance by inflicting her pain upon other parents, whereas Keller is driven by similar desires albeit on a smaller scale as he seeks retribution for Anna's disappearance through a specific third party he deems responsible. *Prisoners* documents these stories at varying stages as Keller begins this transformation in opposition to Holly, a

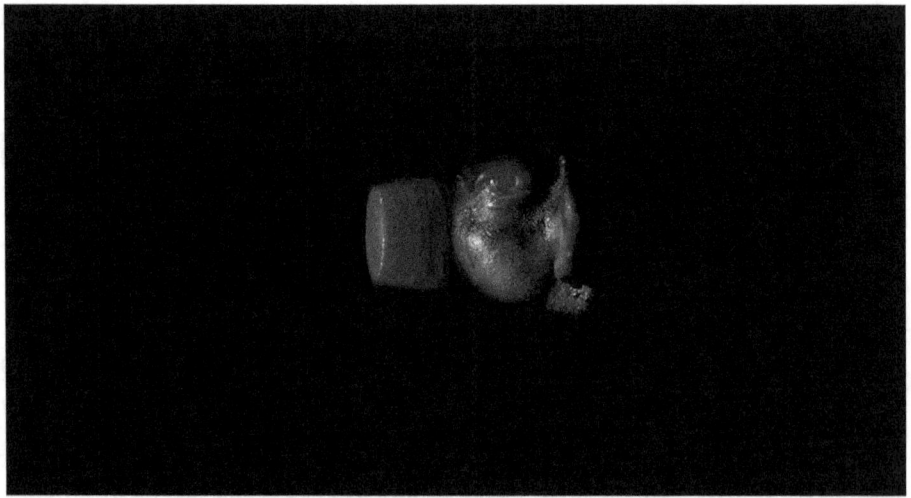

Figure 8.3 Alex (Paul Dano) in Keller's (Hugh Jackman) torture chamber in *Prisoners*.

hidden monster experienced and seasoned in her deception and practice. The transformation of Keller therefore presents insight into the formative processes of Holly's own journey from the ordinary mother her home presents to the murderous abductor hidden beneath her unassuming exterior. Holly therefore represents a natural extension of Keller's behaviour in which an individual is consumed by their thirst for vengeance and resentment for the world around them in the face of tragedy.

For characters in both films, a moral argument is present amongst their violent actions as their trauma is weaponised into a licence to inflict harm with little recompense for those caught in their paths. Just as Alejandro is situated as a necessary evil to restore order amongst cartel forces, Keller's vigilante justice is understood and accepted as a means of purging predatory forces from his community. An appeal to a 'greater good' seen throughout the actions of these characters contributes an additional layer of obfuscation to their moral interstitiality through the presence of contradictory actions and and motivations. It can be assumed that instances of moral justification implied through narratives of retribution may offer some form of repentance for characters pushed to extreme actions, although both Keller and Alejandro find no such redemption through their actions, as seen in the conclusions of both texts. For Keller, his actions result in his ultimate downfall as he is buried alive in the make-shift pit that once contained his daughter, whereas Alejandro must face an existence in which revenge has granted no comfort or closure as he continues in his obscure military capacity, seen as he extorts Kate at gunpoint to corroborate a fabricated account of their missions. As a reward for their actions, both characters are haunted by traces of their respective daughters who still elude their grasp, as seen through Anna's red whistle Keller finds in the pit and through Alejandro's extortion of Kate, a figure akin to his murdered daughter.

An essential hidden monster figure within the story of *Prisoners* and the transformation of Keller lies in the presence of Alex's supposed mother, Holly, a peripheral character for the majority of the film who nonetheless represents the film's most abhorrent monster hidden in plain sight. Holly is first introduced upon Alex's abduction, when Detective Loki visits her home to collect information and she goes on to make sporadic appearances throughout the second act of the film. Keller and Holly eventually come face to face as Keller looks to gain more information to leverage against Alex during his interrogation. During this conversation both characters engage in a friendly yet guarded exchange in which each figure looks to maintain their respective façades whilst probing for insight into the other. For Holly, this act is an extension of a lifetime of deceit, as she imposes her artificial biography demanding sympathy from Keller in order to throw him off her scent. Yet, Keller remains suspicious following this tense exchange and returns to Kate's home to investigate further. During this second exchange, both individuals' acts are initially maintained before revealing their true intentions and Holly revealing her true identity. As Holly holds Keller at gunpoint, the scope and depth of her monstrous nature is slowly uncovered through the abundance of menacing items camouflaged in the unassuming surroundings. Keller is first instructed to pull handcuffs from a cutlery drawer before consuming a drugged liquid contained in a nearby fridge; Holly's experience and confidence with this process are made clear through the meticulous placement of items and the authoritative demeanour in which she guides him. Unlike Keller, who has recently undergone an extended transition into a monstrous figure, Holly is revealed to have been a hidden monster for decades, using an assumed social identity and imposed backstory to hide the crimes and acts of evil she has committed. In carrying out the abduction and murder of children, one of Holly's objectives has also been to create new hidden monsters or 'demons' from the grieving parents, including Keller.

This process is familiar to the hidden monsters observed so far in both *Prisoners* and *Sicario*, with the source of Alejandro's and Kate's monstrous nature originating from a past trauma and the desire for revenge. Existing monsters such as Matt and Holly are then able to foster and manipulate these emotionally vulnerable individuals into accepting and acting upon these feelings in violent and dangerous forms. These individuals can be seen to deviate from figures such as Kate and Alejandro, who have undergone a transformation at the hands of external agents or events and who maintain some forms of resistance to or awareness of their own monstrosity. For Alejandro, this is manifested through the sympathy he has for Kate, offering her mercy and solace in *Sicario*'s closing moments. For Kate, this is observed through her objection throughout stages of her team's missions, including the confrontation with Alejandro during the tunnel sequence. This scene demonstrates both Alejandro's and Kate's capacity for the temporary defiance of their monstrous nature, as Kate attempts to foil the corrupt plan she discovers, and through Alejandro's mercy in sparing Kate despite her threat to his operation. In demonstrating the ability to suspend their problematic behaviours, these characters are distinct from figures such as Matt and Holly, who despite their claims of justification for their actions either in the consolidation of cartel activity, or revenge for the loss of their child, show no remorse for their actions, or attempt to reconcile the consequences of such. This notion of hidden monsters being created and moulded by the events and environments they experience allows for a greater understanding as to the nature of those we define as such. These forms of monsters encourage the analysis of their moral and emotional transformations through observing their interactions and attitudes over an extended period of time. In doing so, the hidden monster figure resists a totalising meaning in its application as this term encompasses the complex relationships and personal contexts of varying individuals. This differs from the process of identifying the source of monsters in films akin to

Carroll's conventional art-horror genre where physiologically threatening beings are tracked to an abstract origin whether that be supernatural, spiritual, or otherwise.

These conclusions demonstrate the transformation these figures have undergone from regular citizens to morally corrupted monsters at the hands of external events or actors. Our way of understanding and extrapolating these monstrous qualities leads to the formation of the concept of hidden monsters as a way of conceptually grounding characters such as Matt, Keller, Holly and Alejandro. This process takes places within a narrative framework in accordance with the actionable moral criterion informed by the representational aesthetics and narrative conventions of art-horror genres Carroll describes as complex discovery plots (*Philosophy* 126). Complex discovery plots are argued to feature four essential narrative stages, referred to as 'onset, discovery, confirmation, and confrontation', which can be modified to various effects. A relevant example in *Sicario* and *Prisoners* refers to the mystery story, in which 'the drama of proof' plays an essential role in establishing these narratives (Carroll *Philosophy* 126). This approach is observable during *Prisoners*, in which Anna's abduction triggers the onset of events followed by the discoveries of Loki and Keller, resulting in the confirmation of their theories and Keller's confrontation with Holly. Carroll summarises this process as a form of 'phasing', in which information critical to each stage of this structure is communicated asynchronously between characters and the audience (*Philosophy* 99). According to Carroll, the use of these narrative devices produces a particular 'cognitive pleasure' provided through the 'play of reasoning', in which audiences acknowledge these contrary contextual positions and in turn advance through the narrative process either before or ahead of its characters (*Philosophy* 102). Keller's abduction of Alex plays upon this convention, as Keller remains unaware of the case's development through other leads, while Loki remains simultaneously unaware of Alex's involvement in the abduction revealed through his torture. This can usually place the audience in an extremely privileged position as they collect this information from both scenarios, but *Prisoners* chooses to subvert this narrative device through the revelation of new information in its closing scenes. Just as Matt's objective is revealed as the reinstatement of cartel powers, the true identity of Holly and her role in the abduction discredits prior insights and theories as to the moral identities and motivations of key characters.

Both films employ this phasing of information in order to navigate and emphasise the moral intricacies of these characters and their interwoven relationships to each other. The drama of proof present at the conclusion of both texts also unsettles the affectual experiences and reactions of its audience as their perception and interpretations of transpired events are reconfigured as the moral status of characters are either revealed or transformed through their closing scenes. This is a consistent process that relies on the moral ambiguity and obscure identities of central characters who fail to represent normative moral categories or dichotomies. Reimagining the concept and representation of monsters into forms of hidden monsters therefore allows for the development of narratives that thrive amongst the ambiguity of these characters.

In utilising these art-horror narrative devices, *Prisoners* and *Sicario* are both able to operate within the interstitial spaces between Carroll's art-horror and art-dread genres in which the 'ordinary language' of audiences is no longer able to distinguish between the two (Schneider and Shaw 140).[14] As this section has highlighted, by reimagining and adapting this 'entity-based' conception of art-horror, it is possible to create alternative forms of what Carroll refers to as monsters that exist in defiance of the assumed 'fantastic biologies' and physiological representations (*Philosophy* 42). In establishing evil as a moral concept grounded in philosophical accounts of action, affect, and motivation, it becomes possible to extract and apply this idea in order to identify evil antagonistic characters as monsters based upon a criterion of moral judgements. Again, it is important to acknowledge *Sicario* and *Prisoners* not as art-horror, or even art-dread texts; instead, the concept of hidden monsters and role of the adopted conventions from these genres contribute to each film's own interstitial nature which in turn produces their idiosyncratic identity and affectual capacity.

CONCLUSION

In this chapter, I have argued for an alternate approach to the concept of 'monsters' which emphasises a morally grounded philosophical understanding of evil in creating and representing hidden monster characters within the parameters of narrative cinema. In developing this analytical approach to *Sicario* and *Prisoners* this chapter has argued these films are reflective of the narrative conventions of Carroll's art-horror genre as well as the shifting philosophical contexts surrounding the nature and representation of evil or monstrous entities within the contemporary and secular context originally presented through Oppenheimer and Horne. This is not to say that such analysis is exhaustive in scope as outstanding issues remain regarding the development of this concept, especially concerning Hill's aforementioned notion of the aesthetic representation of horror cinema's narrative events. The concern for narrative cinema from this perspective remains that if monsters are no longer understood and represented purely through conventional physiological representation, how then can abstract psychological or morally evil monstrous figures be communicated as such? In response to such concerns, I address the notion of ambiguity present through *Prisoners* and *Sicario* as a process in which the identification of monsters has developed beyond conventional representations unique to a particular genre or subgenre of fiction. Hidden monsters therefore represent an emergent iteration of the 'monster' figure within narrative cinema shaped by social, cultural, and epistemological attitudes towards increasingly secular and morally grounded accounts of evil. As a concept, the hidden monster is a useful tool in our analysis of texts and characters who behave outside of the normative patterns of fixed moral dichotomies as it offers a consistent inclusive approach to the representation and definition of complex, interstitial, and contradictory figures. In the case of *Sicario* and *Prisoners,* this analysis is able to use concepts borrowed from Carroll's art-horror writings in order to identify and extrapolate a number of characteristics and behaviours to develop a coherent account of the moral status of key characters who otherwise elude such evaluations. As a result, this analysis generates an alternate reading of these texts in which characters such as Matt, Alejandro, Keller and Holly, exist not as forms of conventional 'anti-heroes' or 'complex characters' but as defined monsters who exhibit evil tendencies or behaviours according to an established moral criterion. This process initially contributes to the identification of the text's 'true' moral protagonist, as we are no longer concerned with questioning the affiliation or motivation of the hidden monster's present. As a result, the tragic stories of characters such as Kate or Loki are able to develop as the true identity of their assumed allies are revealed allowing for further sociopolitical discussions as to the plight and trauma of the protagonists.

In utilising the concept of hidden monsters, it is also possible to conduct further analysis into hidden monster characters and figures within positions of political or social authority, as seen in *Sicario* through Matt's influence within branches of the military-industrial-complex, or through the social influence of the demonic cult in *Prisoners*. In striving for a transparency as to the nature of hidden monster characters these texts are granted greater access to these discourses in which the observations extracted from this chapter can be transposed into a multitude of alternate dialogues. For example, a particularly urgent analysis can be conducted regarding the interstitial spaces or environments which have ultimately facilitated the growth of the interstitial monsters discussed so far. From the problematic dynamics of contemporary military cultures, through to the alienation of rural America, the concept of hidden monsters requires a wider socio-cultural context in order to build upon the initial moral and philosophical insights as well as the criterions utilised in this preliminary analysis. In developing such an approach, it is possible for future research to explore the cultural, social, or environmental dynamics present in the creation of the monsters we find within these texts. Through future consideration of these factors, it is also possible to extend this analysis to other texts within Villeneuve's filmography in order to interrogate the representation of other characters through this concept. The development of hidden monsters can therefore lead to alternate approaches to untangling the complex political dynamics present through *Arrival* (2016), or a disambiguation of the moral or ontological status of Anthony and Adam (Jake Gyllenhaal) in *Enemy* (2013). As mentioned at the beginning of this chapter, Villeneuve's catalogue carries with it many idiosyncrasies and considerations for one to grapple with. In synthesising genres and their conventions, dissimulating the moral status of key characters, and misleading audiences through narrative structures, Villeneuve is successful in creating an abstruse aura to his films. Yet, the concept of the hidden monster equips the viewer with a mode of analysis in which one can disambiguate the effects of these qualities with the potential to contribute to the growing academic and fan-driven discussions of Villeneuve's filmography.

NOTES

1. Lambie, Ryan, 'Denis Villeneuve Interview: *Sicario*, Kurosawa, Sci-Fi, Ugly Poetry', *Den of Geek*, 24 September 2015, available at: www.denofgeek.com/movies/denis-villeneuve-interview-sicario-kurosawa-sci-fi-ugly-poetry (last accessed 3 March 2021).
2. Carroll, Noel, *Philosophy of Horror: or Paradoxes of the Heart*, Routledge, 1990.
3. Hills, Matt, 'An Event Based Definition of Art-Horror', *Dark Thoughts: Philosophic Reflections on Cinematic Horror*, edited by Steven Jay Schneider and Daniel Shaw, Scarecrow Press, 2003.
4. Nys, Thomas, and Stephen De Wijze, *The Routledge Handbook of the Philosophy of Evil (Routledge Handbooks in Philosophy)*, Routledge, 2019.
5. Horne, Brian, 'On the Representation of Evil in Modern Literature', *New Blackfriars*, vol. 84, no. 983, 2003, pp. 30–42.
6. Oppenheimer, Paul, *Evil and the Demonic: A New Theory of Monstrous Behavior*, New York University Press, 1996, pp. 1–9.
7. Carroll, Noel, 'The Nature of Horror', *The Journal of Aesthetics and Art Criticism*, vol. 46, no. 1, Fall 1987, pp. 51–9.
8. Freeland, Cynthia, *The Naked and the Undead: Evil and the Appeal of Horror*, Westview Press, 1999.
9. Thomas, Laurence, *Vessels of Evil: American Slavery and the Holocaust*, Temple University Press, 1993.
10. McGinn, Colin, *Ethics, Evil and Fiction*, Clarendon Press, 1997.
11. Calder, Todd, 'The Concept of Evil', *The Stanford Encyclopaedia of Philosophy*, Summer 2020, edited by Edward N. Zalta, available at: https://plato.stanford.edu/archives/sum2020/entries/concept-evil (last accessed 20 March 2021).
12. Bordwell, David, *Poetics of Cinema*, Routledge, 2007.
13. Knight, Deborah, and George McKnight, 'American Psycho: Horror, Satire, Aesthetics, and Identification', *Dark Thoughts: Philosophic Reflections on Cinematic Horror*, edited by Steven Jay Schneider and Daniel Shaw, Scarecrow Press, 2003, pp. 212–30.
14. Schneider, Steven Jay, and Daniel Shaw, *Dark Thoughts: Philosophic Reflections on Cinematic Horror*, Scarecrow Press, 2003.

CHAPTER 9

Beyond Complexity: Narrative Experimentation and Genre Development in *Enemy*

Melanie Kreitler

'Chaos is order yet undeciphered': this opening line looms over Denis Villeneuve's *Enemy* (2013), implying a meaningful interpretation beneath an entangled surface. Among Villeneuve's feature-length films – from *Un 32 août sur terre* (1998) to his 2021 remake of the science fiction classic *Dune* – *Enemy* offers like no other a fascinating conflation of modes of filmmaking, storytelling strategies and genre conventions. Scholarly analyses of Villeneuve's dark drama have yielded vastly different interpretations of the story revolving around the protagonists Adam and Anthony (both played by Jake Gyllenhaal): two men who live different lives but look exactly the same. Nearly all academic endeavours have been dedicated to identifying the 'real' protagonist, understanding the film as a psychoanalytic exploration of a character's subconscious.[1] In this chapter, I address these studies' underlying assumption that the key to untangling *Enemy*'s chaos is the relation between the two protagonists.

Contradictory readings emerge from the question of how to understand the film: is it a psychological game of cat-and-mouse; the fantasy of a man who escapes into another, or possibly even two other lives; or the tragic story of a man who broke down after he lost his wife due to his own failure? *Enemy* is a puzzling mystery for audiences to engage with as Villeneuve cleverly keeps different interpretations in balance, offering affirmation, ambiguity and contradiction to different hypotheses at the same time. The story of Adam and Anthony allows mimetic, (magical) realist, psychoanalytic and allegorical readings that balance each other out, leaving spectators wondering at the order behind the implied chaos.

In order to address *Enemy*'s intricacy, this chapter foregrounds the film's narrative structure that is best described by its experimental features. Since the early 2000s, scholars in film studies and narrative theory have analysed such productions in the broader context of narrative complexity in cinema, a tendency in filmmaking and storytelling that has flourished since the 1990s. Scholars attempted to describe the diverse corpus of complex cinema as a phenomenon, trend, tendency and even a (sub- or micro-) genre (Klecker 121; Thon 176).[2] The definitional common ground of these different approaches is a shared notion of the productions' properties: they introduce experimental narrative strategies, characters or events that defy conventions of cinematic storytelling and audiences' viewing habits. *Enemy* appears to be no exception to this design as the opening epigram suggests. However, Villeneuve challenges not only conventions of classical storytelling, but also (by now) conventionalised takes in the quasi-genre of narrative complexity by demanding spectators' formative involvement in the film's meaning-making.

To illuminate Villeneuve's storytelling in *Enemy*, this chapter is divided into two parts. The first part analyses the narrative structure of the film to discern the principles of storytelling and narration that construct this tantalising web of possible interpretations and shed light on the diverging readings of spectators and scholars. The second part aims to situate the movie's storytelling strategies in the context of genre tendencies, especially in relation to contemporary complex cinema.

THE ORDER OF CHAOS: NARRATIVE STRUCTURE IN *ENEMY*

Enemy's enigmatic opening is a quote from the movie's book template, the novel *O Homem Duplicado* (2002) by Portuguese writer José Saramago. Internationally published as *The Double*, the title offers a gateway to untangle the chaos surrounding the protagonists Adam and Anthony. Adam, an introverted history professor, leads a monotonous life only enlivened by his girlfriend, Mary (Mélanie Laurent). His dreary routine changes drastically as he spots his mirror image in a movie and obsesses over finding the other man. His investigations lead him to Anthony, a vain and self-assured actor, who lives in an expensive flat with his six-months-pregnant wife, Helen (Sarah Gadon). Adam convinces Anthony to meet, but as he realises that their sameness is seamless, he flees from the scene. At the same time, Anthony becomes interested in Adam's girlfriend and begins to follow her around Toronto. He extorts a getaway with Mary from Adam, promising to leave the professor alone if he agrees. On the way back from the getaway, Anthony and Mary have a fatal accident and Adam takes Anthony's place as Helen's husband.

Watching *Enemy* for the first time, spectators will likely construct a story under a mimetic premise. Taking classical storytelling as their default starting point, spectators assume that scenes relate to and prompt each other in a chronological way, establishing implicit causal connections. In this way, Adam and Anthony are understood as two distinct characters, for the film introduces information that clearly differentiates between the two: one man is married with a child on the way, the other has a non-committal sexual relationship; one is a moderately successful actor, the other a university professor; one has an expensively furnished flat, the other lives in a sparsely-furnished apartment; one is self-confident, even arrogant, the other is introverted and gauche; one man likes blueberries, the other does not. These pieces of information do not just demarcate one man from another, but establish opposites. Despite their outer appearance, Adam and Anthony do not share a single character trait. Along these interpretative lines, spectators are likely to form the hypothesis that the men are *doppelgänger* of each other, which is an unusual, but not unthinkable scenario in line with Saramago's magical-realist novel.[3] As the characters meet in person and it becomes clear that their appearance is identical rather than outwardly similar, the unusualness turns into impossibility. As the audience attempts to piece together a coherent story, the discourse of the movie provides clues that point spectators in one or the other direction, leading to new hypotheses. The difference between what is shown and how it is shown takes centre stage, implicitly directing spectators' meaning-making processes.

A realistic-mimetic interpretation is liable to break down when spectators are faced with a giant spider looming over Toronto (Figure 9.1), which unfolds its full disruptive potential in the film's final moment, as Helen transforms into a human-sized spider. The imagery of the spider web and the symbol of the spider are recurrent motifs in the film that consistently point beyond a mimetic interpretation without providing viewers a definite direction to follow in their meaning-making efforts. The film introduces the spider motif during the first five minutes when Adam visits a sex club, where a sex worker presents a giant tarantula on a silver platter, only to crush it with her pointy heel. Although this

Figure 9.1 A giant spider looms over the Toronto cityscape in *Enemy*.

scene is alienating, spectators will likely not pay particular attention to possible implications for the entire narrative, as its meaningfulness (although not its meaning) is only disclosed much later. Startled by the sheer impossibility of the final scene, spectators soon realise that a mimetic reading that incrementally constructs the story on the basis of discourse information is unable to address the figurative and literal spider in the room, giving them reason to question the entire narrative and its assumed claim to reality.

Rather than subscribing to a strictly realistic-mimetic premise, the film maintains a balance between possible interpretations. Starting from the information provided in the film's discourse, there are multiple narrative leads to follow, for Villeneuve offers no clues and, at the same time, too many clues pointing in different interpretational directions. Following the revelatory meeting of the two men, Adam/Anthony seeks advice from his mother (Isabella Rossellini). This conversation illuminates *Enemy*'s experimental take on narrative structure. Spectators assume to see Adam due to the missing wedding ring, a feature that clearly distinguishes him from the wed Anthony during the entire movie. Filmed in a classical shot-reverse-shot sequence, the aesthetics of this scene do not indicate a deviation from conventional storytelling. Interestingly, shots linger on characters in mid close-ups which, however, reveal little given the characters' inexpressive emotional responses.[4] As the mother remarks that Adam/Anthony has 'enough trouble sticking with one woman', the camera remains on Adam to reveal an air of fatigue, without him acknowledging the comment any further. The only genuine reaction is Adam's confusion or even surprise when his mother tells him to 'quit that fantasy of becoming a third-rate movie actor' (Figure 9.2). Intriguingly, the scene of the conversation is followed by an establishing shot of a spider out-sizing skyscrapers treading through Toronto, further complicating the construction of a coherent story.

Figure 9.2 Adam/Anthony's (Jake Gyllenhaal) confusion during a conversation with his mother in *Enemy*.

During the scene's unfolding, the play on mimetic story construction becomes apparent, as the line separating the two protagonists starts to blur, establishing difference and sameness at once. The mother's remark on her son's infidelity cannot be tested by spectators, as it is not directly depicted in the movie, but can be aligned with the stereotypical image of a bachelor. However, an earlier conversation between Anthony and his wife likewise insinuates that he has been unfaithful in the past wherefore the comment can be applied to both characters. This faint ambiguity is fuelled by his mother's reassurance, 'You have a respectable job, you have a nice apartment.' This statement does not apply to either one of the men, but seems to address a version that incorporates traits of both characters: the mother appears to address Anthony, as she mentions a nice apartment and his work as actor; however, in contrast to what the film presented so far, it can be inferred that being an actor is not Anthony's main occupation, for he appears to have another, 'respectable' job. This remark likely refers to Adam's profession as history professor at a university.

The dialogue between Adam/Anthony and his mother discloses the oscillation between mimetic and other, more abstract readings. The scene's storytelling mechanisms on the discourse level support a mimetic reading, which is sustained by story information such as the mother's reassurance that 'You are my only son. I am your only mother.' Nonetheless, the mimetic reading forms cracks as logical paradoxes accumulate that cannot be integrated into the story without reconsidering preceding hypotheses and assumptions. If the unwed Adam sits in front of his mother, why does she refer to Anthony's acting job? If it is Anthony, where is the wedding ring he wears for the rest of the film and what is his other occupation? A mimetic reading that establishes Adam and Anthony as two distinct characters, or even a magical-realist reading that understands them as *doppelgänger*, is unable to answer these questions. They remain logical paradoxes that will profoundly disrupt spectators' meaning-making efforts, yielding dissonant cognitions.[5]

Warren Buckland identifies cognitive dissonance as the main effect of narrative complexity, a tendency in filmmaking as of the mid-1990s. Narrative complexity primarily emerges 'from ontological pluralism – the entangling of incompatible (e.g. actual/possible) worlds, the ambiguous boundaries between those worlds, and the cognitive dissonance they generate' (Buckland 6).[6] Positioning *Enemy*'s narrative structure in the framework of complex cinema moves ontological doubts to the fore that call into question the actuality of the men's realities. Abandoning default viewing habits that depend on a mimetic premise, spectators need to 'recentre' their understanding of the film. The process of recentring, the 'readjustment of assumptions and beliefs about the connections between the various parts of the story' (Lavik 56),[7] does not only concern the question of who is sitting in front of the mother. Rather, the conversation can be taken as emblematic of *Enemy*'s entire narrative structure, where the ambiguous boundary separating the characters similarly blurs and eventually vanishes at the end, when Adam takes the place of Anthony as husband and father-to-be.

The process of spectators' recentring is described by Jonathan Culler's concept of naturalisation,[8] meaning the effort to integrate dissonant cognitions into a coherent story. Building on this framework, Jan Alber distinguishes nine strategies of recipients to naturalise logical paradoxes. These strategies include the creation of unnatural frames; generification; subjectification; foregrounding the thematic; reading allegorically; satirisation or parody; positing the narrative in a transcendental realm; 'do it yourself', that is, constructing a story on one's own (Ryan 671);[9] and the Zen way of reading, meaning that paradoxes and incongruities are accepted for what they are (Alber 76–9).[10] Although Alber's model stems from unnatural narratology,[11] these categories prove useful in the analysis of *Enemy*'s narrative structure, providing a rough guideline for understanding the different interpretative trajectories pursued by scholars in their analyses. Abandoning classical storytelling that rests upon the premise of realism and mimesis, I will provide a short overview of scholarship that pursues different approaches to naturalise dissonant cognitions when attempting to untangle *Enemy*'s narrative chaos.

The motif of the *doppelgänger* is the starting point for scholarship delving into psychoanalytic readings that aim to remedy the mimetic interpretation of its inconsistencies. Bernd Leiendecker positions Villeneuve's film in the tradition of unreliable narration as established at the turn of the century by films such as David Fincher's *Fight Club* (1999). *Fight Club*'s narrative structure builds upon a narrational doubling that 'tricks' audiences to overlook the unnamed protagonist's (Edward Norton) mental state, and leads spectators to assume Tyler Durden (Brad Pitt) as a distinct character, rather than an imagined alter ego. Along these interpretative lines, Leiendecker asserts that the same form of narrational doubling can be found in *Enemy*:

> Adam and Anthony are not two separate persons, but two aspects of the same split personality. This personality belongs to the unsuccessful actor Anthony Claire, who makes a living as a history teacher. His wife Helen is pregnant, but Anthony is driven by a terrible fear of commitment. He cheats on Helen, visits seedy nightclubs and creates the personality of Adam Bell. This personality allows him to lead the careless life he thinks he desires. (Leiendecker 202–3)

This interpretation focuses on an inner duality of the protagonist and his wish to escape reality in the form of an alter ego in a similar fashion as in *Fight Club*. The narrative must be understood as a subjective account of events told from the internal perspective of Anthony.[12] There are some indications that further support this reading: Adam is the only character mentioning his own name during a phone call with Anthony; Anthony does not seem to adapt to his role as father, which is suggested by a pull-up bar in the door frame of the nursery or to his role as husband, being unfaithful to his wife and visiting sex clubs. However, this interpretation also leaves some questions unanswered: Why would his wife dodge a confrontation after visiting him at the university, thereby uncovering his double life; why does his imagined alter ego become obsessed with tracking Anthony down, thus deconstructing the fantasy; and why do spiders appear to him? Subjectification may solve some of the riddles posed by the film, yet, again, some logical paradoxes persist in the face of narrative order.

Another psychoanalytic interpretation aims to circumvent these issues by placing the entire story of the film in a transcendental realm. Andrew Rayment and Paul Nadasdy interpret both Adam and Anthony as alter egos:

> [W]hile a real protagonist, a man who lives and breathes in physical (that is, diegetic) space, must exist, he is, in *Enemy*, but a shadowy, occasionally-glimpsed presence secondary to Adam and Anthony [. . .] that dominate the screen as parallel strands of this subject's *fantasy-in-the-diegesis*. [. . .] Taken together, Adam and Anthony represent two sides of [the real protagonist]'s psychic reality: the 'AdamAnt' (his masochistic [viz. Adam] and sadistic [viz. Anthony] sides). (Rayment and Nadasdy 7–8, emphasis in the original)

Placing the entire narrative in a meta-diegetic realm, rather than relegating only scenes to fantasy, allows an integration of any contradictory information. The story thus is turned into an imagery of the real protagonist's psyche, which is populated by reflections of his anxieties and desires: 'the cityscape of buildings is a metaphor for the internal and external webs that entangle [the real protagonist] in his unhappy existence' (Rayment and Nadasdy 9). Similarly, Luis Finol describes the urban cityscape of Toronto as a post-modern fantastic background that constitutes the protagonist's subjective universe (129). In contrast to Rayment and Nadadsy, Finol identifies Adam as the film's protagonist who creates Anthony in a paranoid delusion (120). Along these lines, Toronto is understood as an urban prison that confines Adam, who fights an internal battle against his impulses and desires in a hyper-realist and hyper-connected society (Finol 124). Yet, again, this interpretation is not able to answer all the questions that the film raises. If neither Adam nor Anthony is the protagonist, whose psyche is portrayed and how is it possible to differentiate between the growing number of protagonists? If Adam is the protagonist, why does his girlfriend only realise the mark of his wedding ring toward the end of the film?[13]

Having exhausted the possible relationships between Adam and Anthony, another analytical approach favours interpretative openness by focusing on the symbolical or allegorical meaning embodied by the recurrent motif of the spider. These readings circumvent an immediate integration of logical paradoxes concerning the 'real' protagonist. Along these lines, the motif of the spider has been interpreted as the embodiment of the protagonist's fear of commitment, mothers and motherhood (Foulkes)[14] or women in general (Leiendecker 203). A subtle hint in the film supports this reading, as the movie rental store, where Adam borrows the fateful copy of Anthony's film appearance, showcases a poster of *Attack of the 50ft Woman*, foreshadowing the towering spider over Toronto after the conversation with his mother. This manifestation could also contribute to Adam/Anthony's unconscious construction of a different reality in the tradition of unreliable narration. While these readings stay firmly in the psychoanalytic tradition, another approach identifies the spider as an allegorical signifier of *Enemy*'s narrative openness:

> If the giant spider (in the diegetic content) is a barrier to [the protagonist's] desire and, ultimately, to his 'knowing himself', then the spider is also, in a sense, a barrier to *the viewer*'s desire to 'know the text', to interpret it in a satisfying way. (Rayment and Nadasdy 17, emphasis in the original)

The strategic implementation of Helen's transformation into a spider at the end of the film and after the (assumed) main conflict between Adam and Anthony has been resolved speaks for this global interpretation, but does not account for other instances of the spider motif.

A final reading shatters claims to realism, mimesis and classical storytelling at large. This interpretation aligns the beginning of the film with its end but establishes two narrative strands that play on two different temporal levels. The film begins with Adam/Anthony listening to a recorded message from his mother and ends with him missing a call from her. Again, a form of narrational doubling can be discerned (as in the case of unreliable narration and in the framework of subjectification). This doubling concerns narrative structure and temporal layers lying on top of each other. Following a cyclical understanding, the car accident toward the end of the film is not a metaphorical abandonment of an alter ego or a fantasy, but an actual accident, which caused the scar on Adam/Anthony's torso. Consequently, the two lives and the two women are located on different temporal levels, one life/woman preceding the accident, the other following it. Nonetheless, there is still some difference in approaching the ontological relations of the two lives. While Leiendecker acknowledges the possibility of understanding the story revolving around Adam and Mary as taking place prior to the film's main story surrounding Anthony and Helen (205), Miklós Kiss and Steven Willemsen describe a reading in which Adam lost his pregnant wife during a car accident and fantasises about a different, successful life with an expectant wife after the accident (105). Intriguingly the film offers a possibility to integrate a cyclic reading in a lecture held by Adam:

> And it's important to remember this, that this is a pattern that repeats itself throughout history. [. . .] It was Hegel who said that all the greatest world events happen twice. And then, Karl Marx added, the first time it was a tragedy and the second time it was a farce.

Read from this interpretative stance, Adam's statement can be understood as a meta-referential comment on the narrative structure and cyclic unfolding of *Enemy* in which the protagonist's first life ended in a tragedy, while his current life is a farce, attempting to reconstruct a livelihood that died with the car crash.

As this overview revealed, there is large divergence between approaches for understanding the film, the relationship between the protagonists and the meaning of the spider motif. This ambiguity speaks to *Enemy*'s experimental narrative structure that carefully selects discourse elements to enable these manifold vantage-points for meaning-making. Different strategies delineated by Alber may be adduced to integrate logical paradoxes in a coherent story. However, none of these interpretations seems to yield a reading that is able to answer all the questions the film poses, which was also observed by member of the Toronto Film Critics Association José Teodoro: '*Enemy* abounds with tantalizing suggestions of causality that are always only on the cusp of coherence' (69).[15] In their analysis of *Enemy*, Kiss and Willemsen observe that spectators' diverging interpretations can be ascribed to a disagreement about which 'macro-frame', that is, which interpretative and analytical stance, needs to be adduced to connect scenes meaningfully. Building on Liesbeth Korthals Altes's notion that some texts require 'that we hold in mind alternative conflicting framings and oscillate between them' (33),[16] they concede that films like *Enemy* encourage a hermeneutic play of spectators (Kiss and Willemsen 130) that constitutes a different form of spectator address than can be experienced in classical storytelling.

Disregarding the respective probability of interpretative approaches or macro-frames and without attempting to establish a hierarchy, none of these readings comes naturally to spectators. Rather, they are products of thorough analysis, repeated viewing, and meaning-making efforts. The story has to be reviewed and revised in accordance with the interpretative stance taken; scenes have to be newly contextualised and causal connections have to be (re-)established. In Erlend

Lavik's analysis of M. Night Shyamalan's *The Sixth Sense* (1999), he identifies a similar form of audience engagement:

> *The Sixth Sense* [. . .] starts out like a relatively conventional mixture of drama, horror, mystery, and psychological thriller. It is only after the twist is introduced that we might usefully turn our attention to the process of [story] construction itself (and even more so, I think, on subsequent viewings). (58, emphasis in the original)

Lavik's initial description can easily be transferred to *Enemy*. This film starts out as a (more or less) conventional mixture of drama and psychological thriller. While incongruities keep piling up throughout the narrative, none of these will suspend mimetic story construction as much as the final image of the spider. Consequently, the film's ending introduces a significant element of disruption that not only encourages but demands spectator engagement in the tradition of plot-twist films (Figure 9.3).

In this way, *Enemy*'s narrative structure radically alters audience address, as it moves from active to formative viewer involvement.[17] While classical and Hollywood cinema attempts to avoid logical leaps and incongruities, focusing on a smooth unfolding of the story and character motivation, *Enemy* draws attention to the story's inconsistencies, playing with audience expectation and viewing habits. The careful balance between interpretations may go unnoticed during the immediate (first) viewing, but becomes abundantly clear once engaging with the story more closely:

> The moment of understanding is placed outside the film's initial viewing. [. . .] Some viewers may never understand the unreliable narration at all

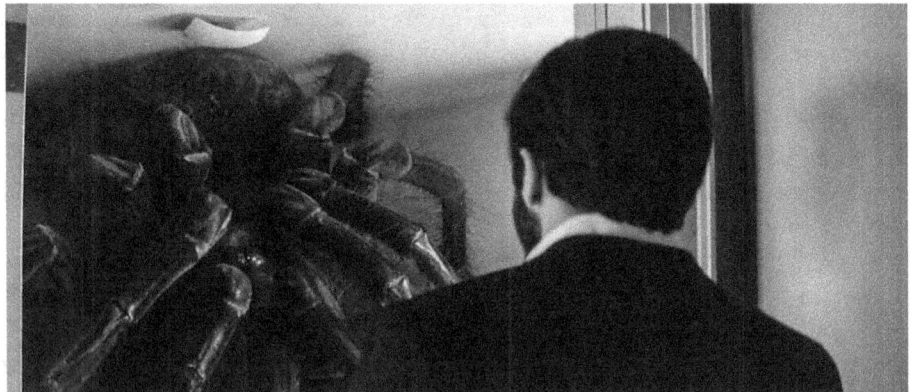

Figure 9.3 Helen's (Sarah Gadon) transformation into a spider at the end of *Enemy*.

because they do not bother to think any further about the film after watching it once. (Leiendecker 204)

The additional work by spectators is what sets *Enemy* apart from classical storytelling and conventional plot-twist films, highlighting its character of narrative experimentation. From the film's introductory quote to the final transformation of Adam/Anthony's wife into a spider, Villeneuve's film hints at a deeper meaning to be deciphered. In contrast to other complex films such as *Fight Club* or *The Sixth Sense*, viewers are left alone to uncover this meaning. The narrative structure places the ultimate moment of paradox at the film's very end, thereby refusing viewers the possibility to incrementally (re)construct the story, reconsider specific scenes and experience characters' reactions to the impossibility of the situation. In contrast to plot-twist films, the final scene does not offer a revelatory moment to guide spectators, but blatantly refuses to be integrated into the narrative. As a realistic-mimetic reading becomes impossible at the end of the film, spectators find themselves in the position of understanding and reconnecting scenes *after* the viewing experience, if they 'bother to think any further' at all.

Enemy's narrative structure demands an investigative and formative involvement with the story as spectators attempt to discern the appropriate macro-frame for understanding the film. This involvement may take multiple forms in subsequent viewings, as a different frame may be adduced each time. However, none of these frames will lead to an interpretation that answers every question the film raises. Kiss and Willemsen's notion of an oscillation between frames that acknowledges different interpretations at the same time (a form of analytical *doublethink*) appears to be the appropriate approach for deciphering the narrative chaos. Along these interpretative lines, discerning the correct answer to whether Adam or Anthony meets his mother moves into the background, foregrounding the possible ways in which this scene can be understood. This stance can be aligned with another principle of naturalisation delineated by Alber, namely Ryan's notion of 'do it yourself'. With reference to Peter Medak's *The Babysitter* (1980), Alber explains that 'this narrative uses mutually incompatible storylines to make us aware of suppressed possibilities and allows us to choose the ones that we prefer for whatever reason' (78). Villeneuve's experimental narrative structure speaks to this formative involvement of spectators, urging them to find their own way of connecting scenes and characters.

After the film's ending, viewers may wave aside the film's story as chaotic, nonsensical and incoherent or they may start a process of uncovering the different layers and meanings implied in the film's discourse. These 'metamusings' (Lavik 58) require a close analysis of structure and story, character construction and motivation as well as different interpretative and analytical frames.

The film's meaning is thus not a fact to be uncovered in the process of viewing. Rather, the search for meaning itself offers a 'participatory experience' (Kiss and Willemsen 16) that best describes *Enemy*'s effect on audiences. In this way, *Enemy* may elicit very different experiences in the course of attempting to understand it, as new clues can be discovered, new ways of relating scenes to each other can be identified and new answers to the question of why the film is told in this way may be found. Ultimately, it is debatable whether Villeneuve intended this movie to be understood in only one way.[18] As the previous analysis suggests, *Enemy* purposefully sows doubts about any interpretative stance. The narrative structure can be characterised by its play on classical storytelling and the exploitation of spectators' default viewing habits. Its openness and ambiguity speak to a careful construction on the level of discourse that allows multiple stories to be inferred. It is a film that demands to be experienced (over and over again) and requires spectators to immerse themselves in the spiderweb of narrative experimentation that entangles Adam/Anthony.

PUZZLING ORDERS: GENRE DEVELOPMENT BEYOND NARRATIVE COMPLEXITY

How can *Enemy*'s narrative idiosyncrasies be situated in the context of contemporary genre tendencies? The preceding analysis of the film's narrative structure introduced two possible frames of contextualisation: plot-twist films and narrative complexity. These theoretical frameworks aim to delineate specific forms of narration in opposition to classical storytelling. In the following, I will sketch out *Enemy*'s points of contact with these modes of narration to highlight how Villeneuve's experimental narrative structure surpasses them. Introducing the framework of impossible puzzle films, I will highlight how a cognitive approach is best suited to capture the interplay of structure and spectator engagement central to the film.

Enemy's ending enhances a disruptive element that invites audience engagement beyond default viewing habits. This is why scholars had grounds to understand the film's narrative structure as building up to a plot twist. In his analysis of unreliable narration in film, Leiendecker claims that *Fight Club*, due to its cult-like status, has established a blueprint for cinematic unreliable narration, which *Enemy* breaks with by omitting overt signposts of subjectivity (203). Lavik's analysis of the narrative structure of *The Sixth Sense* implicitly demonstrates the pivotal difference between conventional plot-twist films and *Enemy*: *Fight Club* and *The Sixth Sense* introduce a twist that lays bare their structure of narrational doubling in a revelatory moment.[19] In this way, these films hand audiences an unambiguous map to guide them through entangled discourse information, and resolve logical paradoxes and cognitive dissonances. A new, coherent story is quickly conceptualised, as the process of recentring is supported by scenes that reveal the protagonists' and films' unreliability. During subsequent viewings, spectators are likely to look for clues that foreshadow the twist or test whether the new reading holds in every scene. In contrast, *Enemy* omits a cathartic moment of realisation, which is why subsequent viewings may yield vastly different experiences that go beyond marvelling at the director's ability to obscure the 'true story' and identifying hidden clues that foreshadow the twist. In *Enemy*, different macro-frames are tested for suitability, which may result in diverging readings and viewing experiences.

By foregrounding the accumulated logical paradoxes and neglecting to resolve its puzzling ending, Villeneuve decisively strays from the blueprint of unreliable narration. Leiendecker implicitly addresses the misfit between plot-twist films and *Enemy*'s narrative structure when he writes: '*Enemy* uses (or at least potentially uses) two other techniques related to perturbatory narration, puzzlement and paradox, and creates an experience for the viewer that is far more challenging than classical unreliability' (203). The element of prolonged puzzlement and the upkeep of logical paradoxes is what sets the film apart from other examples of unreliable narration, as *Enemy*'s narrative idiosyncrasies do not build toward one specific understanding. These deviations from conventional(ised) structures and viewing experiences add an analytical layer that is better characterised by the heterogenous framework of narrative complexity.

Following *The Sixth Sense* and *Fight Club*, the proliferation of narrative complexity in film during the late 1990s can be regarded as the foundational moment of a new genre of film (for example, Klecker 121; Thon 176; Buckland 1).[20] Buckland highlights the common ground of the diverse corpus using the term puzzle film: 'A puzzle plot is intricate in the sense that the arrangement of events is not just complex, but complicated and perplexing; the events are not simply interwoven, but *entangled*' (3, emphasis in the original). He further elaborates that '[p]uzzle films constitute a post-classical mode of filmic representation and experience not delimited by mimesis' (5). *Enemy*'s multiplicity and viability of interpretations that continuously point beyond a realistic-mimetic understanding is testament to the entanglement of its narrative structure and its self-proclaimed narrative chaos.

Nonetheless, Villeneuve's composition again supersedes this analytical framework. Although complex films are perplexing, the puzzlement will eventually be resolved as was the case in plot-twist films. Using yet again a different ascription, namely mind-game film, Thomas Elsaesser describes this resolution as knowing the 'rules of the game':

> What once was 'excessively obvious' [viz. classical storytelling] must now be 'excessively enigmatic', but in ways that still teach (as Hollywood has always done) its audiences the 'rules of the game' of how a Hollywood

film wants to be understood, except that now, it seems, at least as far as the mind-game film is concerned, the rules of the game are what the films are also 'about', even more overtly than before. (Elsaesser, 'Mind-Game' 37)[21]

While one has to agree that *Enemy*'s story is 'excessively enigmatic', this enigma is neither revealed to spectators, nor are the spectators fitted with a map to guide them through the labyrinthine structures of the story. The 'rules of the game' are obscured, not letting viewers in on the way the 'film wants to be understood'. Put differently, the implication of puzzle films is that there may be different ways to arrive at a correct solution, but this solution is predetermined as is the case for completing a puzzle: it does not matter which strategy you pursue in assembling it, every piece will fit eventually, revealing the same picture each time. In *Enemy*, however, the puzzle may take different shapes, revealing a new picture each time, albeit never using every piece of the puzzle. Although the framework of the complex/puzzle/mind-game film is better adapted to the degree of narrative chaos in *Enemy*'s structure, it is unable to attend to the careful balance between interpretations and possible pictures to be uncovered.

Taking this heightened level of complexity into account, Kiss and Willemsen expand the analytical framework of the puzzle film:

> Impossible puzzle films often do not hand their viewers the [. . .] pathways to naturalise their strangeness in an unambiguous manner, nor do they give viewers the ultimate gratification of having 'solved the puzzle'. Instead, they seem to rely on the bewildering and perplexing effects of enduring and pervasive dissonances. (Kiss and Willemsen 127)

Enemy's spectator engagement has continuously proved to surpass other approaches and frameworks, which is why Kiss and Willemsen's cognitive approach introduces a useful vantage-point that acknowledges the effect on viewers' sense-making capabilities. This framework may not resolve logical paradoxes or yield a specific macro-frame for interpretation, but it pays heed to the 'participatory experience' (Kiss and Willemsen 16) that the film offers. Their main claim is that impossible puzzle films:

> . . . maintain *dissonant cognitions* in their viewers through internal incongruities (contradictions in their narration) and projected impossibilities (narrative structures or elements that disrupt the elementary knowledge, logic and schemas that viewers use to make sense of both real life and fiction). (Kiss and Willemsen 6, emphasis in the original)

As the previous analysis revealed, *Enemy* implements both intradiegetic logical paradoxes and an ambiguous narrative structure, thereby maintaining dissonant cognitions during and after the viewing experience. In contrast to other theoretical and analytical frameworks, narrative idiosyncrasies are not resolved or revealed as directorial in(ter)vention, asking spectators to marvel at the careful story construction that tricked them into disregarding clues. Rather, the marvelling itself transpires as the decisive feature that moves the genre of complex film into a different direction.

While *Enemy* is exemplary in its oscillation between modes of narration, this form of structural audience address can also be found in David Lynch's work, especially his LA Trilogy of *Lost Highway* (1997), *Mulholland Drive* (2001) and *Inland Empire* (2006). Lynch is known to offer profoundly puzzling experiences in his films, as his style is characterisable by 'ongoing cinematic experimentalism and a reflexivity about forms' (Elsaesser, 'Actions' 3).[22] In an interview at the 2001 Cannes Film Festival, the year of *Mulholland Drive*'s release, Lynch describes his cinema as visualising ideas rather than stories bound by genre, convention or coherence. Notoriously evasive about giving away clues to his films' understanding, Lynch touches upon the role of the spectator: 'I won't explain it. [. . .] But I think it's going to be a different explanation for, you know, different people. But it's an internal knowing for yourself' (Bombarda 07:44).[23] In his carefully chosen words, Lynch describes a viewing experience that is reminiscent of Kiss and Willemsen's notion of frame switches. In fact, in an analysis of *Mulholland Drive* from 2019, Willemsen and Kiss argue that 'one of the main reasons behind *Mulholland Drive*'s persistent attractiveness [is] a balance that the film maintains between at least two different pulls on viewers' meaning making' (135),[24] establishing a connection between Lynch's enigmatic productions and *Enemy*'s experimental structure. Spectators will read different stories into these compositions, foreground different macro-frames (or ideas), and draw different connections between events. Villeneuve appears to pursue the same premise as Lynch, in that *Enemy* is about several ideas that spectators can uncover and read into the production on an equal footing.

Another film I find instructive to compare to *Enemy* is Charlie Kaufman's Netflix production *I'm Thinking of Ending Things* (2020). Similarly to as they did with *Enemy*, spectators will likely construct a realistic-mimetic story on the grounds of discourse elements. The introduction of paradoxical information, narrative incongruity and sheer impossibility of what is depicted disturbs a coherent story construction. While *I'm Thinking of Ending Things* does not end in a quasi-twist, it introduces other artistic means of representation – such as an adaptation of the dream ballet of the musical *Oklahoma!* (1943) and a verbatim citation of Ron Howard's *A Beautiful Mind* (2001) – that shatter any claim to mimesis and leave spectators in a state of sustained confusion. It remains unclear whether Kaufman intended to adapt Iain Reid's 2017 novel and its twist ending, in which the protagonist Jake (Jesse Plemons) is revealed to imagine the life he could have led with the female protagonist (Jessie Buckley) from her perspective. While Kaufman introduces elements that support this claim, adopting the growing conflation of the two protagonists, he also brings in new elements that complicate the relation between scenes and spectators meaning-making processes beyond the book template, such as the rapid ageing of Jake's parents or the subtle switch between actresses playing the female protagonist during the car ride back to the city. Similarly to *Enemy*, *I'm Thinking of Ending Things* establishes a balance between interpretations that pervades the entire narrative structure and allows the oscillation between several macro-frames to untangle the narrative chaos.

CONCLUSION

In this chapter, I have shown how *Enemy* presents several interpretative paths. The film's audience address is deeply embedded in its narrative structure, offering spectators a participatory experience that exceeds the film's running time. In this way, sense-making relies on the degree of viewer involvement, as the 'rules of the game' are made up by spectators themselves. This experimental narrative structure maintains a careful balance between possible interpretations and allows for an oscillation between analytical stances. The film's structure and narrative ambiguity can be identified as the catalyst enabling formative viewer involvement and the film's engaging effect. I have also drawn comparisons between *Enemy* and other films from different genres and directors to get a sense of where it fits into the context of genre developments. The experience of cognitive dissonance, rather than its resolution, is in line with the analytical category of impossible puzzle films. The comparison to David Lynch's notion of a 'cinema of ideas' and Charlie Kaufman's *I'm Thinking of Ending Things* highlights a tendency in the quasi-genre of complex cinema that is geared toward prolonged, even persistent puzzling viewing experiences.

'Chaos is order yet undeciphered'; Saramago's quote reveals itself to be an analytical hint toward the central role of the spectator in Villeneuve's film. While the film's story may be waved aside as chaotic, I have argued in this chapter that the process of engaging with the complexity of *Enemy*'s narration constitutes the film's decisive feature that involves spectators on a fundamental level of meaning-making. The (continuous) process of uncovering the film's multiple narratives drives means of cinematic narration into a new direction and explores alternative orders of storytelling.

NOTES

1. For example, Leiendecker, Bernd, 'Taking Split Personalities to the Next Level: Perturbatory Narration in *Enemy*', *Perturbatory Narration in Film: Narratological Studies*

on Deception, Paradox and Empuzzlement*, edited by Sabine Schlickers and Vera Toro, De Gruyter, 2018, pp. 199–208; Rayment, Andrew, and Paul Nadasdy, 'The Sphinx and the Bridgekeeper: Denis Villeneuve's *Enemy* as Double-Riddle', *Journal of the Ochanomizu University English Society*, vol. 8, 2018, pp. 5–20; Finol, Luis, '*Enemy*: La Ciudad Como Escenario Fantástico', *Brumal: Revista de Investigación Sobre lo Fantástico*, vol. 5, no. 2, 2017, pp. 107–31.
2. Klecker, Cornelia, 'Mind-Tricking Narratives: Between Classical and Art-Cinema Narration', *Poetics Today*, vol. 34, no. 1–2, 2013, pp. 119–46; Thon, Jan-Noël, 'Mind-Bender: Zur Popularisierung Komplexer Narrativer Strukturen Im Amerikanischen Kino Der 1990er Jahre', *Post-Coca-Colanization: Zurück Zur Vielfalt?*, edited by Sophia Komor and Rebekka Rohleder, Peter Lang, 2009, pp. 171–88.
3. Villeneuve stays mostly true to Saramago's book, and only the ending deviates in content, form, and thus meaning. In the novel, protagonist Tertuliano Máximo Afonso (viz. Adam) reveals his true identity to Helena after her husband António Claro (viz. Anthony) dies in a car accident with Maria. The end of the book presents readers with a clear interpretative framework for the narrative: Tertuliano is called by a man with a voice identical to his, who claims to look exactly like him. This scene mirrors a conversation between Tertuliano and António earlier in the book and suggests that there might be even more doubles. As Tertuliano is faced with the doubling of his self once more, he arranges a meeting with the man to which he brings a gun, assumedly to break the cycle of (narrational) doubling. Although the narrative ends at this point and the outcome of the meeting remains uncertain, Saramago offers a form of closure that is far less ambiguous than Villeneuve's adaptation.
4. For an expanded discussion of close-ups in *Enemy*, please see Marie Pascal's chapter in this same volume.
5. The theory of cognitive dissonance was introduced by Leon Festinger in 1957. For a negotiation of cognitive dissonance in film, see especially Buckland as well as Kiss and Willemsen (Kiss, Miklós, and Steven Willemsen, *Impossible Puzzle Films: A Cognitive Approach to Contemporary Complex Cinema*, Edinburgh University Press, 2017, pp. 65–70). The use of cognitive dissonance in these works relies less on a traditional social-psychological approach as in the case of Festinger, but focuses on the meaning of cognitions that are in dissonant relationship to each other, that is, dissonant cognitions.
6. Buckland, Warren, 'Introduction: Ambiguity, Ontological Pluralism, and Cognitive Dissonance in the Hollywood Puzzle Film', *Hollywood Puzzle Films*, edited by Warren Buckland, Routledge, 2014, pp. 1–14.
7. Lavik, Erlend, 'Narrative Structure in *The Sixth Sense*: A New Twist in "Twist Movies"?', *The Velvet Light Trap*, vol. 58, 2006, pp. 55–64.
8. Culler, Jonathan, *Structuralist Poetics: Structuralism, Linguistics and the Study of Literature*, Routledge, Kegan Paul, 1975.
9. Ryan, Marie-Laure, 'From Parallel Universes to Possible Worlds: Ontological Pluralism in Physics, Narratology, and Narrative', *Poetics Today*, vol. 27, no. 4, 2006, pp. 633–74.
10. Alber, Jan, 'Unnatural Narratology: Developments and Perspectives', *Germanisch-Romanische Monatsschrift*, edited by Ansgar Nünning, vol. 63, no. 1, 2013, pp. 69–84. For an in-depth discussion of these processes in film, see Kiss and Willemsen 110–19.
11. In literary studies, the theoretical framework of unnatural narratology is dedicated to 'texts that feature strikingly impossible or antimimetic elements [. . .] depict[ing] situations and events that move beyond, extend, challenge, or defy our knowledge of the world' (Alber et al. 1–2). See Alber, Jan et al., 'Introduction', *A Poetics of Unnatural Narrative*, edited by Jan Alber, Henrik Skov Nielsen, and Brian Richardson, Ohio State University Press, 2013, pp. 1–15. The advantage of unnatural narratology for this analysis is its focus on 'the insistently fictional' (9), challenging the mimetic bias of narrative theory and the notion that stories 'could be analyzed

12. according to real-world notions of consistency, probability, individual and group psychology, and correspondence with accepted beliefs about the world' (4).
12. This aspect aligns *Enemy*'s protagonist with an untrustworthy or unreliable, or a fallible narrator. See especially Olson, Greta, 'Reconsidering Unreliability: Fallible and Untrustworthy Narrators', *Narrative*, vol. 11, no. 1, 2003, pp. 93–109.
13. Finol acknowledges that the transcendental realm is unable to answer these questions, conceding that the urban space integrates the complexity and multiplicity of the human psyche and the environment in which it exists without attempting to fully comprehend it (129).
14. Foulkes, Sarah, 'On Fertile Ground: The Pregnant Women in Denis Villeneuve's Cinema', *Film School Rejects*, 31 October 2017, available at: filmschoolrejects.com/pregnant-women-in-denis-villeneuves-cinema (last accessed 21 June 2021).
15. Teodoro, José, 'Enemy', *Film Comment*, vol. 50, no. 2, 2014, pp. 69–70.
16. Korthals Altes, Liesbeth, *Ethos and Narrative Interpretation: The Negotiation of Values in Fiction*, University of Nebraska Press, 2014.
17. Empowered modes of viewership have been investigated by numerous scholars yielding categories such as 'pensive' (Bellour, Raymond, 'The Pensive Spectator (1984)', translated by Lynne Kirby, *Wide Angle*, vol. 9, no. 1, 1987, pp. 6–10), 'possessive' (Mulvey, Laura, *Death 24x a Second: Stillness and the Moving Image*, Reaktion Books, 2006) or 'forensic' (Mittell, Jason, '*Lost* in a Great Story: Evaluation in Narrative Television (and Television Studies)', *Reading Lost*, edited by Roberta Pearson, I. B. Tauris, 2009, pp. 119–28). The category of formative viewership should not be understood in opposition to these modes, but as an adaptation that focuses on the outcome of viewers' engagement.
18. In the DVD's bonus material, Villeneuve states that the film is an exploration of actor Jake Gyllenhaal's subconscious, pointing toward a psychoanalytic reading that centres in on a character's inner duality.
19. *Enemy* is not the only film by Villeneuve that has a disruptive ending. *Incendies* (2010) plays with the parallel unfolding of two plot lines. The twins Jeanne (Mélissa Désormeaux-Poulin) and Simon (Maxim Gaudette) uncover their late mother's past to find their ostensibly deceased father and unknown brother, only to realise that they are the same person. Similarly, Villeneuve's first English-language feature film, *Prisoners* (2013), has a revelatory ending, in which the prime suspect in the investigation of the abduction of two young girls is himself a victim of kidnappers, who framed him for their crime. While these endings may constitute a disruptive element, this only pertains to the level of story. The narrative structures may contribute to this effect (such as the parallel unfolding in *Incendies*), but the focalisation in both of these films is unambiguous. In this, spectators are not misled or have to decide between interpretative paths, but engage in the same detective work as the protagonists.
20. There are also opposing voices such as Thomas Elsaesser, who contends 'Mind-Game Films Are Not a Genre' in his posthumously published monograph; Elsaesser, Thomas, *The Mind-Game Film: Distributed Agency, Time Travel, and Productive Pathology*, Routledge, 2021, pp. 25–7.
21. Elsaesser, Thomas, 'The Mind-Game Film', *Puzzle Films: Complex Storytelling in Contemporary Cinema*, edited by Warren Buckland, 2009, pp. 13–41.
22. Elsaesser, Thomas, 'Actions Have Consequences: David Lynch's L.A.-Trilogie', *AugenBlick: Konstanzer Hefte zur Medienwissenschaft*, vol. 59, 2014, pp. 50–70.
23. Bombarda, Olivier, *David Lynch – Mulholland Drive – Sujet: Olivier Bombarda*, YouTube, 2 December 2015, available at: youtube.com/watch?v=xh_AernWIck (last accessed 1 December 2020).
24. Willemsen, Steven, and Miklós Kiss, 'Last Year at Mulholland Drive: Ambiguous Framings and Framing Ambiguities', *Acta Univ. Sapientiae, Film and Media Studies*, vol. 16, pp. 129–52.

CHAPTER 10

Subjectivity and Cinematic Space in *Blade Runner 2049*

Christophe Gelly and David Roche

In spite of its modest box office success upon release, *Blade Runner* (Ridley Scott 1982) has become a model of the dystopian genre and has had a lasting influence on science-fiction film such as *Gattaca* (Andrew Niccol 1997) and television series like *Altered Carbon* (Netflix, 2018–20). The two main aspects of *Blade Runner* that later works revisit are the treatment of the posthuman and of the city, which updated Fritz Lang's *Metropolis* (1927) through a neo-noir lens. The theme of the posthuman and the aesthetics of the city were deeply intermeshed, with foggy, rainy and shadow-ridden Los Angeles constituting a backdrop that mirrored the troubling of identity brought on by the questioning of the border between humans and Replicants. When it was announced that Denis Villeneuve was to helm *Blade Runner*'s long-awaited sequel, whose screenplay Harrison Ford himself had described as 'the best thing [he had] ever read',[1] the question fans of the film raised was how Villeneuve and his cast and crew were going to engage with the pre-existing material. Their tactic was to consider the sequel as a means to update and expand the original, by exploring the world beyond LA, updating the technology and adding AIs to the posthuman equation. This chapter proposes to examine more precisely the relationship between posthuman subjectivity and cinematic space, and thus between *Blade Runner 2049*'s (2017) ethics and aesthetics.

Cinematic space will be considered as a combination of diegetic space and audiovisual space, so that we will engage as much with the topography of the story world as with the surface of the screen. The 1982 film was anchored in a defamiliarised, 'liminal' space' (Brookner 13)[2] that referred to real, though re-arranged settings, but two different spaces appear in the sequel: the unmediated diegetic space explored by K (Ryan Gosling) and other protagonists, and space as it is processed by digital devices. The relations to these spatial categories influence the integration of characters in the diegesis and their relation to reality in general. We argue that *BR 2049* expands the scope of (post)human subjectivity by broadening the spatial configurations and ultimately grounding the debate concerning subjectivity (and thus the possibility of digital subjectivity) in a tension between the condition of inhabiting physical and/or virtual space. Subjectivity in Ridley Scott's 1982 *Blade Runner* revolves around the uneasy distinction between humans and Replicants. Rachael's (Sean Young) relation to Deckard (Harrison Ford) is essentially rooted in the question and the possibility for her to ground her identity in her subjective feelings and memories. Villeneuve's sequel takes up that question and reframes it around the relationship between Replicant K and his AI partner Joi (Ana de Armas), with the same query about the possibility for an artificial being to be constituted as a subjective identity, that is as an independent being endowed with personal feelings, ethics and memory. A crucial element in presenting Replicants as subjective identities in Scott's film (Gwaltney 36),[3] the articulation between empathy and consciousness is redefined in the sequel by making Replicant K the main focaliser.[4] In particular, posthuman entities like Replicants (K) or AIs (Joi) engage with space in ways that renew the human perspective and may testify to their specific identities as autonomous beings. The various modes of inhabiting space will be examined as related to the emergence of this new, posthuman subjectivity, in terms of aesthetics, politics and general representational choices. The concept of 'inhabiting' space refers, here, to the privileging of different perspectives towards material reality, regarding sentience and sensitivity. We will focus on three elements the sequel adds to the original: virtual reality, cinematic space, and the relationship between Replicant and AI. The analysis will bring to the fore *BR 2049*'s relation to its source material, as well as the film's position in Villeneuve's œuvre and in contemporary science-fiction cinema.

VIRTUAL REALITY AND THE VIRTUALISATION OF PHYSICAL SPACE

BR 2049 updates the 1982 film by integrating a twenty-first-century concern with digital technology and virtual reality that expands on the potentialities of the Voight-Kampff test and the Esper computer (which allowed Deckard to explore a 2D image in 3D). The numerous interfaces featured in the 2017 film construct another kind of diegetic space alongside the physical space in which the characters evolve. This virtual space is contingent on the existence of physical reality; it is connected to the latter through the interfaces that allow it to exist and because it serves to explore, recreate or replace it. The virtual allows the figuration and/or exploration of physical space through digital devices, as well as the creation of an imaginary dimension that constitutes an alternative to reality which it is nonetheless modelled on. We will examine these two spaces in order to determine to what extent they differ and interact with (post)human subjectivity.

In *BR 2049*, identity is often verified through or by the virtual; for instance, K's own conformity is validated when he takes the Post-Traumatic Baseline Test upon his return to LAPD headquarters and, later, when he looks for the genetic code that would testify to the survival of Deckard and Rachael's child. If the test only confirms the Replicant's artificiality, the DNA archive suggests that human individuality has been digitalised and reduced to biology in the process; the virtualisation of the human would only confirm the preeminence of physical reality. How exactly do virtual and real space interact in the staging of K's search for a 'missing link' between humans and Replicants? Does their interaction in any way revolutionise the concept of human nature and singularity within the diegesis? And can the virtual create a space in which humanity's position as sole bearer of subjectivity – what Joshi (Robin Wright) calls a 'soul' in the film – would be contested? To answer these questions, we shall first focus on the creation of a virtual space before examining the specific way in which it connects to the question of Replicant procreation.

The 2017 sequel depicts two modes of virtual space: either as a 'pure' fabrication (the memories Ana Stelline [Carla Juri] creates) or as a formalised version of reality (the digital devices utilised by K and Luv [Sylvia Hoeks]). K's visit to Ana Stelline – when he wants to inquire about the authenticity of his own memory – begins with an immersive presentation of virtual space as indistinguishable from actual space; a cut transports us directly from K's discovery of the miniature wooden horse in the furnace at the orphanage to a tropical forest scenery. Ana Stelline fulfills two roles at the same time: she is shown doing her job (creating memories for Replicants to make up for their hardships and enable them to recollect pleasant, albeit fictitious moments) and she is expected to answer K's question about whether his dream is actually a memory – to which she ambiguously answers: 'Someone lived this, yes.' K will deduce, wrongly as it turns out, that he really did live that scene.

Yet if the memory expert's answer initially seems to consolidate the clear-cut distinction between real and virtual spaces, it also ambiguates the very distinction for two reasons. First, K's misreading of her answer reveals that the reality of a given memory by no means guarantees a stable meaning, since he takes it as proof of his own 'special' nature, as Joi puts it later on. The reality of the memory does not preclude the destabilisation of its meaning; like a virtual memory, it can be adapted to various, sometimes opposite contexts. The indistinguishable nature of real versus virtual spaces and their inextricable connection are expressed through the staging of K's meeting with Ana Stelline. This staging is, for the most part, resolutely chiasmatic: Ana Stelline, a human being concerned with virtual creations, inhabits a closed-off space, whereas K, an artificial creature investigating the possibility of Replicant procreation, occupies a more liminal one. Visually, the spectral presence of K's reflection on the window and the absence of Ana Stelline's reflection initially heighten the chiasmatic staging. The position of each character on either side of a glass partition thus seems to assert a series of ontological distinctions (human/Replicant, dream/memory, reflection/reflectionless, virtual/real), which their activities (they are both working) and the faint trace of Ana's reflection at the end of the scene actually undermine.

Secondly, Ana Stelline's successful career as a memory designer is put down to the authenticity of her creations; she believes that 'If you have authentic memories, you have real human responses.' By locating authenticity – and thus (human) subjectivity – in virtuality, her comment further blurs the border between virtual and real space, since reality is equally a source of 'authenticity'. Only the device through which she examines K's face while he is recollecting his dream enables her to tell real memories apart from made-up ones. This device seems to suggest that the interface systems virtualising reality are the only reliable tools to separate reality from its virtual representation.

Real space is often 'duplicated' through devices that produce a virtual copy to help K along in his investigation. This is the case in the opening scene when K sends a drone from his spinner to investigate the surroundings of Sapper Morton's (David Bautista) farm. For Catherine Payne and Alexandra Pitsis,

> The scene is simultaneously constructed as it is viewed through the window of K's spinner. K views the 'real site' (the dead tree on the farm) as it is imaged virtually – extending sight above and below the ground. [. . .] This is one of many archaeological and forensic 'moments' that relaunches the search mechanism and contributes to the construction of the search as part of a mythic narrative. It also provides reference to the film as a digital artefact. (62)[5]

Payne and Pitsis's analysis suggests that, although digital and analog images may be ontologically distinct, their utilisation is grounded in the same ontological myth upon which André Bazin believed cinema was founded: that of 'total cinema', one that would reproduce and preserve reality (23–7).[6] Yet the relation between real and virtual spaces is not always as transparent, as the follow-up scene suggests. When Coco's (David Dastmalchian) forensic analysis of Rachael's bones figures the digitalisation of real clues and space on screen, the process is graphically represented as an opposition between two modes of an object's presence in space: within the same cinematic space, the bones on the examination table in the foreground are contrasted with their magnified, virtual representation on a screen in the blurry right midground (Figure 10.1). This is how the digitalisation of physical space is supposed to explain diegetic findings. Yet the accounting ultimately fails, since the virtual examination only

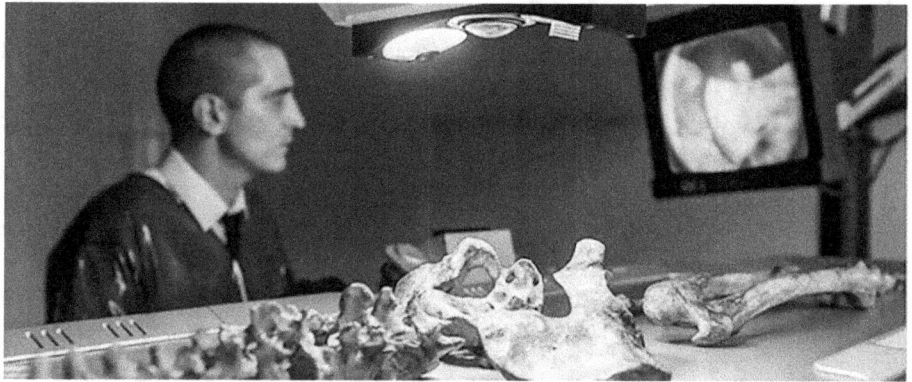

Figure 10.1 Reality and its virtual representation in *Blade Runner 2049*.

raises further questions about the 'miracle' (Sapper Morton's words) of Replicant procreation. The virtualisation of actual space leads to a dead-end, leaving reality just as opaque. K's asking the interface to focus on various parts of the skeleton reprises the 1982 scene in which Deckard successfully uses the Esper computer to locate Pris (Daryl Hannah) in a fold of the photograph. A nod to *Blow-Up* (Antonioni 1966), which similarly dramatises the investigation of a mystery through photographic enhancement, the 1982 scene has been analysed as an anamorphosis, i.e. as a distortion which separates real from virtual space (Shetley and Ferguson 70).[7]

Space is again technologically virtualised when Luv launches rockets at K's assailants at the Los Angeles Municipal Waste Compound and later when K investigates the ruins of Las Vegas in search of Deckard. Both scenes depict the virtualisation of space as a way to control reality but not to explain it. Virtual space is thus confusingly close to the real but unable to explain the whole mystery contained in, and posed by, real space. *BR 2049* insists just as much on the mediatisation of the characters' access to real space through virtualising devices as on the questionable results of this virtualisation. However imperfect, it is these virtualising devices that humans, in the diegesis, constantly resort to in order to control reality. Replicants, computers and AIs are used as tools – a situation Freysa (Hiam Abbass), the leader of the Replicant freedom movement, describes as slavery – sent by humans to explore and excavate physical space on their behalf. Two early scenes, both centred on Replicant reproduction, illustrate this hierarchy. Niander Wallace (Jared Leto), a human being, calls on his army of miniature drones to 'look at' a female Replicant he has just created, and ends up gutting her when he realises she is barren. Two scenes later K, looking for answers concerning the whereabouts of Rachael's offspring, returns to Sapper Morton's farm and finds a baby sock in a tin box.

Though centred on Replicant procreation, the two scenes are polar opposites: Wallace's insensitivity is matched by his dependence on machines, his digital prosthetic eyes situating him somewhere between a Cyborg and an Organorg in Thierry Hoquet's typology,[8] while the Replicants are associated with the organic – covered in liquid, the female Replicant resembles a newborn baby, and Sapper Morton's kitchen is (in the second scene) filled with the smell of garlic boiling on the stove (Green 35).[9] K seems to silently recognise the significance of the sock, as a clue in his investigation, but more fundamentally perhaps, as a sign of the Replicants' humanity; indeed, this cherished item of memorabilia debunks the very idea that memory – along with its emotional power and its link to identity – constitutes a dividing line between real and artificial beings, since Replicants also enjoy the Proustian madeleines that have been designed for them.

By resituating the answer of the posthuman's humanity in subjectivity rather than in biology, *BR 2049* pursues quite faithfully the ethics of the 1982 film; it is the spatial terms that differ. The posthuman beings end up engaging with the problematic line between real and virtual on their own,[10] an ontological question that reflects the question of the nature of their own subjectivity and their potential humanity. The exploitation of Blade Runners like K debunks from the outset Joshi's claim that '[t]he world is built on a wall. It separates kind', since by exploring the real, Replicants like K escape the virtual field human creators mean to contain them in. Hence the baseline test that is inflicted on him when he returns: it suggests that crossing the line between artificial and real is thought to be potentially 'traumatic' for the Replicants.

RECONFIGURING THE VARIABLES OF CINEMATIC SPACE

The opposition between virtual and real is one of many structuring oppositions that inform the handling of space in *BR 2049*; other binaries include verticality/horizontality, inside/outside, lines/curves, optical/haptic. The sequel provocatively highlights its departure from the 1982 film by reprising several elements from the original opening: a series of 'booms' combined with spring reverb; an intertitle providing information on Replicants and the story world; an extreme close-up of an eye; a series of aerial shots of the environment. But the repetition immediately draws attention to the notable differences: the eye appears first; the environment is not urban but rural; the colour scheme is a bright silver rather than darkness streaked with fiery orange. The first shot of what appears to be a dish echoes the circularity and relative flatness of the eye, the bird's eye view preventing the chimney on the right from fully standing out. The chimney's verticality is somewhat highlighted in the subsequent lateral tracking shot, but the presence of five other chimneys in the background is

Figure 10.2 Thwarted verticality in the *incipit* of *Blade Runner 2049*.

dimmed by an overwhelming grey fog. A high-angle track-in, more reminiscent of the 1982 opening shots, highlights the chimneys' puniness, dwarfed as they are by the dozens of circular rows round them. Verticality is altogether eliminated in the next track-in that tilts down to a mosaic of greenhouses harboring insect plantations (Figure 10.2), and it remains in the remote distance in the final (and very similar) shot in which mountains can be glimpsed. If the 2017 opening emphasises the expanse of the agricultural area just as its 1982 model emphasised the urban sprawl, it clearly favours horizontality over verticality.

BR 2049 immediately establishes how it will depart from its model: K's quest will be a far more horizontal one than Deckard's, leading the Blade Runner to depart from the city on three occasions, with visits to the Los Angeles Municipal Waste Processing and Las Vegas, and to fight another Replicant at the foot of the Seawall rather than on the top of a building. K's return to LA represents a return to more familiar territory for viewers of the 1982 landmark film and of its own visual model, *Metropolis* (Mennel 145).[11] Yet the appearance of urban verticality is by no means sudden, certainly not enough to establish a radical dichotomy between urban and rural; it is preceded by high-angle and lateral tracking shots of the LA sprawl whose potential relief is, like the chimneys in the Central Valley, largely attenuated by the dense smog. Only the final track-in – the one that leads us to LAPD headquarters – offers a low-angle view of the downtown area, and it is somewhat contradicted by the subsequent high-angle shot depicting the LAPD rooftop car park, thereby emphasising horizontality. Similarly, the establishing shots of the Wallace Corporation's Earth Headquarters emphasise their height (through the low angle), but their bleak presence (the face of the building is not lit up, unlike the Pan Am building, a nod to the 1982 film which draws attention to the difference in the visuals) is muted by the overarching foggy atmosphere.

BR 2049 departs even more radically from the 1982 film's treatment of indoor spaces. The latter's famous neo-noir aesthetics (low-key lighting, darkness, rain and smoke) pervades both interiors and exteriors, making them equally murky. The lack of boundary between inside and outside is expressed by the set design and the lighting scheme. The corridors and staircases of Sebastian's (William Sanderson) apartment building are outdoors and thus exposed to the elements; Kowalski's (Brion James) hotel room is not sufficiently soundproof to block out the sound of rainfall; and glistening raindrops can be seen running down one of Deckard's windows (in the background) on Rachael's second visit, drawing attention away from the protagonist shot in lateral medium close-up. Deckard's and Sebastian's apartments do provide some shelter, but they are regularly traversed by the city's many shafts of light, which pulsate and sometimes move like searchlights prying into the characters' intimacy, the whiteness even obliterating Rachael's face twice in lateral close-up. By the time Deckard and Roy Batty face off, the mist, rain and mud have seeped into Sebastian's apartment whose wet walls and exposed conduits and wires resemble flesh and entrails, characterising it as a highly Gothic space.

By contrast, the interiors of *BR 2049* are clearly delineated from the outside. Although they remain inhabited by shadows (Sapper Morton's hideout, the orphanage basement, Niander Wallace's quarters) and rain can still be seen running down windowpanes and windshields of Lieutenant Joshi's office and the flying vehicles, these interiors emit a light powerful enough to ward off competing light sources from outside and establish their dominion over the inside space. The hermetic quality of the interiors is reinforced by the colour schemes which emphasise a dominant colour: the whiteness of the LAPD rooms and corridors; the greyness of K's apartment; the golden hue of the Wallace archives and his private quarters; the browness of Gaff's (Edward James Olmos) retirement home; the cold beige of Luv's vehicle. The notable exception is, unsurprisingly, Deckard's Las Vegas quarters, in which the desert city's dusty orange atmosphere not only filters through the huge windows, but penetrates the utmost recesses of the building, including the theatre entrance when Deckard accesses the electrical panel, so that only the Hommage Lounge seems preserved. The opposition between inside and outside is furthered by a second visual device: deep focus composition. Utilised in all shots but the occasional shallow focus close-up, it constructs a precise space in which details remain salient – Morton's dishes and steaming pot, the heater next to Gaff, the soil in the orphanage basement, the web of golden light on Wallace's walls – in spite of encroaching shadows or a harsh backlight. Outdoors, however, the depth of field of the deep focus establishing shots is largely annuled by the opacity produced by a combination of lighting and material atmosphere – it is either too bright (in the Central Valley), too dark and rainy (in LA), too foggy and cluttered (at the Los Angeles Municipal Waste Processing) or too dusty (in Las Vegas) to see in the distance.

This radical change in the handling of cinematic space reflects the major changes made to the *Blade Runner* narrative, and notably to the portrayal of Replicants and the treatment of the posthuman. In the 1982 film, the porosity of indoor spaces reflects the uncertainty as to the boundary between human and Replicant, and of course expresses Deckard's increasing doubts concerning his own identity and the final revelation. In particular, the Replicants are associated with the rain just as much as the human characters, but the connection is reinforced as the narrative progresses (it accompanies the deaths of the four runaways) and culminates most memorably in Roy Batty's 'Tears in Rain' soliloquy, which emphasises that humanity is less about biological essence (developing in a uterus, being made up of 60% of water, etc.) than about being capable of emotions. In *BR 2049*, the humans are more or less contained within the interior spaces, no doubt because the ecological apocalypse has made the outdoors far too hostile – the only exception being, in Orwellian fashion, the social outcasts who live among the refuse of the Los Angeles Municipal Waste Processing. The Replicants (K, Luv and the members of the Replicant freedom movement), on the other hand, are shown to navigate between both interior and exterior spaces. In 2019, their suprahuman status enabled them to work in off-world mining colonies; in 2049, it allows them to walk the Earth itself. The fact that Replicants are not impeded by spatial boundaries is explicitly linked to their physical superiority on the two occasions when K breaks through walls during action scenes (the fight with Sapper Morton and his attempt to escape Luv's drones with Deckard), reprising similar imagery from the 1982 film when Zhora (Joanna Cassidy) dies crashing through a storefront and when Roy rams his head through a tiled wall while mocking and stalking Deckard. Walls can contain neither Roy nor K. Nor can they keep natural forces such as the desert and the ocean entirely at bay, as Deckard's Las Vegas quarters and the overflowing Seawall demonstrate. The film thus depicts a world in which Replicants navigate physical space and virtual space, whereas humans increasingly retreat into virtual space.

Yet it would be wrong to consider the physicality of the Replicant's relationship to space as a mere matter of superhuman strength, with the wall-breaking scenes merely confirming that these humanoid wrecking balls are nothing more than the tools they were designed to be. In *BR 2049*, even more so than in the 1982 film, physicality entails sensuality; it is expressed through a haptic visuality that invites our eye to 'graze rather than to gaze' (Marks 162).[12] We noted the visual paradox whereby images of vast expanses are flattened out by thwarting the depth of field of exterior establishing shots, an indication of the ecological apocalypse's hold over the story world. Two devices are utilised to achieve this effect: certain angles reduce depth of field and, more systematically, the cinematography emphasises the dense materiality of the atmosphere – whether the Los Angeles rain and snow or the Las Vegas sand. One effect of this flattening of the image is that it invites our gaze, which is prevented from plunging into the depths and folds of the image, to graze along its surface. The opening scene's high-angle shots, for instance, fashion diegetic space into a complex geometric pattern that seems to be laid out across the surface of the image, inviting our gaze to lose itself among the multitude of lines of the dishes and greenhouses. This is enhanced by the emphasis Roger Deakins's cinematography puts on the density of the atmosphere. The famous Las Vegas images that were the basis of some of the film's promotional material depict K as a dark silhouette haloed by a luminescent orange blur, who becomes himself a blur when the camera focuses on a metal armature in the foreground. The density of the atmosphere reconfigures the characteristics of diegetic space into an array of shapes and figures with a monochromatic basis. This is also the case in LA, where the buildings looming beyond the Wallace Corporation HQ appear like nothing more than an assortment of spectral parallalepipeds whose distance from the visible building is ultimately unfathomable. Such images insist on the materiality of both the diegetic world and the film image, paradoxically by abstracting the former to a far greater degree than what the 1982 film offered. In this respect, *BR 2049* reflects a contemporary trend, one that is patent in *Arrival* (2016) as well – to explore modes of visuality that go beyond 'models of "optical-systemic space"', i.e. space as 'an autonomous and static physical object, an empty and homogenous receptable structured according to the three axes of Euclidian geometry' (Gaudin 7–8).[13]

DO (POST)HUMANS DREAM OF INHABITING SPACE?

In a narrative whose main focaliser[14] is K, such images come to express his own experience of his environment (for instance, the sense that he is barely progressing through the sandy Las Vegas atmosphere). It is by inviting us to experience the film images sensually that the film expresses K's own sensual experience of the world around him. By insisting on the Replicant's failure to see in spite of his superhuman strength and sight, these images tend to qualify the implications of the surveillance image scenes analysed above; they emphasise, however, his capacity to engage with an environment sensually – to advance into the sandstorm as blindly and cautiously as any human being would in spite of his superhuman strength.

This is where the sequel somewhat departs from the 1982 film. *Blade Runner* famously asserted the Replicants' humanity by depicting their poetic relation to the world through Roy Batty's 'Tears in Rain' monologue; however, the latter was expressed verbally and was above all a question of visual perception[15] ('I've seen', 'I watched', 'glitter'), with the sense of touch evoked exclusively through the motif of rain (both visually in previous images of the Replicants and during the monologue and within the text itself). *BR 2049* maintains the argument of the 1982 film by which humanity is based on one's capacity to experience time and mortality, but it expands on the idea that humanity equally entails an immediate awareness of one's physical presence in and experience of the world. Accordingly, a comparison between K's final moments and Roy's is established through the use of Vangelis's 'Tears in Rain'; the parallel points to similarities in that both Replicants seem to experience an epiphany; K's epiphany, however, is not expressed through language but rather sensually for him and visually for us, when he holds his hand out to catch the falling snow and looks up at the sky before lying down on the snowy steps.

The conclusion of *BR 2049* suggests that being human is not so much a matter of language, whether our use of it or our own codedness; otherwise, as Joi remarks, DNA would demonstrate that '[m]ere data makes a man'. It is about the variety of forms self-consciousness takes. Whereas Roy expresses the transience of time ('All those moments will be lost in time'), K experiences it not merely through the act of dying, but through contact with snowflakes, each one of which is unique. The singularity of each individual composed of the same matter is confirmed when the motif of hands touching is repeated in the final scene, associated with Dr Ana Stelline (a close-up of her hand rubbing virtual snowflakes) and finally Deckard (touching the window that separates us from his daughter), in an image that recalls Louise Banks's (Amy Adams) attempts to communicate with the Heptapods in *Arrival*.

On closer inspection, identity had already been linked to the tactile on several occasions, notably when K examines tiny clues that turn out to be the most significant: the sock and the wooden horse. Singled out in shallow focus extreme close-ups and well-lit in otherwise dark compositions, the two objects stand out visually. K's progression as a sensual being is suggested by the fact that he is not wearing gloves on the second occasion and that the main clue happens to be three-dimensional (a carving) and not two-dimensional (a photograph). His dusting off the surface invites our gaze to similarly graze the carving's contours, to appreciate its shine and texture, an effect reinforced by the rustling sound of him rubbing, until the optical gets the upper hand as the date appears inscribed 6.10.21 and a reverse shot shows us his face. The optical remains more prominent in the first instance than in the second, since it ends on the photograph and not on K's face contorted by emotions.

The suggestion that the Replicants inaugurate a new relation to space thus relies on their capacity to experience space through the regime of the sensible, whose coordinates are not exclusively visual but also tactile (and no doubt involve the senses of hearing, taste and smell as well). It also raises the question of differentiation between K's sentience as an artificial being (a Replicant) and what characterises spatial perception by humans or AIs. If the posthumans inhabit space differently, it should appear comparatively. This is first suggested by Deckard's confrontation with a near-perfect copy of Rachael offered by Wallace to bribe him into cooperation. Initially troubled by the copy, Deckard turns away, muttering, 'Her eyes were green', before Luv shoots the Rachael lookalike dead. If Deckard's reaction initially seems to evince a human attachment to visuals as a defining category of subjective interrelation, it masks a more instinctual reaction that prompts him to lie (any fan of the 1982 film would remember that his lover's eyes were, indeed, brown). The copy's physical perfection cannot make up for the fact that she is not Rachael, and Deckard cannot just pretend that she is.

K has a similar experience in the following scene, a commonality that is highlighted by a graphic match (we transition from a back medium close-up of Deckard to one of K). K is crossing a bridge when he encounters a giant hologram of Joi who looms over him, King-Kong like (Figure 10.3). Joi says: 'What a day. You look lonely. I can fix that. You look like a good Joe', before crouching on all fours and letting out a sexual sigh. The hologram's artificiality is emphasised by its souless black eyes, its pixelated texture, the reverb that renders its voice ethereal, and the blue and pink lines of light that shackle it to its billboard; when it resumes its position on the face of a nearby building, the sales pitch accompanying the advertisement become visible – 'Everything you want to see/hear' – with the last words blinking in turn. On the surface, this scene seems to radically shatter the illusion K had created for himself about the intimate, intersubjective nature of his relationship with the AI. Particularly notable are the use of clichés ('What a day!' is the first sentence we hear K's Joi utter) and the transformation of a cliché into a semblance of identity, especially since Joe is the name Joi suggests K take on to express what he believes to be

Figure 10.3 Joi's (Ana de Armas) giant hologram as the sign of a deceptive subjectivity.

his special nature as a human-Replicant hybrid, but also the emphasis on sight and sound instead of touch (Joi's gesture of pointing at K turns her hand into an instrument of visuality rather than touch). The film here suggests that the very idea of AI subjectivity can be nothing more than an illusion, more precisely a projection of human/Replicant subjectivity; it thus seems to establish an opposition between Replicants and AI on the basis that the latter cannot inhabit space and are thus denied a sensual relationship to the world.

The connection established with the Deckard/Rachael lookalike scene points to similarities in K's and Deckard's experience when confronted with their loved ones' copies: K could very well just be realising that this Joi is not his Joi, just as Deckard realised that this Rachael was not his Rachael, and that the human does not merely inhabit a body, whether physical or virtual. With the K-Joi subplot, the 2017 sequel transplants the drama between artificial posthuman bodies (Replicants) and humans of the 1982 film onto the relationship between Replicants (now reframed as humans) and AIs. The K/Joi reunion scene thus invites us to look back on the rest of the movie for signs (such as eye colour) just as the Deckard/Rachael reunion scene invited us to return to the 1982 film.

From the start, K and Joi's relationship seemed condemned to an audiovisual regime and thus founded on a sort of tactile alienation. By hiring Mariette (Mackenzie Davis), a Replicant prostitute, to act as a stand-in for her and to provide her with a temporary body, Joi seems to recognise the essential role of touch and the necessity to inhabit physical space in order to fully enjoy a romantic relationship. It is through touch that the two female bodies merge in the 'threesome' sex scene between K, Mariette and Joi, whose pornographic acronym draws attention to her ambiguous status as a visual stimulation which is also an enticement to touch. The virtual seems to annex the physical in order to inaugurate a new form of intersubjective relationship. Rather than blurring categories, the love-making scene seems to open new vistas and broaden the channels of perception, associating touch with vision through an aesthetics of synesthesia (the images insist on the hands caressing, the sounds or the gasps elicited by physical contact). The threesome exists in a precarious balance, with the two women's faces, hands and bodies often unmerging, yet in the final close-up of Mariette/Joi, Mariette, walking slowly forward, has been entirely reconfigured into a new and apparently stable body – one that recalls a Deleuzian 'crystal-image', whereby the actual image and its virtual are indistinguishable (Deleuze 69, 93–4).[16]

The sequel seems not so much concerned with the ontological – the destabilisation of human uniqueness is already a given – as with the perceptual; the virtual both unsettles and expands perceptual habits. It also remains profoundly ambiguous. This is suggested first by the track-in on the Joi hologram outside; accompanied by a promotional voice stating 'Joi is anything you want her to be', her look to the camera could express subjectivity as well as a reified woman/consumer product. It is furthered by the derogatory comment Mariette addresses to Joi in the aftermath: 'Quiet now. I've been inside you, not so much there as you think.' On one level, the comment debunks the very purpose of the threesome: that the merging of physicality (by proxy) with a virtual being could allow for a sensual experience of reality (and of K's and Mariette/Joi's body). For Mariette, the experience confirmed the AI's emptiness. Yet against her better judgement perhaps, Mariette nonetheless acknowledges her journey into the AI, and thus recognises the existence of some sort of an inner life, a recognition she lays out in spatial terms ('inside', 'there'). Thus, the possibility that the virtual being inhabits space is paradoxically asserted through its negation. Because Mariette's judgement is based on Replicant (i.e. human) perception, what the scene reveals is not the limitations of the AI, but rather the counter-argument that the Replicant/human cannot perceive the virtual space the AI inhabits. In the 2017 sequel, then, posthuman potential may very well lie in the novelty of Joi's subjective engagement with space, one that does not rely on physicality and three-dimensionality; it relies on the valuation of something eminently human, physical contact, as well as on the subversion of the very notion of depth.

If K is apparently condemned to an audiovisual relationship with Joi, it is also through her that the 'optical-systemic model of space' is interrogated and possibly debunked. This was already the case in an earlier scene, when K's spinner is attacked at the Los Angeles Municipal Waste Compound. Because she has been damaged in the crash, Joi begins to glitch, holding up her right hand as if to touch K, before appearing suddenly outside the vehicle, and finally through K's rainy window. Inside then/and outside, Joi demonstrates a non-Euclidian relationship to space, but this ubiquity points to the more fundamental paradox that she is both here (the emulator on the spinner floor) and there. Her distress, however, is expressed through an eminently human gesture: that of her holding her hand out, the same motif that, in the film's final moments, will unite K and Deckard in a common (post)humanity. And her final moment is framed in a flattened image (because of the lack of perspective produced by the rain on the window) that encourages the haptic visuality discussed above.

A similarly ambiguous configuration resurfaces in Joi's final moments. When Joi intervenes in K and Luv's fight, the 'Stop!' she addresses to Luv who has just noticed K crawling toward the emulator can be seen as a plea to spare K or herself. Yet by pitting the expression of love (Joi's last words are clearly addressed to K) against the sadism of a posthuman ironically named Luv, the scene tends to dispel such ambiguity. It is not so much Joi's reaction that endows her with humanity since, after all, she may just have been programmed to produce romantic clichés. Luv's response, however, is just as ambiguous as Mariette's words, since by looking at Joi instead of K, she is positioning the AI as the consumer subject and the emulator as the product that expanded her spatial range. Subjectivity is no more limited to a body than it is to language or one's name.

The AI's connection to the physical realm interrogates the degree to which human subjectivity is a matter of inhabiting space and experiencing it sensually. The epistemological and ontological inquiry raised by the sequel takes up where the 1982 film left off, as the emulator K purchases allows Joi to have her own 'Tears in Rain' epiphany. As in the final scene with K in the snow, Roy Batty's monologue makes way for the staging of a tactile experience. If Joi cannot 'feel' the rain on her skin, the rain nonetheless disrupts the contours of her virtual body, touches her. The 'authenticity' of this sensual experience is rendered ambiguous, since the clichéd romantic scene of two estranged lovers kissing in the rain is interrupted by a call from K's boss, Joshi. Joi is on the verge of accessing subjective identity and feelings when she is brought back to her status as a virtual being, as a 'product' dependent on an emulator and ultimately on her owner. Yet this conclusion is countered on two levels. First, K's surprise at her 'freezing' body (confirming that she is only an image) indicates that, in spite of the glitch, she remains the bearer of a subjective identity in his eyes. Second, Joshi's phone call is a reminder of K's own status as a product subjected to an employer who also exploits him sentimentally and possibly sexually. If K remains a human subject in spite of these hierarchies maintained by power (Joshi declares at one point that the revelation of a Replicant giving birth would 'break[s] the world'), then surely Joi should benefit from the same consideration. The AI's ambiguous nature, its existence as a hologram and as hardware, also recalls the Deleuzian crystal-image, a special case of the time-image that Deleuze argues is a pure expression of time, and thus subjectivity (110).

CONCLUSION

BR 2049 thus pursues the 1982 film's exploration of (post)human subjectivity by taking into account new technological developments (virtual reality and artificial intelligence), but its spatialisation of the problem is perhaps even more deliberate than in its predecessor. The environment K navigates not only mirrors the ethical question central to both films; it implicates a primal mode of being – the sensual inhabiting of physical space. The Replicant is fleshed out as a sensual being, something that the film aims to express not so much through language (as in the 1982 film) as through its haptic visuality, pointing to a conception of subjectivity grounded in a more primal relation to the world than language or consciousness. The boundary between the material and the virtual thus appears immutable and incontestable, with the latter often representing a copy of the former, fundamentally alienated from the virtual; such a domain would remain essentially inaccessible for the digital subject. And yet, just as the 1982 film questioned the dividing line between Replicants and humans, the 2017 film questions the division between AI and Replicants; the binary established between the physical and the virtual is undercut by the multiple parallels established between the apparently opposite modes of being. In this respect, *BR 2049* pursues the exploration of borders and their relationship to identity in Villeneuve's previous films (*Incendies*, *Sicario*, *Arrival*), while ultimately coming to a similar conclusion as that drawn by *Her* (Spike Jonze 2013). It ultimately falls on us humans (including Replicants) to acknowledge the digital other as a subject or to reject her as the radical other that stabilises our own identity.

NOTES

1. Khatchatourian, Manne, 'Ridley Scott: *Blade Runner* Sequel is Best Script Harrison Ford Has "Ever Read"', *Variety*, 13 December 2014, available at: https://variety.com/2014/film/news/harrison-ford-loves-blade-runner-2-script-1201378743/ (last accessed 27 February 2021).
2. Brookner, Will (ed.), *The Blade Runner Experience*, London and New York, Wallflower Press, 2005.
3. Gwaltney, Marilyn, 'Androids as a Device for Reflection on Personhood', *Retrofitting Blade Runner: Issues in Ridley Scott's Blade Runner and Philip K. Dick's Do Androids Dream of Electric Sheep?* (1991), edited by Judith B. Kerman, University of Wisconsin Press, 1997, pp. 32–40.
4. An element that distinguishes humans from Replicants is the capacity for 'heterocoital' reproduction, which Replicants lack. Despite the fact that Rachael, Roy – and K in the sequel – save Deckard, their potential access to procreation represents a threat to humanity. See Fedosik, Marina, 'The Power to "Make Live": Biopolitics and Reproduction in *Blade Runner 2049*', *Adoption & Culture*, vol. 7, no. 2, 2019, pp. 169–75.
5. Payne, Catherine and Alexandra Pitsis, 'On Nature and the Tactility of the Senses in *Blade Runner 2049*', *Journal of Asia-Pacific Pop Culture*, vol. 3, no. 1, 2018, pp. 55–74.
6. Bazin, André, 'The Myth of Total Cinema' (1946), *What Is Cinema*, 2 vols, translated by Hugh Gray, University of California Press, 1967, pp. 23–7.
7. Shetley, Vernon and Alissa Ferguson, 'Reflections in a Silver Eye: Lens and Mirror in *Blade Runner*', *Science Fiction Studies*, vol. 28, no. 1, March 2001, pp. 66–76.
8. For Hoquet, an Organorg can survive without his equipment – Batman is one such example. Hoquet, Thierry, 'Cyborg, Mutant, Robot, etc.: Essai de typologie des presque-humains', *Post Humains: Frontières, évolutions, hybridités*, edited by Elaine Després and Hélène Machinal, Presses Universitaires de Rennes, 2014. pp. 99–118.
9. Green, Michael, 'The Replicant Singularity in *Blade Runner 2049*', *Film International*, vol. 17, no. 1, March 2019, pp. 33–9.
10. This situation whereby the relation to the real is taken away from humans by artificial beings is described as 'parasitism' by Sharon Kim (13), who notices that it is humanity's own weakness that allows Replicants to take over. Kim, Sharon, '*Pale Fire*: Human Image and Post-human Desire in *Blade Runner 2049*', *Journal of Science Fiction*, vol. 3, no. 3, November 2019, pp. 8–19.
11. Mennel, Barbara, *Cities and Cinema*, Routledge, 2008.
12. Marks, Laura U., *The Skin of the Film: Intercultural Cinema, Embodiment, and the Senses*, Duke University Press, 2000.

13. Our translation. Gaudin, Antoine, *L'Espace cinématographique*, Armand Colin, 2015.
14. By this we mean that K is the 'cognitive point of view of the story' (Gaudreault and Jost 130, our translation), present in practically every scene. See Gaudreault, André, and François Jost, *Le Récit filmique: Cinéma et récit II*, Paris: Nathan, 1990.
15. Apparently, an earlier version of David Peoples' screenplay contained a longer monologue in which other senses were invoked ('with sweat in my eyes', 'I've felt wind in my hair', 'I've seen it, felt it'). See Myers, Scott, '*Blade Runner* dialogue analysis', *Go Into The Story: The Official Screenwriting Blog of the Black List*, 3 December 2009, available as: https://gointothestory.blcklst.com/blade-runner-dialogue-analysis-ff0e306a7630 (last accessed 8 January 2021).
16. Deleuze, Gilles, *L'image-Temps, Cinéma 2*, Éditions de Minuit, 1985.

CHAPTER 11

Mere Data Makes a Man: Artificial Intelligences in *Blade Runner 2049*

Kingsley Marshall

> Mere data makes a man. A and C and T and G. The alphabet of you. All from four symbols. I am only two: 1 and 0.
>
> Joi, *Blade Runner 2049*

> Once memories and dreams, the dead and ghosts become technologically reproducible.
>
> Friedrich Kittler (1999: 11)

Denis Villeneuve's *Blade Runner 2049* (2017) uses the manner with which near-future technology recreates or feigns consciousness to present a wider discourse around notions of identity, memory, and the formulation of the self and subjectivity. The franchise, which began in 1982 with *Blade Runner* (Ridley Scott), has grown to include three short film stories commissioned by Villeneuve to dramatise moments that take place after the 2019 setting of the original film and before the events of his feature-length sequel, occuring thirty years later. These include the anime *Blade Runner: Black Out 2022* (Shinichiro Wantabe 2017) and two live-action in-world shorts: *2036: Nexus Dawn* (Luke Scott 2017) and *2048: Nowhere to Run* (Luke Scott 2017). Each of these works share similar values, with the short films detailing events significant in Villeneuve's sequel and, to one extent or another, exploring the impact of technological change on society and the anchoring of individual and collective identities to digital or organic memories. This chapter considers how Villeneuve's film represents machine learning or artificial intelligence (AI) as a biocapitalist discourse that considers the philosophical and ethical impacts of real-world applications of technology and the expression of biopolitical power.

COMMON THEMES OF BLADE RUNNER

The *Blade Runner* cinematic universe is orientated around three themes: (1) the development, use, and exploitation of technology; (2) the ethics related to the deployment of this technology by members of the public and corporations; and (3) an exploration of the nature of what constitutes consciousness specifically related to AI and bioengineered technology. In *BR 2049*, these are made manifest through two key characters. K (Ryan Gosling) is the ninth generation of Nexus Replicants, organic lifeforms biologically engineered by the Wallace Corporation. K is an indentured servant of the Los Angeles Police Department tasked to track and 'retire' – a euphemism used in the franchise for the killing of earlier models of Replicant. Joi (Ana de Armas), K's holographic companion, initially occupies K's home through a projection system and latterly explores the world through a portable 'emanator' which K obtains, freeing Joi from the boundaries of his apartment. Joi originates as an off-the-shelf AI, though evolves from this starting entity as experiences are shared and it builds upon its knowledge of their companion. This evolved state is stored either in the cloud or is shown later in the narrative to be downloaded to a local device, such as the emanator. The place of both characters in the world is determined solely through their core function – K as a law enforcement officer tasked to track down Replicants and Joi's role of companion. Both find themselves denigrated by others in society: K is referred to as a 'skinjob' or 'skinner' by fellow cops and in graffiti on the door of his apartment, and Joi is denoted as a 'product' twice within the narrative. All of the other Replicants in the narrative are also in service to others – represented through soldiering, farming, or sex work. K's human boss in the LAPD, Lieutenant Joshi (Robin Wright), observes that the world they occupy is 'built on a wall that separates kind' (Fancher and Green 2017: 22).[1] The fragility of this 'wall' is both physically evident – in the barrier that surrounds Los Angeles from the abandoned wastelands beyond – and in the existential space that distinguishes humans from Replicants, and indeed these physical Replicants from the digitally replicated, multiple iteration AI of the likes of Joi. Though unique, in that personalisation has occurred over time through her accumulated experience with K, Joi is represented as one of any number of customisable 'Joi' iterations made manifest in external shots of holographic advertising billboards, one of which directly addresses K later in the film. K and Joi's 'software', whether organic or digital, is primarily responsive to external information, gathering data to inform their primary purpose – indeed one of the Joi billboards, seen early in the film, makes use of the tagline: 'Whatever you want to see. Whatever you want to hear.' K's Joi helpfully makes this explicit, distinguishing the organic nature of K from their own digital or binary self. Joi states that K is composed of four symbols – ACTG, representing the nucleotide base chemicals of DNA;

Adenine, Cytosine, Thymine, and Guanine (Adleman 1998)[2] – while Joi comprises of 'only two: 1 and 0'. In a deviation from the original script, a line is removed from the film – Joi stating: 'The alphabet of you. *And them*' (Fancher and Green 44). This omission furthers the distance from the Replicant K and his human masters, acknowledging their biological similarities but placing the philosophical implications of this onto the audience rather than the alliance of the digital Joi and organic K.

Joi's observation reveals what Ian Campbell describes as the holographic character's place in the narrative as one of 'misdirection',[3] in that Joi's sentience is ambiguous and appears limited to serving as feedback to K's thoughts. The audience is reminded that Joi is neither real nor physically present by visual effects applied to their represented body at regular intervals, causing the holographic image to flicker or become translucent (Figure 11.1). More importantly, and in reference to Joshi's observation of the wall that separates Replicants from humans, though the space between Joi and K is made explicit through Joi's visual representation, throughout the *Blade Runner* universe this separation between human and Replicant is far less clear. The distinguishing factors grasped by humans are presented not as a wall but a liminal space where the certainties of human identity are constantly being challenged by advanced technologies, and contained by testing and, ultimately, 'retirement'. In Ridley Scott's film, this is shown through an ambiguity around what constitutes consciousness, tested through emotional responses measured by the Voight-Kampff empathy test that appear limited by childlike responses, a consequence of the short lifespan of the film's Nexus 6 model of Replicant. In Villeneuve's sequel, the Wallace Corporation's latest generation of Nexus 9 Replicants understand what they are and remain obedient. The notion of consciousness remains important but is secondary to a narrative centred instead on Wallace and K's parallel searches

Figure 11.1 A pixellated Joi (Ana de Armas) in *Blade Runner 2049*.

for evidence of Replicant procreation. A further layer of discourse is offered in Villeneuve's film by extending the world into the representation of another dimension of this liminal space, familiar to us from the contemporary lived experience, of the represented world occupied by K, and the abstracted digital multiverse occupied by Joi.

BLADE RUNNER AND BIOPOLITICAL POWER

Sean Guynes observes that the *Blade Runner* franchise, as in so much science fiction, presents itself as 'neoliberal dystopianism' (143).[4] Guynes notes that the economic drivers of the Replicants' creator, the Wallace Corporation's CEO Niander Wallace (Jared Leto), provide a continuation of what motivated the first film's Replicant creator, Eldon Tyrell (Joe Turkel), and his own titular Tyrell Corporation. In both films, these men are driven to terraform and colonise planets beyond Earth through the development and deployment of Replicant labour. In a monologue to his Replicant executive companion and enforcer Luv (Sylvia Hoeks), Wallace explains his frustration at the Wallace Corporation's reliance on Tyrell's inefficient Replicant assembly methods and his belief that this has curbed his ambition in building off-world colonies, disdainfully referring to the low number of the 'nine new worlds' occupied by humans. He is aware that Tyrell had perfected Replicant procreation but notes that this 'last trick [. . .] was lost' (Fancher and Green 37). K's search for identity then is wrapped up in a biopolitical discourse of the breeding of an enslaved people for economic gain, indirectly referencing the real-world practices of children of slaves inheriting the status of servitude from their parents and of the place of these groups to challenge such structural oppression.[5] Wallace explicitly refers to the significance of biopolitical slavery in previous Eurocentric colonisations familiar through history. These references to slavery are prevalent both in Wallace's diatribe and supported through the repeated use of allegory. As Syed Mustafa Ali notes, the Sepulveda Sea Wall shown to surround Los Angeles takes its name from Juan Ginés de Sepúlveda, a Spanish philospher and defender of colonialism of the Americas.[6] Mustafa Ali explains that Sepúlveda 'argued against Dominican friar Bartolomé de las Casas that the "New World natives" encountered by Columbus in 1492 CE were not humans, but rather animals and therefore should be treated as chattel' and argues that the sea wall serves as a 'metaphor for contemporary concerns associated with the latest manifestation of "White Crisis" – concerns about "rising tides of colour"'.

When K searches for records of the Replicant child, he discovers they suffer from a 'genetic abnormality, Galatians Syndrome' (Fancher and Green 46). This fictional condition reaches beyond the colonial through an extratextual biblical reference to the enslaved, to a people freed from the burden of slavery

Figure 11.2 The inscription 6.10.21 that K (Ryan Gosling) remembers as his birth or incept date.

through faith: 'But when the right time came, God sent his Son, born of a woman, subject to the law. God sent him to buy freedom for us who were slaves to the law, so that he could adopt us as his very own children' (4 Galatians, 4:5, NIV). These biblical references in the film are both explicit and implied, literal in Wallace's address to Rick Deckard (Harrison Ford) when they meet: 'And God remembered Rachel. And heeded her, and opened her womb' (Genesis, 30:22, NIV), and more obliquely elsewhere in the narrative. An inscription of 6.10.21 on a wooden horse and on the tree at Sapper Morton's farm that K remembers as an incept or birth date (Figure 11.2), suggests a citation of scripture, the book, chapter and verse appearing entirely relevant: 'For our struggle is not against flesh and blood, but against the rulers, against the authorities' (6 Ephesians, 10:21, NIV). These references do not advance the story but provide a wider context for the experience of the Replicants as one seeded in *human* history, providing an origin story for them, a faith on which to hook a rebellion from bondage limited not to a handful of individuals as in the original film, but an entire people.

THE CONCEPT OF CONSCIOUSNESS

K's origin story forms the heart of the narrative for Villeneuve's film and extends the scope of what it constitutes to attain consciousness in the *Blade Runner* franchise. Ben Tyrer notes that in Philip K. Dick's 1968 novel, on which the films draw, the dreams of the book's androids are more an aspiration – as much about the nature of the pursuit of happiness via consumerism, than consciousness. As Tyrer puts it, the original story focuses on 'the individual's pursuit of happiness (via commodities) rather than the encounter with unconscious desire' (14).[7] This observation is certainly also true of *BR 2049*, in the manner with which K engages with practices of consumerism: namely, his purchase of Joi, and the emanator to lend her a form of freedom – in this case of the physical boundaries of the apartment – that is held from him, in terms of the boundaries of his mind. In response to being asked if an upbringing is essential to the formation of consciousness, psychologist Chris Frith recalls a conversation with a Lacanian psychoanalyst:

> We were talking about whether machines could be conscious. He got very cross and said, 'No, of course they can't,' and I said, 'Why not?' He said, 'Because they don't have a mother.' This is almost what I'm beginning to think might be an interesting point.[8]

Emma Louise Backe argues this 'promise of transformation through childbearing is a tired trope of science fiction'[9] aligned with similarly familiar traits of the existential limits of human creation and can be traced from *Frankenstein*[10] through to more recent fictional production including *Black Mirror* (2011–), *Westworld* (1973, 2016–) and *Ex Machina* (Alex Garland 2014).[11] Indeed the wall that Joshi identifies could also be extended to gender in the narrative. K appears as male while Joi's projected self presents as female, with many of the represented female characters in some form of service role. Julie Muncy notes that this objectification of women throughout the film represents continuity from the first film, evident in Wallace's executive assistant and enforcer Luv, who shares traits with the first film's Zhora (Joanna Cassidy), and the pleasure Replicant Mariette (Mackenzie Davis) – who echoes Pris's (Daryl Hannah) role.[12] By picking up on the world of *Blade Runner* thirty years beyond the events of the original film, Villeneuve can further advance the ideas of identity explored in the first film to consider the implications of procreation to the Replicants, and the humans that rule over them. K himself identifies what he considers the distinction between the manufactured and the physically created – 'To be born is to have a soul', he says in response to a question Joshi poses which considers the difference between Replicants born in a lab, and those born through natural gestation. This both expands the ongoing ambition of Replicants to be truly independent of their human masters, but also the risks of a technological singularity made physically manifest – as Michael Green deems a 'material transcendence, in which achieving their human control depends on them becoming more like physical humans, rather than less like them' (34).[13] Though this is true of the film, Calum Neill questions the validity of reading the Replicants this way, suggesting that it results in an anthropomorphism where 'we read human traits into the nonhuman [. . .] as much as we read them into the human' (222).[14] The question left open in so many science fiction representations of new intelligences, including the original *Blade Runner*, forms the starting point of *BR 2049*. With Replicants having both attained singularity and transcended their objectification through spirituality and their capacity to reproduce, in doing so finally realising Tyrell's dream of becoming more human than human, then the power dynamic has unalterably reversed and it is humanity that appears prone to subjugation. It is this fear that drives Villeneuve's film.

Mireille Hildebrandt observes that although both automation and autonomic machine learning processes rely on algorithms, the distinction between the two is that automation is static, while autonomic machine learning is 'adaptive, dynamic and more or less transformative' (57).[15] As such both K and Joi can be determined as autonomic – or self-governing systems – where their respective bioengineering or machine learning is autonomous, allowing them the space to develop and, in some readings of Villeneuve's film, fully form what appear to be emotions from their memory whether implanted or experienced. Each of these characters satisfies Martin Heidegger's notion of 'Dasein' in that both entities are present and able to directly relate to the world around them albeit through their differing forms. In Heidegger's terms however, there is a distinction that can be made between the two through their relative ability to demonstrate 'an openness-of-being'. The Replicant manifestation of K is capable of the openness of independent thought, while Joi's limitation to mirroring K's thoughts suggests that the virtual being is 'merely [a] self-conscious being knowing himself only as an instrument ready for use', encumbered only in a service, or reactive role – a simulation of thought and consciousness.[16] When K's newly gestated identity is torn from him with the revelation that his implanted memories were in service of his own and other surrogates' role in covering the traces of the true survivor of Rachael's childbirth, Deckard's daughter Ana Stelline (Carla Juri), he is told that his place is to serve as 'a piece of a puzzle' by the Replicant rebel leader – and witness to Stelline's birth – Freysa Sadeghpour (Hiam Abbass) (Fancher and Green 100).

Andrew Schopp notes that proponents of transhumanism such as Ray Kurzweil commonly represent new technologies as a catalyst for change with a positive outcome or ideal.[17] Kurzweil's idealistic notions of an advanced spirituality borne of technological change engendering an epoch of 'greater knowledge, greater intelligence, greater beauty, greater creativity, and greater levels of subtle attributes such as love' (*Singularity* 344)[18] are called into question by the *Blade Runner* cycle. The films align with common fictional transmedia representations of artificial intelligence, whether digital or biological, though still non-human, characters, but present the ethical and socio-political challenges of technological change, channeled through a lens of the contemporary lived experience, shifting away from Kurzweil's ideas, that have been likened by Michael E. Zimmerman to a Western salvation narrative.[19] In doing so, such stories cast light on how and where technological change presents a *challenge* to humanity or the *experience* of being human (Schopp 66). In the original *Blade Runner*, this is represented as a search for self-identity by the principal characters Rick Deckard and Rachael (Sean Young). For the bioengineered Replicants Deckard is tasked to hunt down and retire – Roy (Rutger Hauer), Pris, Leon (Brion James), and Zhora – their goal is initially more simple: to extend their artificially shortened lifespan beyond the four years from their original, and fixed, 'Incept Date', with each of these characters holding a mirror to Deckard's understanding of selfhood. In *BR 2049*, these ideas of identity and artificially engendered life are coupled with philosophies of belief – in oneself, one's values, and faith in the continuity of one's world which, as Robin Bunce notes, has experienced 'ecological and societal collapse'.[20] These beliefs are anchored to subjective truths that the audience experiences in a closed narrative advanced by the discoveries of the film's protagonist K. As in the HBO series *Westworld* (2016–), both stories present an escape of the subjugated from corporate repression through faith – itself inspired by trauma and loss – where the Replicants and hosts hope to jump-start their consciousness through the trauma they have experienced and, in doing so, will 'work themselves free of their subjugation' (Marshall 98).[21]

The implications of birth, death, and grief are understood by K as the impact of his work in 'retiring' Replicants, with the effects of this activity on his psyche regularly measured by a Post-Traumatic Baseline Test. This test requires K to repeat a series of lines to an unseen interviewer in a room at the LAPD headquarters to determine if he has strayed from his baseline. It first features in the film when K returns from retiring the Replicant Sapper Morton (Dave Bautista) in the opening sequence. A baseline test is typically the benchmark of performance against a known standard of reference used in science and education and, in *BR 2049*, replaces the Voight-Kampff test of the earlier film though is no longer used to distinguish humans from Replicants. Instead – though still based on measuring empathy, response time, and intonation – the purpose of the test is to ensure Replicants remain emotionally passive in their response to trauma.

As K is led to believe some of his memories of childhood are part of a lived experience, rather than his original understanding of them having been implanted, he is shown to deviate from his baseline in a second test. This seed of belief, planted by Stelline in his visit to the lab in which she crafts the memories to be programmed into Wallace's Replicants, inspires K to lie to Joshi about having found and killed the naturally born Replicant. Luv suggests later in the film that Replicants should be incapable of lying to humans, though K's admission could be understood to be a form of existential truth where he is referring to himself when he explains to his supervisor: 'He was set up as a standard Replicant, put on a service job. Hidden in plain sight [. . .] even he didn't know what he was' (Fancher and Green 67). The death of K's old self is the death of his belief in implanted memories replaced and reborn by K as the child of Rachael and Deckard. Either way, K displays agency in this moment, the first step towards self-actualisation and free will.

It is interesting that K fails the Baseline Test at all, his increasing faith in this alternative identity – that he was born rather than made – being the catalyst for his emotional response. K's encounter with Stelline reveals that faith can instill emotion in all Nexus 9 Replicants, ratifying their creation myth rather than being limited by their programming or inception dates. This notion of Replicant inception is referred to in the original film but shown in Villeneuve's sequel through a sequence in a room described as the 'Creche' in the script. In this scene, a Replicant falls fully formed to the ground from plastic sheeting, taking their first breath as they are exposed to air and inspected and eventually dispatched by Wallace by way of a scalpel cut to the abdomen. The 'retirement' of the unnamed and voiceless female Replicant moments after its manufacture in Wallace's creche, and the subsequent dispatch by Luv of a remade simulacrum of Rachael – presented by Wallace to Deckard, and 'retired' by Luv on Deckard's rejection – present Replicants as product – disposable, characterless, repeatable – chattels solely for corporate gain. When Deckard rejects the recreated Rachael, his own lived memory of her challenges Wallace's genetic replica. Continuing an obsession with the eyes as a window to humanity present throughout *Blade Runner*, Deckard comments that 'her eyes were green'. The screenplay adds a line in the description of Rachael as she is presented in the scene: 'Flesh and blood. Young again. Remade. Authentic. Inauthentic' (Hampton and Green 96) (Figure 11.3). As in the original, in Villeneuve's film, the identity of the titular *Blade Runner* is initially challenged, causing K to question himself and his beliefs and seek certainty in his own memories. As K's true identity is explained to him by Freysa, his narrative arc mirrors that of Roy Batty in the first film in that he sacrifices himself in service of Deckard's continuing life – Freysa suggesting to K that this is 'the most human thing we can do' (Fancher and Green 99).

As the story progresses, characters explain the impact of a digital blackout following an electromagnetic pulse that had occurred over twenty years before the events of the film. The resultant crash of finance and trade markets lead to famine, ended through advancements in genetically-modified food. The cause of the pulse is ascribed to Replicants, who are subsequently prohibited for two decades until they are reintroduced by the Wallace Corporation with the Nexus 9, a model which has an open-ended lifespan but is deemed successfully subservient. This renewed control over this later iteration of Replicant is framed in the live-action short *2036: Nexus Dawn*, where Wallace demonsrates to a panel the obediance of the Nexus 9 in a sequence where he asks a Replicant to choose between his own life, and that of his maker.

Figure 11.3 Niander Wallace (Jared Leto) and the simulacrum of Rachael (Sean Young).

The lines repeated by K in the Baseline Test are drawn from the poem at the centre of Vladimir Nabokov's *Pale Fire*.[22] The significance of this text is underlined in a later scene where the attention is drawn to the book by its appearance in K's apartment – described in Hampton Fancher and Michael Green's script as 'well-thumbed, noted, creased' (14) – and presented by Joi, who asks K to read from it for her. That K owns a copy of the book from which the content of the test is drawn is ambiguous but suggests an attempt to contextualise and trick the baseline test, or offers evidence of K's engagement with cultural production for its own benefit – and a search for a soul that predates his discovery of the remains of the Replicant mother. Perhaps more significantly, the use and display of a metafictional novel makes explicit extratextual links to the narrative of the film – the book is narrated by an unreliable narrator who shifts the framing of the poem within it. This refers to drafts of the poem burnt in an incinerator, reflecting K's own memories and the Replicant records destroyed in the blackout, and the lines K repeats from the poem allude to evidence of an afterlife. Through this framing, the appearance of the book in K's apartment suggests very early in the film that he may well also serve as an unreliable narrator for an audience alert to such intertextual subtleties.

These ideas are in line with the notion of Replicants and replication within the original film. Elena Gomel suggests that if *Blade Runner* was to be considered revolutionary, the sequel is more reactionary – situating Villeneuve's later film in a cycle of nostalgic recycling – something that she connects with Svetlana Boym's observation of this phenomenon serving as a by-product of globalisation and late capitalism's use and reuse of existing materials.[23] Gomel suggests that this play allows science fiction to move simplistic binary representations of utopia and dystopia into an age of a more radically – as she puts it, 'unevenly distributed' future – which is closer to our own experience of gradual change. The film certainly folds in the influences of what came before both in terms of its diegetic and non-diegetic material. The noir aesthetic is evident in dress and lighting, its prevalent use of Nabokov's 1962 novel, and a reference to Robert Louis Stevenson's *Treasure Island*[24] that serves as an intertextual callback to a deleted scene in the original film when Deckard visits his injured colleague Holden in hospital. It is present too in the diegetic music (and the holographic representation) of Elvis Presley seen in K's visit to Las Vegas, and the use of Sergei Prokofiev's 'Peter's Theme' (1936), which appears several times within the film when Joi is activated as a Wallace brand identifier. Self-reflexivity also extends to the non-diegetic score, where Vangelis' themes from the original film are reimagined by Villeneuve's composers Hans Zimmer and Benjamin Wallfisch, an approach that James Denis McGlynn describes as 'a primary compositional referent for their whole score'.[25] Throughout the film, this look to the past – narratively, but also in the aesthetics of sound and image – when facing the challenges created by the technological 'progress' of the present could be considered naïve. This nostalgia presents instead as a denial, rather than questioning, the implications of technological change in the post-industrial, techno-fetishistic present day.

Indeed, Ali Rıza Taşkale suggests that Villeneuve's film represents a 'dearth of imagination' (118)[26] in that the death of Elden Tyrell in the first film and the subsequent bankruptcy of his Tyrell Corporation only allows Niander Wallace and his Wallace Corporation to thrive within a world divested of ethics. While K appears to understand that the purpose of the state apparatus of the LAPD is to maintain Joshi's wall, and Wallace appears driven solely by the economics of corporate growth through his ambitions towards colonisation, the ramifications of the Replicant childbirth are unquestioned beyond providing a catalyst for the Replicants struggle. Without procreation, the film suggests, the Replicants have no rationale for rebellion. Brian R. Jacobson has described cinema as presenting a 'technocritical' role in culture through its capacity to represent stories within artificial worlds that play an important role in engaging with the 'popular discourses about technological change' (24),[27] particularly concerning near-future or future worlds. Writing about *Ex Machina*, he observes that the film is at its best when reflexively

> ... probing cinema's world-making, life-simulating capacity – and its limits – [...] the medium's critical role in allowing its publics to imagine and think through the realities that science, technology, and cinema itself might make possible in a biocybernetic world. (33)

Sherryl Vint suggests that this criticality does not occur in *BR 2049*, however. She draws a connection between Wallace's ambition and the contemporary commodification and capitalisation of life sciences, specifically genetic research and biotechnologies, where she describes 'the reorganisation of life processes on a cellular level in order to make them better serve capital' (15),[28] specifically the capital invested by global corporations. Vint argues that the enslaved Replicants and the 'life' enabled by the Wallace Corporation are not only an embodied indentured labour-power, but 'a unit of fixed capital' (27) that serves to represent the neoliberal drive to control and commodify nature not for a wider societal good, but of capital gain. Through his actions and exposition, Wallace suggests that the manufactured Replicants are free of the human qualities of empathy and are therefore excluded of any ethical consideration. This is only challenged by the evidence of K's self-realisation beyond his formation as a bioengineered machine. It is the implication, rather than any firm evidence, of a Replicant birth through procreation that serves as the catalyst for K's self-actualisation as a conscious being. Though, as K puts it, a natural childhood enables Replicants to 'have a soul' (Fancher and Green 27), the notion of this 'miracle' as having occurred is referred to by Sapper Morton early in the film and ratified in Freysa's revelations to K, serves as the establishing principle of faith for the rebel Replicants. Mirroring human religious belief systems it is the Replicant's belief in this miracle birth that instigates their faith (and, in this case, sentience), over and above any evidence of the event. The idea that serves as a gossamer thread from Philip K. Dick's source material through Scott's film, Villeneuve's commissioned shorts and his feature sequel is that consciousness is born of faith and an engagement in culture. In Deckard's case this is evident throughout the franchise in his references to music and literature, something he commends to K when they meet within *BR 2049*.

HOLDING A MIRROR TO CONTEMPORARY LIFE

This cult of billionaire tech personality is familiar to contemporary audiences, holding a mirror to today's 'digital dominance'[29] of companies including Google, Amazon, Meta and their founders Larry Page and Sergey Brin, Jeff Bezos, and Mark Zuckerberg. Like the Wallace Corporation, the software interests of these companies have come to creep to include everything from retail, entertainment, farming, manufacture, defence, and tech infrastructure. This work is often framed as in service of society, but is motivated by a capitalist discourse centred around the accumulation of capital. Like the legal and regulatory facilitators of these companies, Joshi represents the complicit enabling of figures such as Wallace. Joshi, and the law she represents, that serves to maintain these biopolitical structures. She is fully aware that Replicants are capable of untruths and presumably have developed emotions beyond their work-related agency – her revelation that protocols demand that K would typically be retired following his baseline test failure suggesting there had been a precedent prior to K's own awakening.

Taşkale's critique of contemporary science fiction denies the form as a technocritical art, instead suggesting that 'dystopian cinema has already accepted the currently reigning political imaginary of corporate capitalism as an inevitable part of our future' (118), reinforcing rather than challenging existing biopolitical or thanatopolitical structures of racism, colonialism, and patriarchy. Hans Ulrich Gumbrecht describes the familiarity of such understandings, arguing that cinematic projections into the future occupy a philology of 'the complex present' in which representations of the future are 'occupied by threats that are inevitably moving towards us – one thinks of global warming as an example' (276).[30] There is much of the complex present to recognise in Villeneuve's sequel. The toxic and decaying world, part of the background of the original film, is brought to the foreground in several set pieces. The toxic post-industrial 'trash mesa', complete with scavenging bedouins, that replaces the San Diego coastline resembles Asian shipbreaking yards such as the Bangladesh city of Chittahong. The radiation-strewn Las Vegas borrows from the abandoned landscapes surrounding the Chernobyl and Fukushima nuclear plants, and cinematographer Roger Deakins and production designer Denis Gassner acknowledged the real-world influences of the Beijing smog and the Eastern Australian dust storm of 2009.[31] In the film's climax, the impact of climate change is represented by the giant Sepulveda Sea Wall protecting Los Angeles from the 'risen ocean' (Fancher and Green 102).

The *Blade Runner* cinematic universe presents a narrative orientated around the perception of technological change which is perhaps not as extreme as it first appears. Many of its themes are familiar to our own personal, social, economic and political circumstances. The deployment of the technologies that characterise the fourth industrial revolution – AI, big data, and the amalgam of physical and digital spaces – is repeatedly chastised around a lack of globally agreed ethical guidelines or regulation, while the ethics of tax avoidance form a well-reported central principle of global corporate accounting.[32] As in the filmic world, we are increasingly reliant on such services, despite their impact on our shared environment and social obligations of the nation-state. Regardless of our awareness of their power to denigrate and resist national and global regulatory frameworks, we maintain a complex relationship with the values of corporate capitalism and neoliberalism, while mirrors of the popularism and cult of personality manifest in the *Blade Runner* billionaires Tyrell and Wallace are evident in our political, cultural and business leadership.

Science fiction has long presented worlds in which mechanisation, automation and digitisation have disrupted individual identity, as well as social and economic structures and traditions. Perhaps in the familiar positioning of so many aspects of *BR 2049* to our own contemporary world and a sense of inevitability in a future dominated by corporate power, unbridled consumerism, and biopolitical influence, Villeneuve presents the audience with the possibility of becoming more like K, prompting us to question our own relationship with the environment, understanding of society, and place and responsibilities within that society. BR 2049 challenges us to develop our own technocritical faculties, rather than presenting neat solutions. We stare headfirst at the ambivalent potentiality of technologies that threaten the imposition of a totalising reduction of human beings to a stock of manipulable resources. As K is inspired to seek self-realisation and develop empathy through his encounters with inaccuracies, conflicting or incomplete information, and the subjugation of the self by corporate power enabled by weak institutions, so his realisation harbours the promise of opening up a transformed way of inhabiting the technological world more thoughtfully. Indeed critiques of *Blade Runner* could be seen as a MacGuffin, with the film's themes serving as a catalyst for the audience to question the complex implications of what we do not understand – of the ethical implications of the erosion of privacy, national regulatory governance, and tax regimes together with the parallel deployment of emergent technologies such as artificial intelligence and machine learning, quantum computing, the internet of automation and internet of robotics. The lessons of the *Blade Runner* universe are to pay more attention to the technological and global changes occurring in the twenty-first century through the mechanisms of the fourth industrial revolution, and our place within these changes as complicit enablers.

NOTES

1. Fancher, Hampton and Green, Michael, *Blade Runner 2049: Final Shooting Script*, The Script Savant, 2017, available at: https://thescriptsavant.com/pdf/blade_runner%20(2049).pdf (last accessed 15 September 2020). Fancher and Green's screenplay provides some explicit context for narrative information implied in the film itself.
2. Adleman, Leonard M., 'Computing with DNA', *Scientific American*, vol. 279, no. 2, 1998, pp. 54–61.
3. Campbell, Ian, 'Metafiction and *Pale Fire* in *Blade Runner 2049*', *The Projector: A Journal on Film, Media, and Culture*, 2020, available at: https://www.theprojectorjournal.com/campbell-metafiction-and-pale-fire (last accessed 15 September 2020).
4. Guynes, Sean, 'Dystopia fatigue doesn't cut it, or, *Blade Runner 2049*'s utopian longings', *Science Fiction Film and Television*, vol. 13, no. 1, 2020, pp. 143–8.
5. For a detailed consideration of this, see Brion, David Davis 'Slavery, Sex, and Dehumanization', *Sex, Power, and Slavery*, edited by Gwyn Campbell and Elizabeth Elbourne, Ohio University Press, 2014, pp. 51–3.
6. Mustafa Ali, Syed, 'Of Sea Walls And Rising Rides: Critical Race/Religion Readings Of "White Crisis" in Science Fiction Dystopia',*Critical Muslim Studies,* available at: https://www.criticalmuslimstudies.co.uk/of-sea-walls-and-rising-rides-pt1 (last accessed 20 May 2021).
7. Tyrer, Ben, 'Do Filminds Dream of Celluloid Sheep? Lacan, Filmosophy and *Blade Runner 2049*', *Lacanian Perspectives on Blade Runner 2049*, edited by Calum Neill, Palgrave Macmillan, 2021, pp. 13–39.

8. Gomes, Victor, 'The Science Behind *Blade Runner*'s Voight-Kampff Test', *Nautilus*, 15 July 2019, available at: https://nautil.us/blog/-the-science-behind-blade-runners-voight_kampff-test (last accessed 1 September 2020).
9. Backe, Emma Louise, 'Replicants and Reproduction: *Blade Runner 2049* and Sci Fi's Obsession with Motherhood', *The Geek Anthropologist*, 19 October 2017, available at: https://thegeekanthropologist.com/2017/10/19/Replicants-and-reproduction-blade-runner-2049-and-sci-fis-obsession-with-motherhood (last accessed 15 September 2020).
10. Shelley, Mary, *Frankenstein; or, The Modern Prometheus*, London, Lackington, Hughes, Harding, Mavor, & Jones, 1818.
11. For an analysis of reproductive futurism in *Blade Runner 2049*, please see Brenda Longfellow's chapter in this volume.
12. Muncy, Julie, '*Blade Runner 2049* Director Opens up about the Film's Treatment of Women', *Gizmodo*, 26 November 2017, available at: https://io9.gizmodo.com/blade-runner-2049-directoropens-up-about-the-films-tre-1820747134 (last accessed 20 February 2020).
13. Green, Michael, 'The Replicant Singularity in *Blade Runner 2049*', *Film International*, vol. 17, no. 10, 2019, pp. 33–9.
14. Neill, Calum, 'Do Electric Sheep Dream of Androids? On the Place of Fantasy in the Consideration of the Nonhuman', *Lacan and the Nonhuman*, edited by Gautam Basu Thakur and Jonathan Dickstein, Palgrave Macmillan, 2018, p. 213–25.
15. Hildebrandt, Mireille, 'The New Imbroglio: Living with Machine Algorithms', *The Art of Ethics in the Information Society*, edited by Liisa Janssens, Liisa, Amsterdam University Press, 2016, pp. 55–60.
16. Heidegger, Martin, *The Question Concerning Technology and Other Essays*, Harper and Row, 1977.
17. Schopp, Andrew, 'Making Room for Our Personal Posthuman Prisons: *Black Mirror*'s "Be Right Back"', *Through the Black Mirror: Deconstructing the Side Effects of the Digital Age*, edited by Terence McSweeney and Stuart Joy, Palgrave Macmillan, 2019; Kurzweil, Ray, *The Age of Spiritual Machines*, Viking Books, 1999; Kurzweil, Ray, *How to Create a Mind: The Secret of Human Thought Revealed*, Viking Books, 2012.
18. Kurzweil, Ray, *The Singularity is Near*, Viking Books, 2005.
19. Zimmerman, Michael E., 'The Singularity: A Crucial Phase in Divine Self-Actualization?', *Cosmos and History: The Journal of Natural and Social Philosophy*, vol. 4, no. 2, 2008, pp. 347–70; Zimmerman, Michael E., 'Religious Motifs in Technological Posthumanism', *Western Humanities Review*, special issue on Nature, Culture, Technology, edited by Anne-Marie Feenberg-Dibon and Reginald McGinnis, vol. LXIII, no. 3, Fall 2009, pp. 67–83.
20. Bunce, Robin, '*Blade Runner 2049*'s politics resonate because they are so perilously close to our own', *The New Statesman*, 16 October 2017, available at: https://www.newstatesman.com/culture/film/2017/10/blade-runner-2049-s-politics-resonate-because-they-are-so-perilously-close-our (last accessed 15 September 2020).
21. Marshall, Kingsley, 'Music as a Source of Narrative Information in HBO's *Westworld*', *Reading Westworld*, edited by Alex Goody and Antonia Mackay, Palgrave Macmillan, 2019, pp. 97–118.
22. Nabokov, Vladimir, *Pale Fire*, GP Putnam's Sons, 1962.
23. Gomel, Elana, 'Recycled Dystopias: Cyberpunk and the End of History', *Arts*. vol. 7, no. 3, 2018; Boym, Svetlana, *The Future of Nostalgia*, Basic Books, 2001.
24. Stevenson, Robert Louis, *Treasure Island*, London, Cassell & Co, 1883.
25. McGlynn, James Denis, 'Revisiting Vangelis: Sonic Citation and Narration in the Score for *Blade Runner 2049*', *SonicScope: New Approaches to Audiovisual Culture*, vol. 1, 6 October 2020, available at: https://www.sonicscope.org/pub/iatko5dg/release/4 (last accessed 6 October 2020).

26. Taşkale, Ali Rıza, 'Thoughts Interlinked: Corporate Imaginaries and Post-Capitalist Futures in *Blade Runner 2049*', *Critique*, vol. 48, no. 1, 2020, pp. 113–19.
27. Jacobson, Brian R., *Ex Machina* in the Garden', *Film Quarterly*, vol. 69, no. 4, Summer 2016, pp. 23–34.
28. Vint, Sherryl, 'Vitality and reproduction in *Blade Runner 2049*', *Science Fiction Film and Television*, vol. 13, no. 1, pp. 15–35.
29. Moore, Martin and Tambini, Damian, *Digital Dominance: The Power of Google, Amazon, Facebook, and Apple*, Oxford University Press, 2018.
30. Gumbrecht, Hans Ulrich, 'Philology and the Complex Present', *Florilegium*, vol. 32, 2015, pp. 273–81.
31. Grobar, Matt, '*Blade Runner 2049* Cinematographer Roger Deakins Made Light "Feel Alive" With Computer-Controlled Rigs', *Deadline*, 26 February 2018, available at: https://deadline.com/2018/02/blade-runner-2049-roger-deakins-oscars-cinematography-interview-1202280774 (last accessed 20 February 2020).
32. Babuta, Alexander and Marion Oswald, 'Data analytics and algorithms in policing in England and Wales: Towards a new policy framework', *Royal United User Services Institute Occasional Paper, Commissioned by the Centre for Data Ethics and Innovation*, 23 Feb. 2020, available at: https://researchportal.northumbria.ac.uk/en/publications/data-analytics-and-algorithms-in-policing-in-england-and-wales-to (last accessed 23 February 2020).

CHAPTER 12

Shortening the Way: Villeneuve's *Dune* as Film and as Project

Trip McCrossin

'This is only the beginning', Chani (Zendaya) muses, bringing a shyly knowing expression to Paul's (Timothée Chalamet) face, his gaze lowered ever so slightly (Figure 12.1), his mind's eye revealing the prescient vision of her as his soulmate, and so bringing to a provocative conclusion Denis Villeneuve's initial 2021 adaptation of Frank Herbert's celebrated novel *Dune* (1965). Subtitled *Part One*, reflecting Villeneuve's insistence that he could not hope to capture in a single film the scope and grandeur of more than the first two parts of the novel, the overwhelming consensus is that it is indeed 'the version we've all been waiting for', as Ben Child predicted.[1] It stands to reason, then, that we will feel similarly about *Part Two*, set to appear in 2023, reflecting at least the concluding third part of the novel, and about what, as Villeneuve has hinted, may follow in turn.

For *Dune* fans who are also fans of one or more of its seven sequels, Chani's is not a simple cliffhanger-style provocation. There's the film, that is, and then there's the *project*, a distinction of Villeneuve's own, which begs, in the spirit of her more *layered* provocation, two related questions. What will animate the project overall? What may we glean of this already from the first film?

CHANI'S PROVOCATIONS

'This project is, as the book is, a tragedy', Villeneuve tells us, 'the story of a young man', Paul Atreides, who bears 'the burden of a terrible religious heritage'.[2] Paul's tragedy is not just the burden itself, however, but its tragic consequences for humanity, which *Dune: Part One* effectively teases with snippets of Paul's 'a war in my name' visions of the future. Chani's first and most obvious provocation, then, has us looking forward to being in the audience again when this future

Figure 12.1 Paul's (Timothée Chalamet) lowered gaze and knowing expression at the conclusion of *Dune*.

comes more fully into view. To this extent, we cannot help but be additionally provoked to look forward to witnessing it develop further still, in *Dune: Part Two* and what may follow, not only in the spirit of *Dune*'s third and final part, but of its first sequel, *Dune Messiah* (Herbert 1969).

The tragedy of Paul is also that of his descendants coming to bear the same burden, his and Chani's son in particular, with newly tragic, and this time far longer-lasting consequences for humanity. And so we are again provoked, a third time, to look forward to what Villeneuve may have in store for us in depicting Paul's broader tragedy, as we have experienced it in reading the five subsequent sequels, *Children of Dune* (Herbert 1976), *God Emperor of Dune* (Herbert 1981), *Heretics of Dune* (Herbert 1984), *Chapterhouse: Dune* (Herbert 1985), as well as *Hunters of Dune* (Brian Herbert and Kevin Anderson 2006) and most of the seventh and final novel, *Sandworms of Dune* (Herbert and Anderson 2007), both based on Herbert's posthumously discovered outline for a concluding 'Dune 7'.[3]

Those of us who have read through to the end, however, through the concluding fourteen chapters of *Sandworms* and its epilogue, are provoked a fourth time, or perhaps we are provoked differently just once to begin with, to look forward to a project that portrays Paul's tragedy in more subtle and complex terms. As *Sandworms* concludes, that is, Paul and his beloved Chani, 'bathed in the golden rays of sunset' (Epilogue), having returned to Arrakis, forty plus publishing years and five plus millennia in storyline years after the 'warm night at Castle Caladan' (*Dune*, Chapter 1) that *Dune* opened on originally, he finds himself now '[i]nstilled with fresh optimism' (*Sandworms*, Epilogue).

Remembering that night, we recall Paul overhearing a fateful possibility. '[I]f he's really the Kwisatz Haderach . . .', Reverend Mother Gaius Helen Mohiam murmurs to Lady Jessica, Paul's mother, 'well . . .' (*Dune*, Chapter 1). We recall his curiosity and consternation. We recall the Reverend Mother administering, and Paul surviving, defiantly, her terrifying humanity test. And we recall that, before he learns more of what he overheard, he suffers a related premonition, that he has been 'infected with terrible purpose', even while he does 'not know yet what that terrible purpose [i]s' (*Dune*, Chapter 1). *Dune* and its sequels weave in intricate detail the story of the realisation and tragic aftermath of Paul's 'terrible purpose', including the last two novels, *Hunters* and *Sandworms*, realised eventually by Herbert and Anderson. Trusting their reverence for 'the genius who created this incredible series' (*Sandworms*, Dedication), the legitimacy of 'Dune 7', and the faithfulness of its realisation, we must also trust in Paul's 'fresh optimism', as he looks back on the defining burden of his earlier life.

'In the bygone days', we are reminded, which are bygone millennia really, five in all, 'he had been the legendary Muad'Dib, leading a Fremen army' (*Sandworms*, Epilogue). Now, however, he and Chani settled again on Arrakis, he's 'content to be a modern-day Fremen, a leader of 753 people who had established austere homes in the rocks, which were on the way to becoming thriving sietches' (*Sandworms*, Epilogue). And in the language of *Dune*, he looks forward to their offspring enjoying 'great potential, without the curse of terrible purpose' (*Sandworms*, Epilogue), which had infected their original children, Alia and Leto II, as it had infected him. Over and above our intrinsic interest in the completion, finally, of one of the most celebrated science-fiction stories ever told, Paul's optimism begs for attention. After all, neither the word 'optimism', nor any of its cognates figure in the first seven novels, even while its condition, 'fresh', suggests that it's not unprecedented, but rather renews prior sentiment.

Edith Wharton wrote memorably, in *French Ways and Their Meaning* (1919), of a conversation with William Dean Howells regarding 'that strange exigency of the American public which compels the dramatist (if [they] wis[h] to be played) to wind up [their] play, whatever its point of departure, with the "happy-ever-after" of the fairy-tales' (65).[4] It's the way of the culture, she offered, 'our audiences want[ing] to be harrowed (and even slightly shocked) from eight till ten-thirty, and then consoled and reassured before eleven' (65), to which he agreed and added, 'what the American public wants is a tragedy with a happy ending' (65). Perhaps something like this is all that's going on here.

Then again, Wharton's eight-to-eleven, three-hour timespan corresponds by analogy to one that for Herbert is decades in the making, from the appearance of *Dune*, on 1 January 1965, through the period in between the appearance of *Chapterhouse*, on 1 April 1985, and Herbert's death, on 11 February 1986, during which time he presumably wrote the 'Dune 7' outline. This together with the underlying role of religion, albeit *à la Dune*, leads one to wonder whether Paul's optimism is more than merely colloquial, something with deeper philosophical roots? Put another way, however right we may be in calling *Dune* a tragedy, we can't help but wonder whether it is at least a more complex one than we first anticipated.

The importance of Villeneuve's *Dune*, recognised as 'the version we've all been waiting for', and so the beginning of a developing project, is the opportunity it affords to explore in newly spectacular ways the ever-thorny intersection of tragedy and optimism.

THE FUTURE OF ILLUSIONS

'These are illusions of popular history which a successful religion must promote', we learn from the *Instruction Manual* of the Bene Gesserit's Missionaria Protectiva, as cited at the outset of chapter twelve of *Children*:

> Evil men never prosper; only the brave deserve the fair; honesty is the best policy; actions speak louder than words; virtue always triumphs; a good deed is its own reward; any bad human can be reformed; religious talismans protect one from demon possession; only females understand the ancient mysteries; the rich are doomed to unhappiness [. . .]. (*Children*, Chapter 12)

'[C]harged with sowing infectious superstitions on primitive worlds, thus opening those regions to exploitation by the Bene Gesserit' (*Sandworms*, 'Terminology of the Imperium'), the Missionaria Protectiva developed on Arrakis in particular, over centuries, the broadly religious 'prophecy [of] the one foretold as the Lisan al-Gaib, the Voice from the Outer World' (*Dune*, Chapter 13). Central to *Dune*'s original storyline and, eventually, to that of the ensuing saga, Paul comes to fulfil the prophecy, becoming the mahdi, or messiah Paul-Muad'Dib – the Kwisatz Haderach, that is, which we learn from an exchange between Lady Jessica and Liet-Kynes when they first meet, means 'the shortening of the way' (*Dune*, Chapter 16). The way *to where*, however, is left provocatively unclear.

What's clearer is that success depended on the promotion of the above 'illusions'. At first glance, without knowing what the ellipsis concluding the above passage stands in for, the illusions are admittedly a bit of a hodgepodge. Appearances notwithstanding, there's nonetheless a certain pattern to the first, fifth, and tenth illusions in particular, not unprovocative in its own right, having to do with the long fraught intersection of evil, virtue, and happiness. Most would say, in other words, that in the world as it appears to *us*, evildoers *often* prosper, virtue only *sometimes* triumphs, and however doomed they may be, the rich are happy enough in the meantime. Bad things happen to good people, that is, and good things to bad, a very old and enduring problem known as the 'problem of evil' – the perniciously difficult to satisfy 'need to find order within those appearances so unbearable that they threaten reason's ability to go on' (41), as Susan Neiman has described it.[5]

In promoting the three illusions in question, the Missionaria Protectiva is effectively promoting, in the aggregate, the idea that the problem of evil itself is an illusion, not really a problem. We may be offended by happy evildoers and unhappy welldoers, yes, but still, we can't help but believe, however inscrutable the evidence, that respectively, they're either not *really* happy and unhappy, or they'll be punished and rewarded *eventually*, or finally, their happiness and unhappiness serve some *greater* good, some *higher* purpose. In spite of appearances, that is, virtue and happiness and vice and unhappiness do *somehow* come together, generally speaking.

There's no record of when precisely the Bene Gesserit put the Missionaria Protectiva into effect, but in the vicinity of a dozen-plus millennia into the future, it seems that by promoting the illusions in question they're promoting a version of a familiar philosophical doctrine from out of our own past, one called 'Optimism'. Crafted in response to the problem of evil, it dates at least as far back as the Enlightenment, conventionally associated with Gottfried Leibniz's *Theodicy*, which appeared in 1710. In reality, not by name, and in a variety of more modest forms, it's in the Enlightenment water supply generally speaking. What do we do when things are bad, really bad, reason-paralysingly bad, and so on, but we don't want to blame God, in this instance a God-like ruler? We remind ourselves, however sincerely or insincerely, that they're all-powerful and all-knowing and so the world they govern must surely be the best it can be, the best outright even. However bad things may be, then, they're also contributions to this greater good, and so, in the end, we mustn't blame, or for that matter complain.

Optimism's popularity waxed and waned through the mid-nineenth century, mostly waning by the mid-twentieth, the era's accumulated atrocities making the view increasingly difficult to stomach. In this spirit, the mid-1960s saw the beginnings of Melvin Lerner's 'just world hypothesis', its first results appearing the year after *Dune*'s appearance, its standard-bearer, Lerner's more pessimistically titled *The Belief in a Just World: A Fundamental Delusion*, appearing in 1980, in between *Messiah*'s appearance and *Children*'s.[6] Does Herbert share Lerner's view? Are the *Dune* novels ultimately optimistic, as in 'the arc of the [Imperium's history] is long, but bends toward justice', or are the Missionaria Protectiva's illusions ultimately the order of the day? Which returns us to the question: the Kwisatz Haderach is 'the shortening of the way' *to where*?

While it mysteriously eschews the phrase, Villeneuve's *Dune* helps nonetheless to shape an answer early on, in the context of the Reverend Mother testing Paul for humanity.[7] Villeneuve's Reverend Mother (Charlotte Rampling) is far sterner than Herbert's, than David Lynch's (*Dune* 1984) even, who was already sterner, and he also made her, as neither had, complicit in the Emperor's machinations against House Atreides. She tests Paul brutally, cruelly even, eliciting Jessica's (Rebecca Ferguson) challenge, and the Reverend Mother's rebuke in turn. '[Y]ou in your pride thought you could bring forth the Kwisatz Haderach', she chides, but even if 'he *is* the One, he has a long way to go, his sight is barely awakened, and now he goes into the fire [and may yet] fai[l] his promise'. The script indicates that hearing this was to 'drain the defiance from Jessica's eyes', as she asks 'Do you see so little hope?', in response to which the Reverend Mother was to 'soften' in farewell, consistent with the general tenor of their exchange in the novel.[8] In spite of these directions, however, the scene is shot in a distinctly different manner, seemingly void of anything so conciliatory. In particular, Jessica's question's delivery is such that the 'Do' is all but inaudible; even if we're aware of it, from the script or subtitles, it seems clearly meant as a rhetorical question, a rebuke of the Reverend Mother's seemingly dismal appraisal of Paul as Kwisatz Haderach, and so a tacit assertion of her own hopefulness.

Shortly afterward, the Reverend Mother leaves Caladan, and Paul confronts his mother. 'What does it mean that I could be the One?', he asks. 'For thousands of years, we've been carefully crossing bloodlines', she explains, 'to bring forth a mind powerful enough to breach space and time, past and future, who can help us into a better future' (Figure 12.2). The former bit, 'a mind powerful enough to breach space and time, past and future', reflects well enough the novel's 'one who can be many places [in space and time] at once' (*Dune*, Chapter 1). What comes after, however, 'who can help us into a better future', is helpfully new and, while at risk of being among the Missionaria Protectiva's 'illusions of popular history', suggests a premonitory future in the spirit of the Kwisatz Haderach as 'shortening of the way'.[9]

Figure 12.2 Paul, shrouded in mist, as seen by his mother, Lady Jessica (Rebecca Ferguson).

In precisely this spirit, the *Dune* universe's history unfolds punctuated by the sort of appearances in question, ones 'so unbearable that they threaten reason's ability to go on' (Neiman 41). It does so in three broad stages, over the course of the roughly fifteen millennia of the overall storyline.

The first stage begins with the prehistory reflected indirectly in Paul's initial exchange with the Reverend Mother (and more directly in the 'Brief Timeline of the Dune Universe' in *Hunters* and its authors' various prequel novels). It continues with Paul's story, as reflected in *Dune* and *Messiah*, Kwisatz Haderach turned Emperor, freeing the Fremen, but powerless to prevent the carnage of the ensuing Fremen Jihad across the Known Universe. It continues in turn with the story of Paul and Chani's son, Leto II, as reflected in *Children* and *God Emperor*, a second Kwisatz Haderach who, turned God Emperor this time, institutes a millennia-long, carnage-ridden tyranny over it.

The second stage, as reflected in *Heretics* and *Chapterhouse*, is the story of the 'Scattering' of humanity outside the Known Universe, which results from Leto II's eventual assassination, and the famine and chaos that ensues. More specifically, it's the story of the resulting interstellar conflict that ensues as forces arise that aspire to 'return' to conquer the Known Universe.

The third stage, finally, as reflected in *Hunters* and *Sandworms*, is the story of the long-ago Butlerian Jihad revealed as not having been altogether successful after all, and the return of an old enemy, also vying for domination of the Known Universe, and the rise of a *third* Kwisatz Haderach, and a definitive answer, finally, to the 'shortening of the way [to where?]' question.

'The Good Lord is in the detail', though, as Gustave Flaubert is said to have said, and in this instance in particular, as Villeneuve moves the project forward, it is in those that make for transitions from the first stage to the second, and then from the first and second stages to the third. In laying this out in a bit more detail, perhaps we shorten the way for him in a different sense, even if only a bit.[10]

WHEN A LONG TRAIN . . .

Ten-plus millennia before Paul's birth, the League of Nobles and its Butlerian Jihad overthrew 'centuries of thinking-machine oppression' (*Hunters*, 'Brief Timeline of the Dune Universe'), leaving the Imperium and the Known Universe to be ruled by the Great Houses of the Lansraad, most notably House Atreides and House Harkonnen, ruled in turn by the Padishah Emperor. In the immediate aftermath of the final battle of the Butlerian Jihad, the Battle of Corrin, led by Vorian Atreides and Abulard Harkonnen, the latter is banished for cowardice, establishing the enduring animosity between their respective Houses that is *Dune*'s immediate backdrop.

The longer aftermath sees the 'formation of [the] Bene Gesserit, Suk doctors, Mentats, [and] Swordmasters' (*Hunters*, 'Brief Timeline'). Finally, the 'Foldspace Shipping Company takes the name of Spacing Guild and monopolises space commerce, transport, and interplanetary banking' (*Hunters*, 'Brief Timeline'), resetting recorded time to '1 A.G.', that is 'After Guild', approximately 13,000 AD, a little over a century after the end of the Butlerian Jihad, 201–108 B.G. The same year, in light of the Jihad's 'horrors' (*Hunters*, 'Brief Timeline'), especially the Battle of Corrin, the use of nuclear and biological weaponry against human populations is banned, and the 'Council of Ecumenical Translators releases that Orange Catholic Bible, meant to quell all religious divisions' (*Hunters*, 'Brief Timeline'). In the still longer, indeed millennia-long aftermath, Spacing Guild navigators' reliance on Arrakian 'spice', produced by Arrakis's sandworms, and so only there, means the planet's subjugation and the systematic oppression of its people, the Fremen.

As the storyline reflected in *Dune* and *Messiah* begins, as reflected spectacularly, majestically even, in Villeneuve's film, fifteen years after Paul is born, in the forty-seventh year of the Padishah Emperor's rule, in 10,191 A.G., the Emperor directs House Atreides to relieve House Harkonnen of its stewardship of Arrakis, orchestrating the latter's murderous reprisal, and triggering the revelation that Paul, now Paul-Muad'Dib, is the Kwisatz Haderach. He quickly becomes Emperor Paul-Muad'Dib, liberating the Fremen from Harkonnen bondage, but in the process unleashing a broader Freman Jihad, which conquers the Known Universe, at the expense of tens of billions of lives, which Villeneuve vividly reflects in the snippets from Paul's prescient visions.

In 10,207 A.G., Paul-Muad'Dib and Chani's twins, daughter Ghanima and son Leto II, are born. Having foreseen Chani's death in childbirth, his palpable trauma over the realisation of his prescience triggers a preprogrammed Hayt – a 'ghola' created by Tleilaxu Master Scytale from the remains of Duncan Idaho, legendary warrior of House Atreides and Paul's beloved mentor, fallen in the above conflagration – to attempt to assassinate him. The attempt fails, Hayt regaining his former memories, and so becoming effectively Duncan once again, the first in a long line of Duncan gholas. Paul is blinded and, renouncing his title, walks into the desert to his apparent death, leaving the twins in his sister Alia's care, and her to rule.

As the storyline reflected in *Children* and *God Emperor* begins, roughly a decade has elapsed since Paul-Muad'Dib walked into the desert to die. His promised rehabilitation of Arrakis proceeds, but, at the eventual expense of the worm population, it is realised, and so of spice production. He also did not die, we learn, but is now a mysterious religious figure called 'Preacher', railing against religious governance and unwelcome transformations among the Fremen.

Various machinations lead eventually to renegade Fremen, infiltrated by Gerney Halleck, at now Reverend Mother Jessica's instigation, capturing Leto II. He's forced to drink the 'water of life' and undergo the 'agony' (*Children*, Chapter 39), which heightens his already significant powers of prescience, revealing a 'Golden Path' as the only one of all the possible paths available to humanity that allows for its survival. Sacrificing his own humanity, in 10,217 A.G., by merging with a school of 'sand trout', he becomes a seemingly invincible human/worm hybrid, declaring himself God Emperor. And so begins his three-and-a-half-millennia-long, prescience-driven tyranny, for the sake of the Golden Path, with a succession of Duncan gholas ever by his side, facilitated by his possession of a secret cache of spice, all that's known to remain in the wake of the near-extinction of Arrakis's sandworm population, and the effective cessation of the spice industry that depended on it. Unlike the Fremen Jihad, there's no recorded death toll, but given the Golden Path's duration, we can't help but imagine it exponentially worse.

The millions upon millions of lives lost to earthbound atrocities since the beginning of the last century of *our* second millennium AD make those of us who carry on yearn 'to find order within those appearances so unbearable that they threaten reason's ability to go on' (Neiman 41). Surely, then, the billions upon billions lost across the Imperium, during the eleventh through fourteenth millennia A.G., as a result of the Fremen Jihad and Golden Path, must make for yearning more urgent still. How to 'find order'? In a not untraditional way, it seems.

'It seems to most observers', Spacing Guild Navigator Edric challenges Paul, for example, 'that you conspire to make a god of yourself', which is not obviously 'something that any mortal can do . . . safely?' (*Messiah*, Chapter 9). Having 'asked himself time and again' (*Messiah*, Chapter 9) precisely this, however, 'he had seen enough alternated Timelines to know of worse possibilities. Much worse' (*Messiah*, Chapter 9). Later, in the introductory chapter of *God Emperor*, Leto II describes his Golden Path, which his spice-induced prescience makes available to him, but only to him, as 'the survival of humankind, nothing more nor less' (Chapter 1). No longer merely the better-than-worse-alternatives path, but the best and only one.

Roughly two dozen millennia into the future, it seems that what order's available is broadly Optimistic, as described above. Bad, really bad, reason-paralysingly bad things are happening; we don't want to blame the Emperor, even less the God Emperor, but we don't have to because powerful and prescient as they are, the Imperium must surely be the best it can be, perhaps even the best outright. However bad things may be, then, in our suffering we're contributing to this greater good, and so, in the end, we mustn't blame him, or for that matter complain. But is this merely an illusion, propagated long ago by the Missionaria Protectiva?

PURSUING INVARIABLY . . .

As the storyline reflected in *Heretics* and *God Emperor* begins, a millennium and a half has elapsed since the latest Duncan ghola, with the assistance of Siona, a distant descendant of Ghanima, assassinated Leto II, in 13,725 A.G., leading to widespread famine and the Scattering, an Imperium-wide diaspora of humanity beyond the confines of the Known Universe. Arrakis's climate has reverted in part to its original state, and sandworms have returned, and with them, spice production. As portions of the Scattering begin to return, the Imperium is rife with the interstellar political tension and conflict, primarily between the Bene Gesserit, still committed to some version of the Golden Path, and three forces that have arisen to prominence out of the Scattering.

The Bene Tleilax, on the one hand, a totalitarian theocracy bent on conquering the Known Universe, are known and also reviled for their genetic manipulation. Most conspicuously, and most troublingly, this involves 'axlotl tanks', which are transformed bodies of women who ostensibly volunteer, with which not only gholas are produced, but limited quantities of spice. The Honored Matres, on the other hand, a matriarchal society trained in combat and the sexual domination of men, a technique called 'imprinting', are also bent on conquering the Known Universe. In particular, they want to wipe out the Bene Tleilax, for the obvious affront they and their axlotl tanks represent, and want to assimilate the mystical talents of the Bene Gesserit and do away with them as well. The Ixians, finally, are more pecuniary than political in their designs, able to fabricate so called 'no-ships', capable of spice-less interstellar travel, and in the process of remaining invisible to almost all forms of detection.

The conflict evolves into one primarily between the Bene Gesserit and the Honored Matres, leading to an Honored Matres attack that decimates Arrakis, and so the sandworm population. But a single one remains, which the Bene Gesserit escape with, planning to introduce it into the terraformed landscape of their secret planet, Chapterhouse, in order to recreate there a newly thriving and productive population of sandworms.

Eventually, the Bene Gesserit and the Honored Matres merge under a single leader, Murbella, one of two presumptive Bene Gesserit Mother Superiors, not so much deliberately, as from a confluence of unlikely or at least unpredictable contingencies. And not before more tens of billions perish. Again, the question we can't help but imagine plaguing the Imperium, in the apparent absence of a Kwizatz Haderach – how to 'find order' to preserve 'reason's ability to go on' (Neiman 41).

At first glance, it seems that the Scattering and its deadly aftermath have made a mockery of the optimistic spins Emperor Paul-Muad'Dib and God Emperor Leto II put on the Fremen Jihad and Golden Path. But then we recall Leto II's dying words, that the Scattering was an eventual phase of the Golden Path all along. However credible this may be for the Scattering itself, its aftermath can't help but make for more mockery of Optimism. Unless, that is, this struggle too, however atrocious, is ultimately part of 'shortening [t]he way'.

EVINCES A DESIGN . . .

The final stage in the overall *Dune* storyline begins as *Chapterhouse* ends, with its famous two-pronged cliffhanger, resolved finally, twenty-one maddening years later, in *Hunters* and *Sandworms*.

The Bene Gesserit and Honored Matres's merger wasn't to everyone's liking. In particular, in the final three chapters of the novel, a small group flee in a captured no-ship, led by the latest, and ultimately final Duncan ghola, and Sheeana, the other presumptive Bene Gesserit Mother Superior. With them are a contingent of similarly disaffected Bene Gesserit, the ghola of famed Bene Gesserit military commander Myles Teg, the last of the Ixians, Master Scytale, who has traded his knowledge of azlotl tanks for Bene Gesserit sanctuary, and finally, a Rabbi and his congregation. That's one prong: 'the next phase', as former Mother Superior Darwi Odrade says to her successor, Murbella, 'Muad'Dib to Tyrant to Honored Matres to us to Sheeana . . . to what?' (*Chapterhouse*, Chapter 47).

The other prong, more mysterious still, involves the realisation, at the very moment of escape from Chapterhouse, of an obscure vision Duncan's been having, of a 'shimmering net undulating like an infinite borealis [. . .] and the elderly couple defined by criss-crossed lines' (*Chapterhouse*, Chapters 10 and 21), Daniel and Marty, as we come to know them in the final chapter, 'sens[ing] godlike stability in these people, but [also] something common about them [in their] by-now-familiar garden landscape stretched out behind them[, who] belonged to no one but themselves' (*Chapterhouse*, Chapter 21). Clearing the surface, '[t]here they were: the old couple in their garden setting [and] the net shimmering in front of them, the man gesturing at it, smiling in round-faced satisfaction[, his] lips shap[ing the] words [. . .] "*We expected you*"' (*Chapterhouse*, Chapter 46). They move to capture the *Ithaca*, as the ship will come to be known, on the assumption that among them is the Kwisatz Haderach, but Duncan manages to fold space, albeit unusually, leaving them safe, but an 'unidentifiable ship in an unidentifiable universe' (*Chapterhouse*, Chapter 46).

What we're treated to as we move into the concluding 'Dune 7' sequels, *Hunters* and *Sandworms*, amid the cast-of-thousands world-building we've come to expect, is a surprising return to the Dune Universe's prehistory. The Butlerian Jihad didn't succeed definitively after all, that is, Daniel and Marty being in reality surviving thinking machines Omnius and Erasmus. Omnius was the central figure in the subjugation of humanity in the pre-Jihad era, and Erasmus, originally Omnius's subordinate, later an 'independent robot' (*Hunters*, Chapter 97), was ultimately responsible for sparking the Jihad in the first place, by killing Serena Butler's child. They survived, reassembled the 'Synchonized Empire', and have returned, millennia later, overwhelming forces arrayed, to annihilate, or at least re-subjugate, humanity.

At risk of slighting the fantastic complexity of the lead-up, what's most important in this context, in coming to grips with whether the overall *Dune* storyline is more optimistically than conventionally tragic, is the resolution and aftermath of 'Kralizek', referred to in passing in *Children* as a foretold 'Typhoon Struggle', which 'live[s] in [Fremen's] hearts' (*Children*, Chapter 12) and now as the actually occurring 'battle at the end of the universe' (*Hunters*, Chapter 2). Murbella, now fully in control of the now fully consolidated Bene Gesserit and Honored Matres, stages a momentous last stand, which, sabotaged, fails. A mysterious figure appears again, however, who we'd seen return the *Ithaca* to regular space three years after it left Chapterhouse, the Oracle of Time, formerly Norma Senva.

Born shortly before the Butlerian Jihad, Norma Senva is responsible for much of the scientific and technological discovery the Guild's space-travel prowess is built upon, even while Tio Holtzman ultimately took credit for it. In the years following the Guild's creation, as a result of both her discovery and use of it, as the first fold-space navigator, together with her Sorceresses of Rossak lineage, she evolves into the disembodied, mystically powerful, and seemingly eternal Oracle of Time, the Guild's protector, its navigators in particular. She reemerges now, to save Murbella's resistance, decimating the thinking-machine forces arrayed, and departing then for Synchrony, the planet capital of the Synchronized Empire, where Omnius and Erasmus reside, and where they've brought the finally captured *Ithaca*, which has come to include a wider assortment of gholas, many of whom have been central to the overall storyline, including in particular those of Paul, Chani, and Lady Jessica.

The immediate thinking-machine threat thwarted, thanks to the Oracle of Time, the overarching one from the Synchonize Empire persists, Kralizek's resolution still pending, depending on what Erasmus does now, in Omnius's absence, in particular with respect to the long-sought Kwisatz Haderach, long thought by Omnius to be essential to thinking-machine victory. At the risk, again, of slighting the storyline, what is revealed is that the assumption that Paul's ghola would be the new Kwisatz Haderach, as the original Paul had been, and as his son Leto had been afterward, is mistaken. It turns out that Duncan, the latest in a long line of Duncan gholas is the Kwisatz Haderach, the 'ultimate and final' one (*Sandworms*, Chapter 76), the one who's *finally* the 'shortening of the way', the *to where* question final answered.

Erasmus's long fascination with the what's-it-like-to-be-human question, the answer forever eluding him in his current form, and Duncan's desire to end machine-human antagonism leads to their merger, the death of Erasmus as he has existed, but his persistence in Duncan, now no longer strictly human, a human-machine-hybrid Kwisatz Haderach, as Leto II had been a human-sandworm-hybrid Kwisatz Haderach. Arrakis's sandworms, thought to have been destroyed as a result of an Honored Matres attack on the Bene Gesserit, survived after all, a 'pearl' of Leto II's consciousness in each of them, and so of his prescience, anticipating the attack, burrowing far below the surface of the planet, and emerging now to the 'desert planet' we were introduced to in *Dune*. Duncan, as Kwisatz Haderach, exponentially more powerful than his predecessors, all the more for having assimilated Erasmus, and so assuming command of thinking machines across the Synchronized Empire, busies himself remaking and otherwise making peace across the Known Universe. Paul and Chani return to Arrakis, to live out their 'content to be [m]odern-day Fremen' lives (*Sandworms*, Epilogue). 'My Shihaya', Paul says to her, concluding the overall storyline, 'I have loved you for five thousand years' (*Sandworms*, Epilogue).

IN THEIR END IS THEIR BEGINNING

With this, the project's final scene cannot help but begin to take shape. Moved by Paul's testimony, Chani lowers her gaze ever so slightly, a shyly knowing expression developing on her face, and we see in their mind's eye the prescient vision of the way finally shortened, of their lives together, to the end, in this 'better future' (Figure 12.3). Fade to optimistic black.[11]

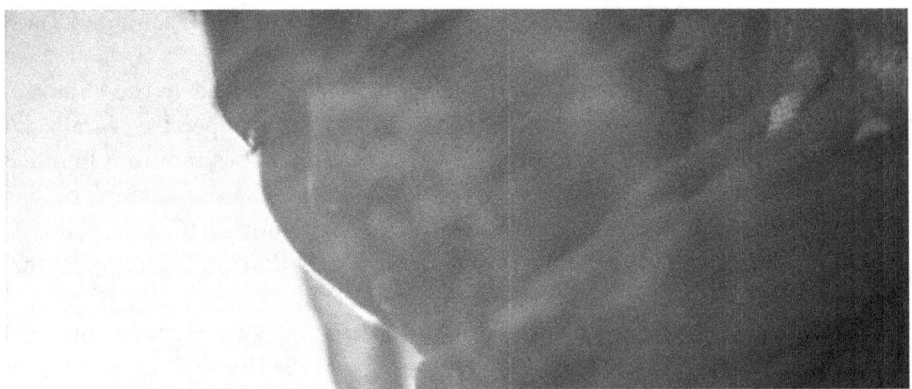

Figure 12.3 Chani (Zendaya) as imagined by Paul in the final scene.

NOTES

1. Child, Ben, 'Denis Villeneuve's Dune could be the version we've all been waiting for', *The Guardian*, 10 September 2020.
2. Page, Thomas, 'It's Denis Villeneuve's *Dune* Now', *CNN Style*, 22 October 2021.
3. The editions used here are, for the first six, New York: Ace Books, and for the seventh and eighth, New York: Tor Books, all in ebook form. For ease of reading, in what follows sequel titles are referred to in abbreviated form, as *Messiah*, *Children*, *God Emperor*, *Heretics*, *Chapterhouse*, *Hunters*, and *Sandworms*. Passages included are identified by abbreviated title and by the chapter in which the passage occurs.
4. Wharton, Edith, *French Ways and Their Meaning*, New York/London, D. Appleton and Company, 1919, available at: https://www.gutenberg.org/files/57786/57786-h/57786-h.htm (last accessed 12 December 2021).
5. Neiman, Susan, 'What Is the Problem of Evil', *Rethinking Evil: Contemporary Perspectives*, edited by Maria Pia Lara, University of California Press, 2001, pp. 27–45. The view is laid out more comprehensively in *Evil in Modern Thought: An Alternate History of Philosophy*, Princeton University Press, 2002.
6. Lerner, Melvin, *The Belief in a Just World: A Fundamental Delusion*, New York, Springer, 1980.
7. The closest Villeneuve's *Dune* comes is Jessica's phrase 'preparing the way', but the reference is not to the Kwisatz Haderach, but to what 'the Bene Gesserit have been at work' doing, that is, fomenting anticipation of the Lisan al-Gaib.
8. Spaihts, Jon, Denis Villeneuve and Eric Roth, Dune: *Screenplay, Based on the Novel Dune by Frank Herbert*, Salmon Revisions, Final Shooting Script, 19 June 2020, available at: https://www.duneinfo.com/caladan/script-index (last accessed 2 December 2021).
9. Villeneuve's film departs from Herbert's novel in other substantive ways as well, some relevant to the present perspective, but left out for economy's sake. The banquet scene, for example, in chapter sixteen, roughly two-thirds of the way through part one, which Villeneuve must have known was an omission from Lynch's earlier adaptation that Herbert disapproved of, but repeated nonetheless. For another, Liet-Kynes's death occurs in a more complex way in the novel, tied to the prescience and ecology themes that course through the original more overtly than Villeneuve himself reflects.
10. No assumption is made here as to how many of the sequels Villeneuve has read, nor his fellow scriptwriters, Eric Roth and Jon Spaihts. For Villeneuve's part in particular, there's reason to believe that he's more likely to have read the earlier ones than the later ones, the last two in particular. 'The idea', he tells Page elsewhere in the above interview, 'was to try to bring back to the surface those images that I had in my mind when I (first) read the book – those uncorrupted images that I had at thirteen years old', which he turned on 3 October 1980. By then, *Messiah* and *Children* had appeared, as *God Emperor* would as well soon, on 28 May 1981, roughly midway between his thirteenth and fourteenth birthdays. Given the impression that *Dune* clearly made on him, it is easy enough to imagine that he read the available sequels as well at the time, perhaps also *Heretics* and *Chapterhouse* when they appeared, in 1984 and 1985. It seems less likely that he read *Hunters* and *Sandworms*, however, when they appeared at least, in 2006 and 2007, midway through the five-year process of writing the screenplay for *Incendies* (2010), based on Wajdi Mouawad's play of the same name (2003), during which time he also directed three films, the first and third of which he also wrote: *120 Seconds to Get Elected* (2006), *Next Door* (2008), and *Polytechnique* (2009).

11. I am as ever profoundly grateful to Susan Neiman for my interest in, understanding of, and commitment to the problem of evil. I am also grateful to the Pacific Ancient and Modern Language Association (PAMLA), and its Executive Director in particular, Craig Svonkin, for allowing me to organise for the 2021 Annual Convention a '*Dune*: From Herbert's to Villeneuve's' panel, and to my fellow presenters, Mercedes Diaz, Andrea Marshall and Jerry Piven, for their fascinating contributions. I am grateful as well to the folks in my Fall 2021 'The Problem of Evil in Philosophy and Popular Culture' seminar, for their insights into the film and in general, Elie Kapengut, Amay Mehta and Tomaima Yousef in particular. Finally, I am very grateful to this volume's editors for their patience, far above and beyond the call.

Filmography

Villeneuve, Denis, director, *Un 32 août sur terre*, France Film, 1998.
--- *Maëlstrom*, Alliance Atlantis, 2000.
--- *Polytechnique*, Remstar Media Partners/Alliance Vivafilm, 2008.
--- *Incendies*, Les films Christal, 2010.
--- *Enemy*, Entertainment One, 2013.
--- *Prisoners*, Warner Bros Pictures, 2013.
--- *Sicario*, Lionsgate, 2015.
--- *Arrival*, Paramount Pictures/Sony Pictures Releasing International/Stage 6 Films, 2016.
--- *Blade Runner 2049*, Warner Bros Pictures, 2017.
--- *Dune: Part 1*, Warner Bros Pictures, 2021.

Bibliography

Adleman, Leonard M. (1998), 'Computing with DNA', *Scientific American*, vol. 279, no. 2, pp. 54–61.
Alber, Jan (2013), 'Unnatural Narratology: Developments and Perspectives', *Germanisch-Romanische Monatsschrift*, edited by Ansgar Nünning, vol. 63, no. 1, pp. 69–84.
Alber, Jan, Stefan Iversen, Henrik Skov Nielsen and Brian Richardson (2013), 'Introduction', *A Poetics of Unnatural Narrative*, edited by Jan Alber, Henrik Skov Nielsen and Brian Richardson, Columbus: Ohio State University Press, pp. 1–15.
Albrecht-Crane, Christa (2005), 'Style/Stutter', in *Deleuze: Key Concepts*, edited by Charles J. Stivale, Montreal: McGill-Queen's University Press.
Alioff, Maurie (1998), 'Denis Villeneuve's *Un 32 aout sur terre*: Lost in the Desert', *Take One: Film & Television in Canada*, no. 21, pp. 29–31.
--- (1997), 'Cosmos: The World According to Frappier', *Take One*, no. 17, Fall, pp. 24–33.
Amsdem, Cynthia (2001), '*Maelström* – Much Ado about a Fish', *Take One*, no. 29, Winter, pp. 22–4.
Andrade, Pilar (2008), 'Cinema's Doubles, their Meaning and Literary Intertexts', *Comparative Literature and Culture*, vol. 10, no. 4, article 8.
Atwood, Margaret (2003), *Oryx and Crake*, Toronto: McClelland & Stewart.
Babuta, Alexander and Marion Oswald (2020), 'Data analytics and algorithms in policing in England and Wales: Towards a new policy framework', *Royal United User Services Institute Occasional Paper*, commissioned by the Centre for Data Ethics and Innovation, 23 February, available at: https://researchportal.northumbria.ac.uk/en/publications/data-analytics-and-algorithms-in-policing-in-england-and-wales-to (last accessed 23 February 2020).

Backe, Emma Louise (2017), 'Replicants and Reproduction: *Blade Runner 2049* and Sci Fi's Obsession with Motherhood', *The Geek Anthropologist*, 19 October, available at: https://thegeekanthropologist.com/2017/10/19/replicants-and-reproduction-blade-runner-2049-and-sci-fis-obsession-with-motherhood (last accessed 15 September 2020).

Barrette, Pierre (1998), 'Le désert de l'âme/ *Un 32 août sur Terre* de Denis Villeneuve', *24 images*, no. 95, p. 51.

--- (2006), 'Made in Québec: Le cinéma québécois, entre imitation et critique du modèle hollywoodien', *24 images*, no. 128, pp. 17–18.

Baugh, Bruce (1992), 'Transcendental Empiricism: Deleuze's Response to Hegel', *Man and World*, vol. 25, no. 2, April, pp. 133–48.

Bazin, André (1946), 'The Myth of Total Cinema', *What Is Cinema*, 2 vols (1967), translated by Hugh Gray, Berkeley: University of California Press, pp. 23–7.

Beaulieu, Simon (2004), '*Ma voisine danse le ska*' (review), *Séquences*, no. 229, January–February, p. 54.

Bellour, Raymond (1987), 'The Pensive Spectator (1984)', translated by Lynne Kirby, *Wide Angle*, vol. 9, no. 1, pp. 6–10.

Berardi, Franco, Gary Genosko and Nicholas Thoburn (2011), *After the Future*, Chico, CA: AK Press.

Bertin, Raymond (2010), 'Prendre une pièce pour un scénario: entretiens avec Philippe Falardeau et Denis Villeneuve', *Jeu*, no. 134, pp. 65–72.

Blais, Mélissa, Francis Dupuis-Déri, Lyne Kurtzman and Dominique Payette (eds) (2010), *Retour sur un attentat antiféministe: École Polytechnique de Montréal, 6 décembre 1989*, Montreal: Remue-ménage.

Bombarda, Olivier (2015), 'David Lynch – Mulholland Drive – Sujet: Olivier Bombarda', YouTube, 2 December, available at: https://www.youtube.com/watch?v=xh_AernWIck (last accessed 1 December 2020).

Bordwell, David (2007), *Poetics of Cinema*, New York: Routledge.

Bouchard, Gérard (2005), 'L'imaginaire de la grande noirceur et de la révolution tranquille: fictions identitaires et jeux de mémoire au Québec', *Recherches sociographiques*, vol. 46, no. 3, pp. 411–36.

Bouchard, Gérard, and Richard Lalou (1993), 'La surfécondité des couples québécois depuis le XVIIe siècle, essai de mesure d'interprétation', *Recherches sociographiques*, vol. 34, no. 1, pp. 9–44.

Brookner, Will (ed.) (2005), *The Blade Runner Experience*, London/New York: Wallflower Press.

Boym, Svetlana (2001), *The Future of Nostalgia*, New York: Basic Books, 2001.

Brinkema, Eugenie (2021), 'Form', in *A Concise Companion to Visual Culture*, edited by A. Joan Saab, Aubrey Anable and Catherine Zuromskis, Wiley Blackwell, pp. 259–76.

--- (2014), *The Forms of the Affects*, Durham, NC: Duke University Press.
Brion, David Davis (2014), 'Slavery, Sex, and Dehumanization', in *Sex, Power, and Slavery*, edited by Gwyn Campbell and Elizabeth Elbourne, Athens, OH: Ohio University Press.
Brookes, N. Christine (2018), 'South of the 49th Parallel: Denis Villeneuve's *Sicario* (2015)', *Québec Studies*, vol. 65, no. 1, pp. 149–67.
Bryant, Levi R (2008), *Difference and Givenness: Deleuze's Transcendental Empiricism and the Ontology of Immanence*, Evanston: Northwestern University Press, 2008.
Buckland, Warren (2014), 'Introduction: Ambiguity, Ontological Pluralism, and Cognitive Dissonance in the Hollywood Puzzle Film', *Hollywood Puzzle Films*, edited by Warren Buckland, New York: Routledge, pp. 1–14.
Bukatman, Scott (1997), *Blade Runner*, British Film Institute, p. 17.
Bunce, Robin (2017), '*Blade Runner 2049*'s politics resonate because they are so perilously close to our own', *The New Statesman*, 16 October, available at: https://www.newstatesman.com/culture/film/2017/10/blade-runner-2049-s-politics-resonate-because-they-are-so-perilously-close-our (last accessed 15 September 2020).
Bunce, Robin and Trip McCrossin (eds) (2019), *Blade Runner 2049 and Philosophy: This Breaks the World*, Chicago: Open Court.
Calder, Todd (2020), 'The Concept of Evil', *The Stanford Encyclopaedia of Philosophy*, Summer, edited by Edward N. Zalta, available at: https://plato.stanford.edu/archives/sum2020/entries/concept-evil (last accessed 20 March 2021).
Campbell, Ian (2020), 'Metafiction and *Pale Fire* in *Blade Runner 2049*', *The Projector: A Journal on Film, Media, and Culture*, available at: https://www.theprojectorjournal.com/campbell-metafiction-and-pale-fire (last accessed 15 September 2020).
Caron, André (2017), '*Blade Runner 2049*: Si seulement tu voyais le même film que j'ai vu', *Séquences*, no. 311, p. 23.
Carroll, Noel (1987), 'The Nature of Horror', *The Journal of Aesthetics and Art Criticism*, vol. 46, no. 1, Fall, pp. 51–9.
--- (1990), *Philosophy of Horror: or Paradoxes of the Heart*, London: Routledge.
Carruthers, Anne (2018), 'Temporality, Reproduction and the Not-Yet in Denis Villeneuve's *Arrival*', *Film-Philosophy*, vol. 22, no. 3, October, pp. 321–39.
Castiel, Élie (1997), '*Cosmos*: les risques du métier', *Séquences*, no. 188, January–February, pp. 22–4.
Chan, Edward (2020), 'Race in the *Blade Runner* cycle and demographic dystopia', *Science Fiction Film and Television*, vol. 13, no. 1, Spring, pp. 59–76.

Chartier, Daniel (2009), 'Le Cinéma du pays de la neige devient pluriculturel', *Études romanes*, vol. 59, pp. 141–53.
Chiang, Ted (2016), 'Story of Your Life', in *Stories of Your Life and Others*, New York: Vintage, pp. 91–146.
Child, Ben (2020), 'Denis Villeneuve's Dune could be the version we've all been waiting for', *The Guardian*, 10 September.
Comte, Joanne (1994), 'Denis Villeneuve – Portrait surréaliste d'un cerveaunaute en vol', *Séquences*, no. 175, p. 11.
Coulombe, Michel (1997), 'De quelques histoires inventées, ou le cinéma québécois des années 90', *Ciné-Bulles*, vol. 16, no. 2, pp. 30–5.
Creed, Barbara (1986), 'Horror and the Monstrous-Feminine: An Imaginary Abjection', *Screen*, vol. 27, no. 1, January/February, pp. 44–71.
— (1993), *The Monstrous-Feminine: Film, Feminism, Psychoanalysis*, London/New York: Routledge.
Culler, Jonathan (1975), *Structuralist Poetics: Structuralism, Linguistics and the Study of Literature*, London: Routledge, Kegan Paul.
Czach, Liz (2020), 'The Quebec Heritage Film', *Cinema of Pain: On Quebec's Nostalgic Screen*, edited by Liz Czach and André Loiselle, Waterloo, ON: Wilfrid Laurier University Press, pp. 41–60.
De Zwann, Victoria (2009), 'Slipstream', in *The Routledge Companion to Science Fiction*, edited by Mark Bould, New York: Routledge, pp. 500–4.
Debruge, Peter (2017), 'Film Review: *Blade Runner 2049*', *Variety*, 29 September, available at: https://variety.com/2017/film/reviews/blade-runner-2049-review-1202576220 (last accessed 28 June 2021).
Defoy, Stéphane (2010), 'Denis Villeneuve, scénariste et réalisateur d'*Incendies*', *Ciné-Bulles*, vol. 28, no. 4, pp. 42–7.
— (2009), 'Exorciser le mal: *Polytechnique* de Denis Villeneuve', *Ciné-Bulles*, vol. 27, no. 2, pp. 22–3.
Deleuze, Gilles (2001), *The Fold*, translated by Tom Conley, London/New York: Continuum.
— (1983), *L'Image-Mouvement*, Paris: Éditions de Minuit.
— (1985), *L'image-Temps, Cinéma 2*, Paris: Éditions de Minuit.
Dequen, Bruno (2010), 'Au mauvais endroit: *Incendies* de Denis Villeneuve', *24 images*, no. 148, p. 62.
— (2011), 'Table ronde sur le renouveau du cinéma québécois', *Nouvelles Vues: revue sur les pratiques et les théories du cinéma au Québec*, edited by Jean-Pierre Sirois-Trahan and Thomas Carrier-Lafleur, no. 12, Spring–Summer.
Dick, Philip K. (1968), *Do Androids Dream of Electric Sheep?*, New York: Doubleday.
Doane, Mary-Ann (1999), 'Technophilia: Technology, Representation and the Feminine', *Cybersexualities: A Reader on Feminist Theory, Cyborgs and*

Cyberspace, edited by Jenny Wolmark, Edinburgh: Edinburgh University Press, pp 20–33.
--- (2003), 'The Close-up: Scale and Detail in the Cinema', *Differences: A Journal of Feminist Cultural Studies*, vol. 14, no. 3, pp. 89–111.
Dupont, Louis (1995), '*L'américanité* in Quebec in the 1980s: Political and Cultural Considerations of an Emerging Discourse', *American Review of Canadian Studies*, vol. 25, no. 1, pp. 27–52.
Dyer, Richard (1997), *White: Essays on Race and Culture*, London/New York: Routledge.
Eco, Umberto (1985), '*Casablanca*: Cult Movies and Intertextual Collage', *Substance*, vol. 14, no. 2, issue 47, pp. 3–12.
Edelman, Lee (2004), *No Future: Queer Theory and the Death Drive*, Durham, NC: Duke University Press.
Elsaesser, Thomas (2009), 'The Mind-Game Film', *Puzzle Films: Complex Storytelling in Contemporary Cinema*, edited by Warren Buckland, Malden: Wiley-Blackwell, pp. 13–41.
--- (2014), 'Actions Have Consequences: David Lynch's L.A.-Trilogie', *AugenBlick: Konstanzer Hefte zur Medienwissenschaft*, vol. 59, pp. 50–70.
--- (2021), *The Mind-Game Film: Distributed Agency, Time Travel, and Productive Pathology*, London/New York: Routledge.
Epstein, Jean (1921), *Bonjour Cinéma*, Paris: Éditions de la Sirène.
Escobar, Matthew (2016), *The Persistence of the Human: Consciousness, Meta-body and Survival in Contemporary Film and Literature*, Lieden: Brill Rodopi.
Fancher, Hampton and Green, Michael (2017), *Blade Runner 2049: Final Shooting Script*, The Script Savant, available at: https://thescriptsavant.com/pdf/blade_runner%20(2049).pdf (last accessed 15 September 2020).
Fedosik, Marina (2019), 'The Power to "Make Live": Biopolitics and Reproduction in *Blade Runner 2049*', *Adoption & Culture*, vol. 7, no. 2, pp. 169–75.
Finol, Luis (2017), '*Enemy*: La Ciudad Como Escenario Fantástico', *Brumal: Revista de Investigación Sobre lo Fantástico*, vol. 5, no. 2, pp. 107–31.
Fleming, David H. (2020), 'Race and World Memory in *Arrival*', *Science Fiction Film and Television*, vol. 13, no. 2, Summer, pp. 247–67.
Fleming, David H. and William Brown (2018), 'Through a (First) Contact Lens Darkly: *Arrival*, Unreal Time and Chthulucinema,' *Film Philosophy*, vol. 22, no. 3, October, pp. 340–63.
Fletcher, Rosie and Sam Ashurst (2017), 'Can we talk about *Blade Runner 2049*'s problem with women?', *DigitalSpy*, 9 October, available at: https://www.digitalspy.com/movies/a839916/blade-runner-2049-gender-issues (last accessed 28 June 2021).

Foulkes, Sarah (2017), 'On Fertile Ground: The Pregnant Women in Denis Villeneuve's Cinema', *Film School Rejects*, 31 October, available at; https://filmschoolrejects.com/pregnant-women-in-denis-villeneuves-cinema (last accessed 21 June 2021).
Fournier, Daniel (1989), 'Pourquoi la revanche des berceaux? L'hypothèse de la sociabilité', *Recherches sociographiques*, vol. 30, no. 2, pp. 171–98.
Fournier, Marcel (2001), 'Quebec Sociology and Quebec Society: The Construction of a Collective Identity', *The Canadian Journal of Sociology*, vol. 26, no. 3, pp. 333–47.
Freeland, Cynthia (1999), *The Naked and the Undead: Evil and the Appeal of Horror*, Boulder: Westview Press.
Freud, Sigmund (1919), *The Uncanny*, New York: Penguin [2003].
Gaudin, Antoine (2015), *L'Espace cinématographique*, Paris: Armand Colin.
Gaudreault, André and François Jost (1990), *Le récit cinématographique*, Paris: Nathan.
Gendron, Thierry (1997), '*Cosmos*' (review), *Ciné-Bulles*, vol. 15, no. 4, pp. 57–8.
Gervais, Stéphan (2016), Christopher Kirkey, and Jarrett Rudy (eds), *Quebec Questions: Quebec Studies for the Twenty-first Century*, 2nd edition, Toronto: Oxford University Press.
Glazier, Michael and Monika Hellwig (2004), *The Modern Catholic Encyclopedia*, vol. 13, rev. and exp. ed., Collegeville: Liturgical Press.
Gomel, Elana (2018), 'Recycled Dystopias: Cyberpunk and the End of History', *Arts*, vol. 7, no. 3.
Gomes, Victor (2019), 'The Science Behind *Blade Runner*'s Voight-Kampff Test', *Nautilus*, 15 July, available at: https://nautil.us/blog/-the-science-behind-blade-runners-voight_kampff-test (last accessed 1 September 2020).
Green, Mary-Jean (2012), 'Denis Villeneuve's *Incendies*: From Word to Image', *Québec Studies*, vol. 54, Fall 2012/Winter 2013, pp. 103–10.
Green, Michael (2019), 'The Replicant Singularity in *Blade Runner 2049*', *Film International*, vol. 17, no. 1, March, pp. 33–9.
Grobar, Matt (2018), '*Blade Runner 2049* Cinematographer Roger Deakins Made Light "Feel Alive" With Computer-Controlled Rigs', *Deadline*, 26 February, available at: https://deadline.com/2018/02/blade-runner-2049-roger-deakins-oscars-cinematography-interview-1202280774 (last accessed 20 February 2020).
Gumbrecht, Hans Ulrich (2015), 'Philology and the Complex Present', *Florilegium*, vol. 32, pp. 273–81.
Guynes, Sean (2020), 'Dystopia Fatigue Doesn't Cut It, or *Blade Runner 2049*'s Utopian Longings', *Science Fiction Film and Television*, vol. 13, no. 1, Spring, pp. 143–8.
Gwaltney, Marilyn (1991), 'Androids as a Device for Reflection on Personhood', *Retrofitting Blade Runner: Issues in Ridley Scott's* Blade

Runner *and Philip K. Dick's* Do Androids Dream of Electric Sheep?, edited by Judith B Kerman, Madison: University of Wisconsin Press, 1997, pp. 32–40.

Haraway, Donna (1987), 'Manifesto for Cyborgs: Science, Technology, and Socialist Feminism in the 1980s', *Australian Feminist Studies*, vol. 2, no. 4, pp. 1–42.

--- (2016), *Staying With the Trouble: Making Kin in the Chthulucene*, Durham, NC: Duke University Press.

--- (2016), 'Tentacular Thinking: Anthropocene, Capitalocene, Chthulucene', *E-flux*, no. 75, September, available at: https://www.e-flux.com/journal/75/67125/tentacular-thinking-anthropocene-capitalocene-chthulucene (last accessed 28 June 2021).

Harel, Simon (2014), 'Sur la banquette arrière d'un taxi montréalais: à propos de *Cosmos* (1996)', *Études littéraires*, vol. 45, no. 2, pp. 63–72.

Herbert, Brian and Kevin Anderson (2006), *Hunters of Dune*, New York: Tor Books.

--- (2007), *Sandworms of Dune*, New York: Tor Books.

Herbert, Frank (1965), *Dune*, New York: Ace Books.

--- (1969), *Dune Messiah*, New York: Ace Books.

--- (1976), *Children of Dune*, New York: Ace Books.

--- (1981), *God Emperor of Dune*, New York: Ace Books.

--- (1981), *Heretics of Dune*, New York: Ace Books.

--- (1985), *Chapterhouse: Dune*, New York: Ace Books.

Heersmink, Richard and Christopher Jude McCarroll (2020), 'The Best Memories: Identity, Narrative and Objects', in *Blade Runner 2049: A Philosophical Exploration*, edited by Timothy Shanahan and Paul Smart, London/New York: Routledge, pp. 87–107.

Heidegger, Martin (1977), *The Question Concerning Technology and Other Essays*, New York: Harper and Row, 1977.

Hildebrandt, Mireille (2016), 'The New Imbroglio: Living with Machine Algorithms', *The Art of Ethics in the Information Society*, edited by Liisa Janssens, Amsterdam: Amsterdam University Press, pp. 55–60.

Hills, Matt (2003), 'An Event Based Definition of Art-Horror', *Dark Thoughts: Philosophic Reflections on Cinematic Horror*, edited by Steven Jay Schneider and Daniel Shaw, Lanham: Scarecrow Press.

Hjort, Mette and Duncan Petrie (2007), 'Introduction', in *The Cinema of Small Nations*, edited by Mette Hjort and Duncan Petrie, Indiana: Indiana University Press, pp. 1–19.

Holden, Stephen (2002), 'Film Review: Fathoming Meaning From a Talking Fish', *The New York Times*, 25 January.

Hoquet, Thierry (2014), 'Cyborg, Mutant, Robot, etc.: Essai de typologie des presque-humains', *Post Humains: Frontières, évolutions, hybridités*, edited by Elaine Després and Hélène Machinal, Rennes: Presses Universitaires de Rennes, pp. 99–118.

Horne, Brian (2003), 'On the Representation of Evil in Modern Literature', *New Blackfriars*, vol. 84, no. 983, pp. 30–42.

Huskinson, Lucy (2016), 'Introduction: The Urban Uncanny', *The Urban Uncanny: A Collection of Interdisciplinary Studies*, edited by Huskinson, London/New York: Routledge, pp. 1–17.

Jack's Movie Reviews (2018), '*Blade Runner 2049* – The Evolution of Humanity', YouTube, 6 January, available at: https://www.youtube.com/watch?v=LxIBv_XS3ls&ab_channel=Jack%27sMovieReviews (last accessed 28 June 2021).

Jackson, Zakiyyah Iman (2020), *Becoming Human: Matter and Meaning in an Antiblack World*, New York: New York University Press.

Jacobson, Brian R. (2016), '*Ex Machina* in the Garden', *Film Quarterly*, vol. 69, no. 4, Summer pp. 23–34.

Jameson, Fredric (1991), *Postmodernism, or The Cultural Logic of Late Capitalism*, Durham, NC: Duke University Press.

Khatchatourian, Manne (2014), 'Ridley Scott: *Blade Runner* Sequel is Best Script Harrison Ford Has "Ever Read"', *Variety*, 13 December, available at: https://variety.com/2014/film/news/harrison-ford-loves-blade-runner-2-script-1201378743 (last accessed 27 February 2021).

Kim, Sharon (2019), '*Pale Fire*: Human Image and Post-human Desire in *Blade Runner 2049*', *Journal of Science Fiction*, vol. 3, no. 3, November, pp. 8–19.

Kiss, Miklós, and Steven Willemsen (2017), *Impossible Puzzle Films: A Cognitive Approach to Contemporary Complex Cinema*, Edinburgh: Edinburgh University Press.

Klecker, Cornelia (2013), 'Mind-Tricking Narratives: Between Classical and Art-Cinema Narration', *Poetics Today*, vol. 34, no. 1–2, pp. 119–46.

Knight, Deborah, and George McKnight (2003), 'American Psycho: Horror, Satire, Aesthetics, and Identification', *Dark Thoughts: Philosophic Reflections on Cinematic Horror*, edited by Steven Jay Schneider and Daniel Shaw, Lanham: Scarecrow Press, pp. 212–30.

Kohen-Raz, Odeya and Meiri, Sandra (2018), 'Revisiting Metz: bodiless-character films and the dynamic of desire/fantasy in narrative cinema', *New Review of Film and Television Studies*, vol. 16, no.1, pp. 62–80.

Korthals Altes, Liesbeth (2014), *Ethos and Narrative Interpretation: The Negotiation of Values in Fiction*, Lincoln, NE: University of Nebraska Press.

Kotte, Claudia (2014), 'Zero Degrees of Separation: Post-Exilic Return in Denis Villeneuve's *Incendies*', *Cinematic Homecomings: Exile and Return in Transnational Cinema*, edited by Rebecca Prime, London: Bloomsbury Academic, pp. 287–302.

Kurzweil, Ray (1999), *The Age of Spiritual Machines*, New York: Viking Books.
--- (2005), *The Singularity is Near*, New York: Viking Books.
--- (2012), *How to Create a Mind: The Secret of Human Thought Revealed*, New York: Viking Books.
Lahaie, Christiane (1997), '*Cosmos*: une drôle de promenade en taxi,' *Québec français*, no. 105, pp. 98–9.
Lambie, Ryan (2015), 'Denis Villeneuve Interview: *Sicario*, Kurosawa, Sci-Fi, Ugly Poetry', *Den of Geek*, 24 September, available at: https://www.denofgeek.com/movies/denis-villeneuve-interview-sicario-kurosawa-sci-fi-ugly-poetry (last accessed 3 March 2021).
Lansky, Sam (2016), 'In *Arrival*, Amy Adams Takes a Listening Tour of the Universe', *Time*, 10 November, available at: https://time.com/4565975/amy-adams-arrival (last accessed 28 June 2021).
Latimer, Heather (2021), 'A queer pregnancy: affective kinship, time travel and reproductive choice in Denis Villeneuve's *Arrival*', *Feminist Theory*, vol. 22, no. 3, pp. 429–42.
Lavik, Erlend (2006), 'Narrative Structure in *The Sixth Sense*: A New Twist in "Twist Movies"?', *The Velvet Light Trap*, vol. 58, pp. 55–64.
Lavoie, André (2000), '*Maelström* de Denis Villeneuve', *Ciné-Bulles. Le cinéma d'auteur avant tout*, vol. 19, no. 1, Fall, pp. 61–2.
Leindecker, Bernd (2018), 'Taking Split Personalities to the Next Level: Perturbatory Narration in *Enemy*', *Perturbatory Narration in Film: Narratological Studies on Deception, Paradox and Empuzzlement*, edited by Sabine Schlickers and Vera Toro, Berlin/Boston: De Gruyter, pp. 199–208.
Lerner, Melvin (1980), *The Belief in a Just World: A Fundamental Delusion*, New York: Springer.
Like Stories of Old (2018), 'In Search of the Distinctly Human/the Philosophy of *Blade Runner 2049*.' YouTube, 29 January, available at: https://www.youtube.com/watch?v=O4etinsAy34&ab_channel=LikeStoriesofOld (last accessed 28 June 2021).
Lewis, Helen (2017), '*Blade Runner 2049* is an Uneasy Feminist Parable About Controlling the Means of Reproduction', *The New Statesman*, 9 October, available at: https://www.newstatesman.com/culture/film/2017/10/blade-runner-2049-uneasy-feminist-parable-about-controlling-means-reproduction (last accessed 28 June 2021).
Loiselle, André (2007), *Cinema as History: Michel Brault and Modern Quebec*, Toronto: Toronto International Film Festival Group.
Loiselle, Marie-Claude (1997), 'Téléfilm Canada ou le règne de la bêtise.' *24 images*, no. 88–9, p. 3
--- (2001), 'Au-delà des apparences: *Maelström* de Denis Villeneuve', *24 images*, vol. 105, p. 49.

--- (2005), 'Éditorial.' *24 images*, no. 121, p. 3.
Longfellow, Brenda (2004), 'Counter-Narratives, Class Politics, and Metropolitan Dystopias: Representations of Globalization in *Maelström, waydowntown* and *La Moitié gauche du frigo*', *Canadian Journal of Film Studies*, vol. 13, no. 1, March, pp. 69–83.
--- (2013), 'The practice of memory and the politics of memorialization: Denis Villeneuve's *Polytechnique*', *Canadian Journal of Film Studies/Revue Canadienne d'études cinématographiques*, vol. 22, no. 1, Spring, pp. 86–106.
'Lorsque Pascale est arrivée aux auditions, ça m'a fait chavirer', *La tribune*, 31 October, 1998, p. G5, Collections de BAnQ, available at: https://numerique.banq.qc.ca/patrimoine/details/52327/3887195 (last accessed 1 June 2021).
McDonald, Terrance H. (2022), 'Posthuman Cinema: Terrence Malick and a Cinema of Life', *From Deleuze and Guattari to Posthumanism: Philosophies of Immanence*, edited by Christine Daigle and Terrance H. McDonald, London: Bloomsbury, pp. 129–46.
McGinn, Colin (1997), *Ethics, Evil and Fiction*, Oxford: Clarendon Press.
McGlynn, James Denis (2020), 'Revisiting Vangelis: Sonic Citation and Narration in the Score for *Blade Runner 2049*', *SonicScope: New Approaches to Audiovisual Culture*, vol. 1, 6 October, available at: https://www.sonicscope.org/pub/iatko5dg/release/4 (last accessed 6 October 2020).
MacKenzie, Scott (2004), *Screening Quebec: Québécois Moving Images, National Identity, and the Public Sphere*, Manchester: Manchester University Press.
McLeish, Megan (2014), *Les thèmes nationalistes dans la chanson folk et la chanson québécoise pendant les années 1960 et 1980 au Canada: Une étude de Stan Rogers et de Gilles Vigneault*, University of Waterloo, MS thesis, pp. 83–4.
MacLennan, Hugh (1945), *Two Solitudes*, Toronto: Macmillan.
Mamula, Tijuana (2018), 'Denis Villeneuve, film theorist; or, cinema's arrival in a multilingual world', *Screen*, vol. 59, no. 4, December, pp. 542–51.
Manning, Erin (2005), 'Fluid Relations: Quebec Cinema and the Church', *Nouvelles Vues: revue sur les pratiques et les théories du cinéma au Québec*, no. 4, Fall.
Mandolini Carlo (2000), 'Beauté glacée: *Maelström* de Denis Villeneuve', *Séquences*, 211, p. 35.
Marchessault, Janine (2013), 'Versioning History: *Polytechnique* as vector', *Canadian Journal of Film Studies*, vol. 22, no. 1, pp. 44–65.
Marks, Laura U. (2000), *The Skin of the Film: Intercultural Cinema, Embodiment, and the Senses*, Durham, NC: Duke University Press.
Marshall, Bill (2001), *Quebec National Cinema*, Montreal: McGill-Queen's University Press.

Marshall, Kingsley (2019), 'Music as a Source of Narrative Information in HBO's *Westworld*', *Reading Westworld*, edited by Alex Goody and Antonia Mackay, Cham: Palgrave Macmillan, pp. 97–118.
Marsolais, Gilles (2011), *Cinéma québécois: De l'artisanat à l'industrie*, Montreal: Triptyque.
Mayer, Sophie (2017), 'Girl Power: Back to the Future of Feminist Science Fiction with *Into the Forest* and *Arrival*', *Film Quarterly*, vol. 70, no. 3, pp. 32–42.
Melnyk, George (2014), 'The Gendered City: Feminism in Rozema's *Deperanto* (1991), Pool's *Rispondetemi* (1991), and Villeneuve's *Maelström* (2000)', *Film and the City: The Urban Imaginary in Canadian Cinema*, Edmonton: Athabasca University Press, pp. 77–100.
Melnyk, George (2003), 'Quebec's Next Génération: From Lauzon to Turpin', *Ciné-Action*, vol. 61, pp. 10–17.
Mélon, Marc-Emmanuel (1984), 'Quand les fantômes viennent à notre rencontre . . .', *Revue Belge du Cinéma*, vol. 10, Winter, pp. 75–84.
Meerzon, Yana (2013), 'Staging Memory in Wajdi Mouawad's *Incendies*: Archaeolgoical Site or Poetic Venue?', *Theatre Research in Canada*, vol. 34 no. 1, Spring, pp. 12–36.
Memmi, Albert (1972), *Portrait du colonisé, précédé du Portrait du colonisateur et d'une préf. de Jean-Paul Sartre, Suivi Les Canadiens français sont-ils des colonisés?*, Montreal: L'Étincelle.
Mennel, Barbara (2008), *Cities and Cinema*, London/New York: Routledge.
Metz, Christian (1977), *The Imaginary Signifier: Psychoanalysis and the Cinema*, translated by Celia Britton, Annwyl Williams, Ben Brewster and Alfred Guzzetti, Bloomington: Indiana University Press.
Mignolo, Walter D. (2011), *The Darker Side of Western Modernity*, Durham, NC: Duke University Press.
--- (2018), 'The Decolonial Option', *On Decoloniality: Concepts, Analytics, Praxis*, edited by Walter D. Mignolo and Catherine E. Walsh, Durham, NC: Duke University Press, pp. 103–244.
--- (2018), 'Decoloniality and Phenomenology: The Geopolitics of Knowing and Epistemic/Ontological Colonial Differences', *Journal of Speculative Philosophy*, vol. 32, no. 3, pp. 360–87.
Mittell, Jason (2009), '*Lost* in a Great Story: Evaluation in Narrative Television (and Television Studies)', *Reading Lost*, edited by Roberta Pearson, London: I. B. Tauris, pp. 119–28.
Monk, Katherine (2001), *Weird Sex and Snowshoes, and Other Canadian Film Phenomena*, Vancouver: Raincoast Books.
Moore, Martin and Tambini, Damian (2018), *Digital Dominance: The Power of Google, Amazon, Facebook, and Apple*, Oxford: Oxford University Press.

Moss, Jane (2001), 'Passionate Postmortems: Couples Plays by Women Dramatists', *Doing Gender: Franco-Canadian Women Writers of the 1990s*, edited by Paula Ruth Gilbert and Roseanna Dufault, Hackensack: Fairleigh Dickinson University Press.

Mouawad, Wajdi (2003), *Incendies*, Montreal: Actes Sud/Leméac.

Mulhall, Stephen (2020), 'The alphabet of us: Miracles, messianism and the baseline test in *Blade Runner 2049*', *Blade Runner 2049: A Philosophical Exploration*, edited by Timothy Shanahan and Paul Smart, London/New York: Routledge, pp. 27–47.

Mulvey, Laura (2006). *Death 24x a Second: Stillness and the Moving Image*, London: Reaktion Books.

Muncy, Julie, '*Blade Runner 2049* Director Opens up about the Film's Treatment of Women', *Gizmodo*, 26 November 2017, available at: https://io9.gizmodo.com/blade-runner-2049-directoropens-up-about-the-films-tre-1820747134 (last accessed 20 February 2020).

Murphy, Graham J. (2020), 'Cyberpunk's Masculinist Legacy: Puppetry, Labour and *ménage à trois* in *Blade Runner 2049*', *Science Fiction Film and Television*, vol. 13, no. 1, pp. 97–106.

Mustafa Ali, Syed (2019), 'Of Sea Walls and Rising Rides: Critical Race/Religion Readings Of "White Crisis" in Science Fiction Dystopia', *Critical Muslim Studies,* available at: https://www.criticalmuslimstudies.co.uk/of-sea-walls-and-rising-rides-pt1 (last accessed 20 May 2021).

Myers, Scott (2009), '*Blade Runner* dialogue analysis', *Go Into The Story: The Official Screenwriting Blog of the Black List,* 3 December, available at: https://gointothestory.blcklst.com/blade-runner-dialogue-analysis-ff0e306a7630 (last accessed 8 January 2021).

Nabokov, Vladimir (1962), *Pale Fire*, New York: G. P. Putnam's Sons.

Neill, Calum (2018), 'Do Electric Sheep Dream of Androids? On the Place of Fantasy in the Consideration of the Nonhuman', *Lacan and the Nonhuman*, edited by Gautam Basu Thakur and Jonathan Dickstein, Cham: Palgrave Macmillan, p. 213–25.

Neiman, Susan (2001), 'What Is the Problem of Evil', *Rethinking Evil: Contemporary Perspectives*, edited by Maria Pia Lara, Berkeley: University of California Press, pp. 27–45.

--- (2002), *Evil in Modern Thought: An Alternate History of Philosophy*, Boston: Princeton University Press.

Nora, Pierre (1988), 'Between Memory and History: Les Lieux de Mémoire', *Représentations*, no. 26, Spring, pp. 7–24.

'Novum' (2019), '*Blade Runner 2049* *Does Not* Have "A Woman Problem"', YouTube, 11 March, available at: https://www.youtube.com/watch?v=6GsXBh5PGZU&ab_channel=Novum (last accessed 28 June 2021).

Nys, Thomas and Stephen De Wijze (2019), *The Routledge Handbook of the Philosophy of Evil (Routledge Handbooks in Philosophy)*, London/New York: Routledge.

Olson, Greta (2003), 'Reconsidering Unreliability: Fallible and Untrustworthy Narrators', *Narrative*, vol. 11, no. 1, pp. 93–109.

Oppenheimer, Paul (1996), *Evil and the Demonic: A New Theory of Monstrous Behavior*, New York: New York University Press.

Page, Thomas (2021), 'It's Denis Villeneuve's *Dune* Now', *CNN Style*, 22 October.

Payne, Catherine and Alexandra Pitsis (2018), 'On Nature and the Tactility of the Senses in *Blade Runner 2049*', *Journal of Asia-Pacific Pop Culture*, vol. 3, no.1, pp. 55–74.

Pelletier, Esther and Irène Roy (2015), 'Évoquer pour susciter l'imaginaire et montrer plutôt que dire', *Nouvelles études francophones*, vol. 20, no. 2, Fall, pp. 111–28.

Perez-Delouya, Asher (2013), 'L'aboutissement d'une nouvelle démarche: *Prisoners*', *Séquences*, no. 287, p. 55.

Pevere, Geoff (2002), 'Fishy', *North of Everything: English-Canadian Cinema Since 1980*, edited by William Beard and Jerry White, Edmonton: University of Alberta Press.

Pike, David L. (2012), *Canadian Cinema since the 1980s: At the Heart of the World*, Toronto: University of Toronto Press.

Płonowska Ziarek, Ewa (2008), 'Bare Life on Strike: Notes on the Biopolitics of Race and Gender', *South Atlantic Quarterly*, vol. 107, no. 1, pp. 89–105.

Poirier, Christian (2004), 'Le Cinéma québécois et la question identitaire. La Confrontation entre les récits de l'empêchement et de l'enchantement', *Recherches sociographiques*, vol. 45, no. 1, January–April, pp. 11–38.

Ramond, Charles-Henri (2014), 'Entrevue avec Odile Tremblay', *Le Devoir*, 8 March.

--- (2014), 'Méandres identitaires: *Enemy* de Denis Villeneuve', *Séquences*, no. 290, p. 53.

Ransom, Amy J. (2009), *Science Fiction from Quebec: A Postcolonial Study*, Jefferson: McFarland.

--- (2013), 'Deterritorialization and the Crisis of Recognition in Turn of the Millennium Québec Film', *American Review of Canadian Studies*, vol. 43, no. 2, pp. 176–89.

--- (2015), 'The Future of Quebec in SF Film and Television', *Science Fiction Film & Television*, vol. 8, no. 1, pp. 1–28.

--- (2020), 'The Director's Cut: Denis Villeneuve before *Blade Runner 2049*', *Science Fiction Film and Television*, vol. 13, no. 1, pp. 119–27.

Rayment, Andrew, and Paul Nadasdy (2018), 'The Sphinx and the Bridgekeeper: Denis Villeneuve's *Enemy* as Double-Riddle', *Journal of the Ochanomizu University English Society*, vol. 8, pp. 5–20.

Richard, David Evan (2018), 'Film Phenomenology and the "Eloquent Gestures" of Denis Villeneuve's *Arrival*', *Cinephile*, vol. 12, no. 1, pp. 41–7.
Richardson, John, Anna-Elena Pääkkölä and Sanna Qvick (2018), 'Sensing Time and Space through the Soundtracks of *Interstellar* and *Arrival*', *The Oxford Handbook of Cinematic Listening*, edited by Carlo Cenciarelli, Oxford: Oxford University Press, pp. 1–25.
Ricoeur, Paul (1995), *Oneself as Another*, Chicago: The University of Chicago Press.
Robin, Patricia (2015), 'La force tranquille: *Sicario* de Denis Villeneuve', *Séquences*, no. 298, pp. 4–5.
Ruppersberg, Hugh (1990), 'The Alien Messiah', *Alien Zone: Cultural Theory and Contemporary Science Fiction Cinema*, edited by Annette Kuhn, vol. 1, Verso, pp. 32–8.
Ryan, Marie-Laure (2006), 'From Parallel Universes to Possible Worlds: Ontological Pluralism in Physics, Narratology, and Narrative', *Poetics Today*, vol. 27, no. 4, pp. 633–74.
Saramago, José (2004), *The Double*, New York: Houghton Mifflin Harcourt.
--- (2002), *O Homem Duplicado*, Lisbon: Editorial Caminho.
Sartre, Jean-Paul (1946), 'Existentialism is a Humanism', *Existentialism from Dostoyevsky to Sartre*, edited by Walter Kaufman, Meridian Publishing Company (1989), available at: http://www.marxists.org/reference/archive/sartre/works/exist/sartre.htm (last accessed 18 July 2021).
Saul, John Ralston (1998), *Reflections of a Siamese Twin*, Toronto: Penguin.
Schneider, Steven Jay and Daniel Shaw (2003), *Dark Thoughts: Philosophic Reflections on Cinematic Horror*, Lanham: Scarecrow Press.
Schopp, Andrew (2019), 'Making Room for Our Personal Posthuman Prisons: *Black Mirror*'s "Be Right Back"', *Through the Black Mirror: Deconstructing the Side Effects of the Digital Age*, edited by Terence McSweeney and Stuart Joy, Cham: Palgrave Macmillan.
Senécal, Patrick (2002), *Les 7 jours du Talion*, Quebec: Alire.
Shanahan, Timothy (2020), 'We're All Just Looking for Something Real', *Blade Runner 2049: A Philosophical Exploration*, edited by Timothy Shanahan and Paul Smart, London/New York: Routledge, pp. 8–26.
--- (2020), 'What am I to you? The Deck-a-Rep debate and the question of fictional truth', *Blade Runner 2049: A Philosophical Exploration*, edited by Timothy Shanahan and Paul Smart, London/New York: Routledge, pp. 228–47.
Shanahan, Timothy and Paul Smart (eds) (2020), *Blade Runner 2049: A Philosophical Exploration*, London/New York: Routledge.
Sheldon, Rebekah (2013), 'Somatic Capitalism: Reproduction, Futurity, and Feminist Science Fiction', *Ada, A Journal of Gender, New Media & Technology*, no.3, available at: https://adanewmedia.org/2013/11/issue3-sheldon (last accessed 28 June 2021).

Shelley, Mary (1818), *Frankenstein; or, The Modern Prometheus*, London: Lackington, Hughes, Harding, Mavor, & Jones.
Shetley, Vernon and Alissa Ferguson (2001), 'Reflections in a Silver Eye: Lens and Mirror in *Blade Runner*', *Science Fiction Studies*, vol. 28, no. 1, March, pp. 66–76.
Silverman, Kaja (1988), *The Acoustic Mirror: The Female Voice in Psychoanalysis and Cinema*, Bloomington: Indiana University Press.
Singer, Ben (1988), 'Film, Photography, and Fetish: The Analyses of Christian Metz', *Cinema Journal*, vol. 27, no. 4., Summer, pp. 4–22.
Sirois-Trahan, Jean-Pierre (2011), 'Introduction: Du renouveau en terrains connus', *Nouvelles vues: revue sur les pratiques et les théories du cinéma au Québec*, edited by Jean-Pierre Sirois-Trahan and Thomas Carrier-Lafleur, no. 12, Spring–Summer.
Sobchack, Vivian Carol (1987), *Screening Space: The American Science Fiction Film*, 2nd, enl. ed., New York: Ungar.
Spaihts, Jon, Denis Villeneuve and Eric Roth (2020), *Dune: Screenplay: Based on the Novel* Dune *by Frank Herbert*, Salmon Revisions, Final Shooting Script, 19 June, available at: https://www.duneinfo.com/caladan/script-index (last accessed 2 December 2021).
Sterling, Bruce (1989), 'Slipstream', *Science Fiction Eye*, no. 5, pp. 77–80
Stevenson, Robert Louis (1883), *Treasure Island*, London: Cassell & Co.
Stewart, Sara (2017), 'You'll Love the new *Blade Runner* – Unless You're a Woman', *New York Post*, 4 October, available at: https://nypost.com/2017/10/04/youll-love-the-new-blade-runner-unless-youre-a-woman (last accessed 28 June 2021).
Sticchi, Francesco (2018), 'From Spinoza to Contemporary Linguistics: Pragmatic Ethics in Denis Villeneuve's *Arrival*', *Canadian Journal of Film Studies/Revue canadienne d'études cinématographiques*, vol. 27, no. 2, Fall, pp. 48–65.
Taşkale, Ali Rıza (2020), 'Thoughts Interlinked: Corporate Imaginaries and Post-Capitalist Futures in *Blade Runner 2049*', *Critique*, vol. 48, no. 1, pp. 113–19.
Teodoro, José (2014), 'Enemy', *Film Comment*, vol. 50, no. 2, pp. 69–70.
Thain, Alanna (2010), 'A Texture in the Desert of the Real: The Heterotopic Fold of Denis Villeneuve's *Un 32 août sur terre*', *Nouvelles Vues: revue sur les pratiques et les théories du cinéma au Québec*, no. 11, Fall.
Thérien, Gilles (1996), 'La critique et la disparition de son objet', *Cinémas*, vol. 6, no. 2–3, Spring, pp. 142–63.
Thomas, Laurence (1993), *Vessels of Evil: American Slavery and the Holocaust*, Philadelphia: Temple University Press.
Thon, Jan-Noël (2009), 'Mind-Bender: Zur Popularisierung Komplexer Narrativer Strukturen Im Amerikanischen Kino Der 1990er Jahre',

Post-Coca-Colanization: Zurück Zur Vielfalt?, edited by Sophia Komor and Rebekka Rohleder, Berlin: Peter Lang, pp. 171–88.

Treanor, Brian (2020), 'Being-From-Birth: Natality and Narrative', *Blade Runner 2049: A Philosophical Exploration*, edited by Timothy Shanahan and Paul Smart, London/New York: Routledge, pp. 68–86.

Tyrer, Ben (2021), 'Do Filminds Dream of Celluloid Sheep? Lacan, Filmosophy and *Blade Runner 2049*', *Lacanian Perspectives on Blade Runner 2049*, edited by Calum Neill, Cham: Palgrave Macmillan, pp. 13–39.

Vaillancourt, Julie (2015), 'Entretien: Denis Villeneuve', *Séquences*, no. 298, p. 6.

Véronneau, Pierre (2006), 'Genres and Variations: The Audiences of Quebec Cinema', *Self Portraits: The Cinemas of Canada Since Telefilm*, edited by André Loiselle and Tom McSorley, Ottowa: The Canadian Film Institute, pp. 93–128.

Vint, Sherryl (2020), 'Vitality and reproduction in *Blade Runner 2049*', *Science Fiction Film and Television*, vol. 13, no. 1, Spring, pp. 15–35.

Wegner, Phillip E. (2020), 'We, the People of *Blade Runner 2049*', *Science Fiction Film and Television*, vol. 13, no. 1, pp. 135–42.

Weheliye, Alexander G. (2014), *Habeas Viscus: Racializing Assemblages, Biopolitics, and Black Feminist Theories of the Human*, Durham, NC: Duke University Press.

Wharton, Edith. *French Ways and Their Meaning* (1919), New York/London: D. Appleton and Company, available at: https://www.gutenberg.org/files/57786/57786-h/57786-h.htm (last accessed 12 December 2021).

Willemsen, Steven, and Miklós Kiss (2019), 'Last Year at Mulholland Drive: Ambiguous Framings and Framing Ambiguities', *Acta Univ. Sapientiae, Film and Media Studies*, vol. 16, pp. 129–52.

Wynter, Sylvia (2003), 'Unsettling the Coloniality of Being/Power/Truth/Freedom: Towards the Human, After Man, Its Overrepresentation – An Argument', *The New Centennial Review*, vol. 3, no. 3, Fall, pp. 257–337.

Young, Iris Marion (1984), 'Pregnant Embodiment: Subjectivity and Alienation', *The Journal of Medicine and Philosophy: A Forum for Bioethics and Philosophy of Medicine*, vol. 9, no. 1, February pp. 45–62.

Zéau, Caroline (2006), *L'Office national du film et le cinéma canadien (1939–2003): Éloge de la frugalité*, Brussels/New York: Peter Lang.

Zimmerman, Michael E. (2008), 'The Singularity: A Crucial Phase in Divine Self-Actualization?', *Cosmos and History: The Journal of Natural and Social Philosophy*, vol. 4, no. 2, pp. 347–70.

--- (2009), 'Religious Motifs in Technological Posthumanism', *Western Humanities Review*, special issue on *Nature, Culture, Technology*, edited by Anne-Marie Feenberg-Dibon and Reginald McGinnis, vol. 63, no. 3, Fall, pp. 67–83.

Index

Abjection, 63, 118
adaptation, 18, 51, 64, 65, 73, 128, 157, 159n3, 160n17, 194–206, 207n9
aesthetics, 70, 139, 146, 161–2, 168–9, 173, 188
   absence, 76–91
AI *see* artificial intelligence
alien, 14, 16–17, 25, 31, 33–8, 44–5, 55, 60, 63, 64–73, 85, 110; *see also* Heptapod
alienation, 7–9, 12, 17, 18, 105, 112, 146, 173, 175
américanité, 30–8
Arrival, 16–17, 34, 36, 44–5, 55, 60, 63–73, 78, 85–6, 89–90, 110, 170, 171
artificial intelligence, 65, 121, 122, 161, 162, 165, 172–6, 178–91
audience *see* spectator
auteur, 5, 7, 9, 14, 18, 38, 73

Blade Runner 2049, 16, 17, 18, 45, 55–6, 59–63, 73, 110, 111, 120–3, 161–76, 178–91
blindness, 55, 111, 115, 118, 122, 135, 170, 201; *see also* misrecognition
body, 29, 43, 55, 68, 84, 94–5, 97, 112, 114, 116, 118, 120, 122, 180
   female, 59, 68–9, 71, 79, 84, 118, 173, 203
   filmic, 49, 52
   missing, 76–91

pregnant, 43, 64–5, 79, 91, 97, 120
   Replicant, 55, 61, 63, 173–5
border, 5, 9, 13, 14, 16, 29–30, 32, 48, 161, 164, 176
BR 2049 see Blade Runner 2049

capitalism, 62, 93, 95, 96–7, 100–7, 187, 190
child, 9, 13, 15, 27, 29, 30, 31, 33, 34, 35, 44, 45, 46, 60, 61–2, 64–6, 68, 72, 80, 83–6, 89, 110–11, 112–15, 121–3, 135–8, 163, 181–9, 196, 205
childbirth, 24, 45, 61–2, 64–5, 83, 86, 114, 175, 184, 188, 201; *see also* pregnancy; *see also* reproduction
coloniality, 31, 38, 63, 65, 71, 72, 190
consciousness, 60, 64, 69–71, 80, 121, 162, 171, 175, 178–89, 206
Cosmos, 6, 7, 8–9, 15, 23, 24, 33, 37

Deleuze, 7, 41–3, 46, 53, 64, 94–5, 107, 173, 175
deterritorialisation, 5, 7, 9, 11, 13, 16, 17, 18–19
dichotomy, 32, 38, 42, 48–9, 129, 167
doppelgänger, 15, 44, 47, 53–4, 110, 111, 116–20, 145, 147, 148; *see also* double
double, 15–16, 54, 110, 111, 113–14, 117–20, 144, 159n3; *see also* doppelgänger
duality, 18, 54, 88, 148

Dune: Part 1, 18, 110, 194–206
dystopia, 60, 62, 65, 73, 110, 161, 181, 187, 190

Enemy, 15–16, 44–5, 47, 53–4, 110, 111, 116–20, 123, 142, 143–58
ethics, 29, 31, 32, 48, 54, 85–6, 127, 133, 161, 162, 166, 175, 178, 179, 184, 188–91
evil, 99, 126–42, 197–8

fragmentation, 43, 44, 53–4, 55–6
francophone, 9, 11, 17–18, 32–5, 42, 104
French-Canadian, 6, 8–9, 12–13, 17–18, 35–6; *see also* identity, Québécois
French language *see* language, French; *see also* Quebec, French
French-speaking *see* francophone
futurism *see* futurity
futurity, 24, 60, 65
    reproductive, 59–73, 79–80

gender, 12–13, 38, 59, 61, 63, 86, 183
genre, 5–6, 14, 18, 24, 25, 31, 42, 51, 52, 64, 73, 126–8, 139–42, 143–4, 154–8, 161
globalisation, 14, 16, 17, 18, 93, 95–7, 100–7, 187

Heptapod, 16–17, 44–5, 55, 60, 64–73, 85–6, 89–90, 110, 171; *see also* language, Heptapod
Hollywood, 5, 7, 13–14, 18, 31, 34, 35, 36, 42, 52, 59, 64, 152, 155–6
horror, 60, 126–30, 132, 139–41, 152

identity, 5, 17, 51, 54, 107, 110–23, 131, 134–5, 138–41, 159n3, 161–3, 166, 169, 171, 172, 175–6, 178, 180, 183–4, 185–6, 190
    intersubjective, 110–12, 116, 118, 120, 123, 172–3
    narrative, 111–12, 116, 121–2
    Québécois, 5–19, 30–7, 95, 104
    quest, 5, 13, 17, 51, 110–15, 120–3, 167, 181, 185–6
image-affection, 42, 46–8
Incendies, 7, 12, 13, 16, 41, 44, 49, 51, 60, 76, 78, 80, 83–5, 89, 110, 111–16, 118, 122, 123, 176, 207n10

intersubjectivity *see* identity, intersubjective
intertextuality, 18, 41, 64, 187–8

language, 16, 36, 42, 48, 64, 67, 69, 98, 127–8, 140, 171, 175, 196
    English, 14–15, 41–2, 52, 56
    French, 5–6, 8, 17, 32, 41–2, 44, 48–51, 56, 81
    Heptapod, 17, 44–5, 55, 67–8, 70–2, 85–6, 90

Maelström, 6, 7, 9, 11, 17, 41, 43, 49–50, 52, 60, 67, 73, 76, 78, 80–2, 88, 89, 93–108
maternity *see* motherhood
memory, 11, 12, 31, 33, 45, 65, 78, 80, 85–6, 96, 111, 116, 120–3, 125n25, 135, 162, 163–6, 178, 184–7, 201
Metz, 76–9, 88, 90
miracle, 23–4, 25–6, 36–7, 38, 45, 56, 61–2, 65, 111, 122, 165, 189
misrecognition, 110–16, 117, 120–2, 123
monster, 126–42
motherhood, 9, 17, 64–5, 77, 79–86, 90–1, 110, 120, 150

narration, 143–58
    meta, 43, 49–50
    unreliable, 148, 150, 152–3, 154–5
nation, 5–19, 23–38, 79–80, 190–1
nationalism *see* nation

Other, 13, 15, 16–17, 24, 32, 55, 60, 62, 63, 65, 68, 70–3, 94, 110–11, 112, 116–20, 122, 123, 144–5, 147, 176, 179

Polytechnique, 7, 11–13, 17, 41, 43–4, 46–7, 49, 50–1, 52, 60, 73, 76, 78, 80, 82–3, 86, 87–8, 89
possession, 42, 48, 52–3, 55, 56
postmodern, 8, 24, 26–8, 30, 93, 96, 97, 98, 100, 102
poststructuralism, 94, 96–7, 98–9, 100–1, 106

pregnancy, 12, 29, 35, 60, 61–2, 64–5, 79–80, 82–3, 85–6, 91, 97–8, 101–2, 117, 120, 144, 148, 151; *see also* childbirth; reproduction
Prisoners, 12, 14–5, 16, 41, 47–8, 52–3, 64, 76, 85, 126–9, 135–42

Quebec
   Catholicism, 11, 23–4, 32–3, 35, 36
   cinema, 5–19, 23–5, 33–7, 59, 99, 102–6
   culture, 28–9, 34–6, 38, 106
   French, 6, 8, 17, 35
   sovereignty, 5, 7, 15, 16, 18, 23–4, 30–4
   see also religion
Québécois *see* identity
queering, 60, 71–3

racialisation, 60, 63, 68–71
realism, 6, 7, 11, 13, 24, 25, 37, 99, 102–3, 148, 150
rebirth, 23–4, 29–33, 35, 37, 50
reflexivity, 42–6, 157, 188
religion *see* religiosity; *see also* Quebec, Catholicism
religiosity, 24, 25, 33–8, 69, 135, 189, 194, 196, 197–200, 201
Replicant, 17, 46, 55–6, 60, 61–3, 72, 110–11, 120–3, 161–76, 179–91; *see also* body, Replicant
reproduction, 5, 9, 12, 14, 17, 32, 59–73, 79–80, 165, 184; *see also* childbirth; *see also* pregnancy

science fiction, 14, 16–17, 23–38, 42, 55–6, 59–60, 143, 161–2, 181, 183–4, 187, 190–1
secularity, 24, 33, 36, 38, 95, 100, 127, 140–1
Sicario, 12, 14, 16, 41, 48, 54, 76, 85, 126–35, 138–42, 176
space, 27–9, 68–9, 96, 98, 112, 199, 204
   cinematic, 76–8, 161–76

domestic, 95, 96, 168
heterotopic, 9, 30
imaginary, 78, 106, 108
liminal, 79–80, 86, 140–1, 161, 179–81
natural, 27, 105
physical, 161–73, 175, 179, 190
urban, 95, 100
virtual, 161–6, 169, 172–5, 190
spacecraft, 14, 28, 55, 67, 68, 85, 205
spectator, 41–2, 43, 45, 48, 50, 53, 67, 68, 71, 76–8, 88, 113, 115, 118, 143–8, 151–8
subjectivity, 9, 13, 17, 18, 63, 64, 83, 85, 88, 90–1, 94, 100, 110–11, 120–1, 123, 149, 154, 161–4, 166, 173–6, 178

technology, 14, 33, 49, 60, 65, 69, 80, 161, 162, 165, 175, 178–9, 180, 183, 184–5, 188–9, 190–1, 205
temporality, 9–11, 17, 24–9, 51, 60, 64–5, 68, 79–80, 81–2, 85–8, 91, 94–5, 105–6, 110–11, 112, 121, 150–1, 171, 175, 179, 199
territorialisation, 5, 7, 9, 11, 13, 16
thriller, 14, 15, 41, 42, 48, 52–4, 152
time *see* temporality
transcendence, 17, 42, 48, 49–52, 56, 69, 72, 94, 127, 148–9, 183–4
trauma, 9, 13, 78–87, 91, 112, 120, 131, 133, 135, 137–8, 141, 163, 166, 185, 201

Un 32 août sur terre, 7, 9–11, 16, 17, 23–38, 41, 46, 49, 52, 60, 67, 73, 110, 143
uncanny, 111, 118, 123, 126

violence, 7, 12, 13, 16, 35, 36, 37, 60, 61, 80, 82–3, 87, 119, 130–4, 137–8
virtual reality, 162–6, 169, 171, 173–6, 184

whiteness, 28, 30, 31, 33, 34, 60, 63, 65–6, 67, 68–70, 71, 117, 133, 168, 181

EU representative:
Easy Access System Europe
Mustamäe tee 50, 10621 Tallinn, Estonia
Gpsr.requests@easproject.com

www.ingramcontent.com/pod-product-compliance
Lightning Source LLC
Chambersburg PA
CBHW070347240426
43671CB00013BA/2428